A Very B
Muslim Activist
The life of Ghayasuddin Siddiqui

Dedications

From Ghayasuddin Siddiqui:
To my mother, for making it possible;
To my wife, for making it happen.

From C Scott Jordan:
For all of my grandfathers and the grandmothers
who made their stories worth telling.

A Very British Muslim Activist

The life of Ghayasuddin Siddiqui

as told by C Scott Jordan

BEACON BOOKS

First published in the UK by Beacon Books and Media Ltd
Innospace, Chester Street, Manchester M1 5GD, UK.

First paperback edition published in 2019

www.beaconbooks.net

ISBN: 978-1-912356-37-9   International Edition
ISBN: 978-1-912356-38-6   UK Edition
ISBN: 978-1-912356-39-3   eBook

Cover design by John Duggan www.duggan.design/

Cataloging-in-Publication record for this book is available from the British Library

Contents

AUTHOR'S FOREWORD

I have a strange habit of running into people of Pakistani descent.

The first Muslim I ever recall meeting, my school mate Zain, was a second generation Pakistani American. As memory tends to work, I don't remember the first time I met a Muslim—not that it was a monolithic moment of esteemed cinematic value. In fact, I would not have known he was a Muslim if it wasn't for one fateful day that ended the summer of 2001. He was just another bespectacled kid, one of our unique tribe who would meet early in the morning before school in the library to discuss philosophy and comic books. I spent my more formative years in the heart of the region of the United States known as the 'Bible Belt'. Here it was not so much the colour of your skin that set you apart from others, except for obvious racial tensions (which I assure you are alive and well, to much dismay), but which church or denomination you belonged to. For my pubescent self, it was quite the ordeal as I didn't know what denomination my family belonged to and we were not regular church goers. So little did I know that I had a lot more in common with my friend Zain than I could even imagine. And then it happened. 11 September, 2001. And suddenly, for a little kid with a borderline unhealthy obsession with films, I realised that real life was very different from how things played out on the silver screen. I also realised there were other people in this world who were not American. It is silly to recall, but quite existentially disruptive to my young self who could least trust the changes going on in his own body, let alone the stability of the rest of the planet. The people around me were telling me to mourn this great attack, or take heed and trust no one, even to prepare for Armageddon!

I instead took to the family computer. I, having no connection to the attacks, be that an emotional memory of New York or Washington (neither place I had yet been to) or even known anyone close to the carnage, instead was moved in a different way. How had I spent the first twelve years of my life in such ignorance to a whole third of the world? So, I colonised the family computer and sought the wisdom of Yahoo.com, or perhaps it was AskJeeves.com. Much as Ghayas calls upon the young Ghunsham for his knowledge of Hinduism, I took to my friend Zain, demanding the entire history of the Muslim world, asking such profound questions as "what is the difference between an Islam and a Muslim?" Much like Ghunsham, Zain found out that he knew even less about himself and his background than he would care to know. So began our quest for knowledge which continues to this day.

Zain was just the beginning. Later, I would have a professor, born in Pakistan, who once fell asleep while giving a lecture on embryology (which, to be fair, doesn't sound like that difficult of a task). This same man, while working towards his doctorate, was commanded by an adviser to go out in the middle of the Detroit Riots of 1967 to get him a Coca-Cola from the convenience shop across the street. His adviser said, "It isn't that bad out there." Two days and significant police questioning later, my professor returned to the college with the Coca-Cola in hand. This man, who always seemed to exist in his own universe, once turned to me, straight-faced and said, "Why would you want to be a doctor when you have such a talent for writing?" And then, while working at an international summer camp for children aged 12–18 from all around the world, what delegation would I be put in charge of? Of course, the Pakistani delegation which I spent two consecutive summers working with. And then, while completing my master's degree in East-West Studies, my adviser came to me and said we had a special guest coming from London to give a talk at our annual Asian Culture Week event. That speaker was

Ziauddin Sardar and he was going to give a lecture on his new idea, something called Postnormal Times. Following the lecture, we all went to dinner and an idea was sparked. I then travelled to Chicago where I engaged in a polylogue with Zia and his contemporaries. Never had I been more challenged intellectually (and let me tell you, they ate my ignorance for lunch and dinner). An idea became a framework for thinking, and then I would go to London and meet a whole lot more people of Pakistani descent.

In the winter of 2017, I travelled with Zia to Sarum College in Salisbury to attend the Muslim Institute's Winter Gathering. There I gained my introduction to the British Muslim community. The memory I took home from Salisbury was not my visit to the Cathedral or seeing the Magna Carta or even the wonderful intellectual discourse which took place that weekend; rather, it was the warm welcome I was given into the community. I was not seen as anything other than a member of the family. For an American kid with no strong sense of cultural identity or much to distinguish himself from the generic melting pot of America, this was truly heart-warming. The first night of the weekend event, Zia introduced me to several of the people at the gathering. I had been writing for *Critical Muslim*, the Muslim Institute's quarterly journal, so now I could put faces to the names I had been seeing in print and on emails. Then he walked me to a short and thin man with a warm presence. He sat in the front row with a cane at his side and his legs crossed. A natural smile stretched along his jawline, connecting the outer edges of the lenses of his glasses. He sat with the posture of a wise elder man of eminence, yet stared with eager anticipation of what he might learn that night. Zia directed me to sit next to this man. "He is important." And so I sat next to Dr. Ghayasuddin Siddiqui and listened to a lecture from a man essentially telling us the economic crises of the future are only going to get worse and there is little hope for us all.

A little over a year later I would find myself wandering through the hilly streets of Chesham, touting heavy bags behind me on less than ideal sidewalks. Though it was the dead of winter and at an hour somewhere between what modern parlance calls night and morning, I was sweating heavily. Owl noises and the way the moon carved through the wispy clouds made it so that all I could think of was the famous movie line "beware the moors and stick to the road..." A fan of the London Underground and still having an Oyster card, I thought, why not take the tube to Chesham from Heathrow? It shouldn't be a problem. Yet after several hours I finally arrived at the end of the Metropolitan line to a town fully asleep and a less than well-lit series of hills. The station was empty and no Wifi was to be had, rendering my mobile's GPS utterly useless. There was a very rudimentary map of Chesham outside the station and the address I was going to was available on my phone. I attempted to make a navigation of the map.

After one hour of passing quickly amid the pitch-black gaps between the street lights I had come to what I determined was the highest point in Chesham and no closer to my destination, for now Chesham looked like every other village in the UK. What had I gotten myself into? I thought. Thanks to Zia I have travelled the world, and aside from having a tendency to bump into Pakistanis, I also tend to bring with me a hurdle of one sort or another. From climatic cataclysm to geopolitical crisis, it is hard for me to go from one place to another without making some ruckus, but here I was, lost in Chesham of all places, attempting to write a man's biography who I had only met once. A man who had lived for nearly eight decades while I had barely mustered three. The most unlikely guy to insert himself into the great story of British Muslims and to try and commit one of its earliest stories to written word. Doubt tends to flow like the monsoon winds or the sweat cover taking me as I began to speed up my pace around the hills of Chesham (because you know, when you are lost, it seems logical to just move faster, hopefully to become unlost quicker—disregard that you could also just be making yourself more lost.)

But I know my way around a map and the memory dustbin that holds all my old Boy Scout skills hasn't been completely emptied out yet. Biography had always fascinated me from a young age. The heroes I looked up to in my youth were mostly fictional, for my parents taught me that no one is perfect and the films of my formative years taught me that one should never meet their heroes from the world of sports or any other shade of reality. So my heroes were the people of history who I read about through biographies and memoirs often gifted to me when someone couldn't think of a good gift to give me, one of the rare readers in the family. In preparing for my stay in Chesham, I tried to dive into a variety of biographies to see how it was done. Since the subject of this work is still available for a question or two, there was no need to do as the historians or biographers of fame contemporary to this work have done. Long hours in archives reading letters and accounts, drawing conclusions and theses— this would not do here.

Upon speaking with Ehsan Masood, the man who launched me off on this project, it was to be something more engaging. And the writer in me did not seek to make an academic work here. Plenty of those are available for your delicacy and some are listed in the sources of this book for you to begin with. I also have no intention of 'drawing conclusions' or making a 'thesis statement'. This is a tale, simple as that. My challenge, and you, fair reader, are to be the judge of it, is to portray events as accurately as possible and to give each person the dignity and respect afforded in the specific context they arise from. Having said that, I believe that bias needs to be discussed for it is in awareness and preservation of bias that I have gained the most reward and difficulty through the writing of this book.

For those of you who have read other things I have written before, and who knows, maybe even after this, you may make note that I am a pessimist with a penchant for drama and one who walks dangerously close to the river of postmodernism, if not one who thrives in diving in headfirst. I will neither confirm nor deny these notions, but they are the music I face in sitting down to write this work. For each moment I sat to write, I had to recall that this was not my story, but rather their story. But actually, it's everyone's story, so it is my story, but not really. So here's the deal. I don't believe I am a postmodernist because I do very much believe in grand narratives. In fact, so much so that I think that due to the contemporary state of the world, things are so interconnected and complex that we are all part of one giant narrative. You can call it 'the human story' if you feel so bold. What I wanted to do was tell the story of Ghayas, a story that I think needs to be told even if you have never heard of this man. Yet in telling his story, I think there are valuable pieces that relate to each of us in different ways. I try not to pass judgement, except for when Ghayas himself passes judgement at that particular time in his life. Though I hope to challenge the reader critically about both the events and decisions made, in the end it comes down to Ghayas, a man who made choices and bore the results that fol-lowed. Essentially, that is one way you could boil down all of our stories, even the story of humanity you so boldly named earlier. This was one major impediment to this project that had sunk previous attempts at making it so before my entering of the story.

With age, memory can sometimes fade and with Ghayas this is no exception. So, to help fill in the gaps, I did have to act like a professional biographer and watch old interviews and read old writings to find both the missing pieces and the voice through which to tell them. After listening to initial interviews and sitting with Ghayas there was definitely a rich story there, but it only existed in a skeletal form; much tissue and facia needed account-ing for. What also made this exercise all the more enjoyable was that in listening to the stories, looking at photos, and reviewing old videos the amazing plasticity of the brain was revealed with

Ghayas recalling events thought long lost. Thankfully, Ghayas and Talat provided me with a healthy list of people to run around London to interview that winter of 2018/19. I am not a journalist; in fact, I rather despise the whole profession for what it has become. Therefore, I did not fancy myself some hot shot who thought I would be able to ask the perfect question and elicit some inside secret almost lost forever! No. I just wanted stories. What I do more so fancy myself as is a wannabe filmmaker and the first rule of film writing is show, don't tell. My goal in this book is to create more of a novelisation of a film than a book as such. Each interview was intended to help me see Ghayas doing things. I didn't care about people's thoughts on him—which of course were largely positive and vague—but rather, I wanted to hear of him in action. Let the story tell itself to the reader. I leave it to you to draw conclusions, propose theses, and let the story move you as it does. I think it is powerful enough on its own.

The act of collecting information for the book itself played out like the run and gun independent film movement of the 1990s. I conducted interviews in noisy cafés shouting over the background, sometimes face to face, other times through the wonders of telecommunication technologies. In one week, day by day, I would wake up, leave Chesham into Central London and then dive from one station to the next, once getting my foot caught in the door and creating quite the scene on the Jubilee line. In hearing other's stories of Ghayas I walked the roads he did from Bloomsbury to Regents Park. I took a ghostly stroll from Endsleigh Street to Logan Hall and on to the British Museum, picturing what it all looked like forty years earlier. From one museum to the next. From Whitehall to the end of the Northern line in Edgeware. I even held one interview while riding the whole route of the Circle line from Westminster! Each night I would return to sleepy Chesham and met by the Siddiquis, where Talat made sure I never went to bed on an empty stomach or without a quick cup of tea!

The story of writing this book is almost a book of its own in itself. Something happened during my two weeks in Chesham as I prepared to write the first draft. There was going to have to be a two-fold reflection. My anti-postmodernist spirit demanded that I could not simply be a fly on the wall if I expected to do this story justice. No, I needed to, as the philosopher Immanuel Levinas said, face the Other and in so doing, become the Other. I think Aristotle was half-right in saying we are social creatures. We are not social for the sake of being social, as anyone who has lived with an adolescent might be tempted to think is our basic programming, but rather, we are storytelling creatures. It is in telling stories that we relate and communicate. This is where society begins. It is therefore the duty of the best storytellers to tell stories that challenge us to become the Other and cast away ourselves, if but only for a moment, to evaluate and maybe, just maybe, be better.

My challenge was to shed my whiteness, my twenty-something maleness, my Americanness and everything else, so that I could try on the other essences of being that make us unique and individual and put them on trial for myself and see what rises to the top. In the end, the whole process plays out like method acting. Where better to do this than a completely new place? So, after Chesham, I was to be off to Kuala Lumpur, Malaysia, to work on the first draft.

Upon arriving in a new world, I adopted several Ghayas characteristics. Becoming a devout tea drinker, eating egg and toast or porridge for breakfast. Reading *The Guardian* first thing every morning. And then inundating myself in documentaries, television series, and films from the UK between the 1950s and today. It just so happened that my time in Malaysia corresponded with Ramadan, so I thought, well, why not? Into the fast I dived. Headfirst, and it must be said, I'm lucky to have not broken my neck in the process. It helped being in a country where everyone was pretty much all in it together with the fast. I was fortunate to have support all around because hunger has a lot in common with madness. Each day was a new lesson. One day the Raj, the next *The Satanic Verses*. And then another day on Iran. And the next the Halal Food Authority (that chapter had to be written after breaking the fast). As much stood to be learned as stood to be re-learned, either from the bias of having lived through certain events and leaving them to the ignorance of the past, or looking at the past through a different lens. I laughed and cried with the ebb and flow of the life of Ghayasuddin Siddiqui and hope you can have similar experiences. In this state I had to continually keep in mind my own biases, but allow the biases of Ghayas to flavour the pages, from the young boy with dreams of India, to the restless youth seeking justice, to the man who found many causes, and finally, as the father to watch what he helped create mature into something that could always be better than what stood before.

Now I return to doubt. And the foggy moors of Chesham. Creatures of the night about, myself one of them, as I happen to stumble down onto the high street. Alive with light but devoid of movement but for the piece of rubbish blowing along the bricked street. Even the pub was closed by this point. But then I happened upon the Chesham Police Station. It was closed and dark, looking abandoned, but plastered upon the wall outside the station doors was a beautiful and detailed map of this village. And there it was, the very cul-de-sac that the Siddiquis lived on. There might be hope yet!

In the closing pages of *The Autobiography of Malcolm X*, Alex Haley recalls one of the last conversations he had with Malcolm. Malcolm said, "A writer is what I want, not an interpreter." The police station was only a couple of blocks from the Siddiquis' home, a quick climb up the hill from the high street and the turn I didn't take earlier. Lost no more. I had hoped I could uphold Malcolm X's request of Haley, but I don't think that is possible. For it is the writer's task to translate the idioglossias we all live within so that we may experience each other, learn, and be better together. "Don't you dare make him into an epic hero," said one of the individuals I interviewed. Fear not, for as a fan of George R.R. Martin, I take to heart the lessons he teaches us, one of them being that in real life there are no heroes or villains—just people.

The hidden beauty in *A Very British Muslim Activist* is that Ghayas shows us that whatever we may be or whomever we may appear to be, this is not destiny, but something fluid, changeable in an instant, and something we should all work hard to cultivate as he did. Sometimes that requires asking for forgiveness, or dishing out some forgiveness for others. Other times, it just requires helping each other out. As I climbed the hill, the street sign bearing the name of the address in my phone shined brighter than the lights of Las Vegas and in a much more refreshing manner. A car pulled up beside me, the first sign of life other than the nightmares in the shadows revealed itself. A cab driver waved at me. I must have looked quite the sight. A sweaty American kid with two suitcases (one of which was broken so I had it heaved up on my shoulder) and a backpack. "You need help, friend?" To this, one can't help but smile the grin of a madman. "Thank you, but I think I've found where I need to be."

C Scott Jordan
06 September 2019
Kuala Lumpur

ACKNOWLEDGEMENTS

JUST AS THE story of Ghayas is beyond the scope of one man's life, the attempt to find all the lost stories and fragments of memories comprising such a tale took the efforts of many. It is almost certain that I will be incapable of recalling all those who need to be thanked for making sure that this British Muslim's story reverberates into the future, beyond where you, fair reader, stand at this point in time.

In giving thanks, I must begin with Ghayas and Talat Siddiqui, who allowed me to invade their home and their history (not once but twice!) and accommodated my American-sized appetite, especially for coffee, tea and biscuits. Their hospitality and tireless efforts to assist and make me feel comfortable is exemplary of what I've come to find as SOP in the British Muslim community. I must give a very special thanks to Talat for her help in organising people for me to speak with, crafting my navigations through London in search of old memories, and filling in on some of the details lost to all others.

Where the Siddiquis would provide the groundwork both in story and in my process of crafting this story, it is in their children that I obtained much of the meat for the story and to whom I had to rely on for the minutiae. Asim, with his near encyclopaedic knowledge of his father's life and of contemporary British history, was both essential for filling in the skeleton of the story and for creative input from the narrative style to the cover design. Along with Asim, Faiza, Uzma and Salman also helped add colour to the story through their views of the events and were my ultimate Supreme Court of accountability concerning dates and the finer details.

Ehsan Masood must be thanked for being the grand architect behind this project. His tireless efforts to make this book happen are the primary reason you are holding it in your hands. His preliminary interviews with the Siddiquis helped to establish the backdrop of this tale and provided an excellent starting place for organising a life spanning eight decades. His efforts as a master editor are the main reason you can understand this story through my thick American accent.

For details and stories from the life of Ghayas, I spent several weeks in London in the winter of 2018/19. Exceptional coffee and tea accompanied the more traditional interviews conducted while others took place in ancient, beautiful buildings, trying to yell into a phone and listen over the ruckus of other cafégoers in the nearest coffee shop with free Wifi, and through the cyberspace of Skype, fighting the signal's attempts to fade out and undermine the project. One interview even took place spanning the Circle line from Westminster. I owe a special thanks to Amjad Hussain, Lateef Owaisi, Mufti Abdul Kader Barkatulla, Maulana Ovaisi, Riaz Patel, Gita Sahgal, Martin Shaw, Mohammed Moussa, Mohtashim Shaikh, Ahmed Versi, Shaista Gohir, Sarfraz Abidi, Nauman Khan and Raza Ali for lovely conversations and their input for this book.

A thank you is owed to Jamil Chishti and Beacon Books for publishing this book with great speed in order to get it out for Ghayas's 80th Birthday.

I wish to thank Merryl Wyn Davies for being my counsellor through my first Ramadan, the period I thought would be a brilliant opportunity to write the first draft of this book.

I am forever grateful to Ziauddin Sardar who showed me to this door of opportunity like many others before and many others that lie ahead. He is the one to be praised or condemned for waking me from my dogmatic slumber.

I am indebted to the Muslim Institute and the greater British Muslim community for not only making me feel welcomed like a member of the family but allowing me to tell the story that is truly theirs and oh-so very important for all of our futures.

Prologue

JAMSHORO, 1962

A WOMAN'S CRIES echoed through the dusty afternoon streets of the infantile township. The entity born of her wailing sorrows condemned to wander the crowded ruckus of the late afternoon comings and goings. A dinned cacophony dashed to the cadence of the wind, taking its leave where constructs failed to fill voided space. Treading foot and wheel kept the ground firmly in its place below. Drowning within the hubbub of homeward bound traffic, conversations in various stages of a multitude of varieties, random outbursts of man, machine or animal, and the lyrical, yet domineering, *salat al-'asr adhaan*. The woman's anguish would get no auditory justice here. She was a normal woman dressed modestly, her head beneath a *dupatta*, who might have faded into the grand mural of poverty, hunger and desperation. It is the seemingly eternal mural we are all aware of, but all too often our eyes remain shielded in its presence. Shame, embarrassment or what have you; the image is not uncommon, especially in this part of the world. Empathy is numbed before the revving engine of modernity. An ignorant solace might be found in the hope that her collective tears might pass on to the earth, continuing the great cycle, giving life where it had otherwise been denied. As the afternoon traded for dusk, the zephyrs blew the orphaned echoes of a day's struggle off with the Indus into the Arabian Sea, and whatever waited beyond.

The descending sun gave break to the harsh summer heat, signalling the end of another long day's work. The true rush hour would come at the cession of the day's classes at the university.

1

An army of eager minds flooding into the city, surrounding the campus to enjoy their evening meal, relaxation and camaraderie. Jamshoro was what the Westerner would call a 'college town'. Not a decade had passed since the town had proliferated out of a barren stretch along the Western Bank of the Indus River, opposite its sibling city of Hyderabad. Jamshoro was designated as the site for the construction of Sindh University, the river's isolation allowing for study undisturbed by the bustling metropolis to the East. Atop the ruins of a civilisation lost but forever in memory, a town grew alongside the university to provide housing and services for the inflowing student population. Children of a new country with star-studded eyes, hungry for the future; a concept parts of the world such as these had never before given much credence to.

It was almost as if the entirety of Jamshoro was an elaborate plan to bring one particular student to this very point in space and time. Dressed in a suit and tie, the standard professional attire for the young Pakistani university student of this era, he wore well-combed, jet black hair and sported a close and finely trimmed moustache—the male facial fashion in vogue during this time. He was a bit shorter than his fellow students and of an average build. Another day of balancing complicated chemical equations and meticulous experimental design in the books, he looked forward to the reprieve the evenings provided, both from the climate and the mental exhaustion of his studies.

At the gates of the university, he took in a deep breath of liberate air. The public was a series of individuals, waves and particles driven by their own motives towards their subjective ends. The sight of nearly avoided collisions poured out onto the streets, to and fro, most of them completely unaware of those around them, let alone their histories, backgrounds or dreams. Or the consequences, perhaps even the dangers, that lay upon the intersection of any two or more of these trajectories. A nameless member of this ensemble performing its chaotic choreography, our moustached man was just another particle in the cloud, driven by his own valence.

That is, until he wasn't.

The innumerable moments a breath takes from inhalation to exhalation provided the window needed to radically alter our moustached hero's course. A breath begot a name as he stepped from the collective haze of commuters in every direction. His name was Ghayasuddin Siddiqui. Ghayas for short. Just as he was about to go forth into the fray of other individuals, his attention was captured by something stronger than a faint cry above the roar. It was an utterance. An acknowledgement of the Other. Her cries shook distinct from the evening's caterwaul with an irritating dissonance. Ghayas's particle motion was seized before the absolute zero of this Other's need for help.

Breaking from his evening's programme, Ghayas's deadened legs dragged side to side as his head searched for the source of help's need. And just before him, at the street's edge, there sat a normal woman. He approached her and looked down at her. His eyes widening as he closed in, examining what could cause this woman so much pain. *Salaam*, he would have greeted her. What was the matter? Was she okay? Could he help her?

The situation was much more dire than Ghayas could have imagined. This woman's husband had just died and she had no money or means to give him the proper funeral required to set his soul at rest in the hereafter.

The young Ghayas was overcome by compassion, taking on this woman's sorrows. How terrible a fate that a man might die and be unable to have his last wishes fulfilled. More horrible yet, his beloved would remain behind, powerless without the means to see out that last wish. This was an injustice and Ghayas could not abide injustice. For on the surface, he was yet another student in the field of chemical engineering, but beneath this veneer of a scholarly identity, he was of the truly political. An activist. And that spirit could not be denied its appetite, once it had tasted

3

the scent of injustice. This particular individual was of that all-too-rare class of humans who have an inability to sit idle where a wrong would otherwise be allowed to reign rampant. Simply incomprehensible. A contradiction. The division by zero. Nothing else mattered at this moment. Both the nobility of science and the rejuvenation of rest would have no value in an unjust world. His mission in life was to see this poor woman's husband laid to peace and his soul allowed to travel to the great beyond. Only then could the world be set back to something at least more normal, where external and internal peace could attain harmony and the day's work truly be done right.

Ghayas quickly came to learn that this woman and her husband were Hindus. Indeed, a rarer sight this far into Pakistan, this long beyond the partition from India. Though judging by her situation, she was amongst the many unfortunate spirits unable to afford the treacherous journey of the great migration that occurred two decades prior. Of course, there is also the existential crisis of leaving one's home and the tethers of one's historical position. No matter, for something higher than both this woman and Ghayas, and for what it's worth, the whole of old India and the whole world, had set the stage for this collision. Ghayas, you see, was not just an activist in spirit, but had a preternatural talent for connecting the heart and the brain. He could both organise and mobilise people, individuals with their own selfish pursuits, in chase of a collective goal. Ah, but this particular case presented a new challenge for Ghayas. His usual displays of activism had fallen into the realm of ideas he knew well and understood. Ghayas knew others existed in the world; in fact, he had seen and interacted with others of all the diversity of the South Asian world. As all of these people looked and spoke the same, he had assumed that they, like him, had essentially the same historical and motivational foundation. Ghayas was learning the ignorance of his unknowing, none as important as the intricate distinctions of the Hindu religion and its culture.

But ignorance need only be temporary and what is an organiser who does not utilise those whom he organises. Ah! thought Ghayas. He bent down to the woman. Excusing himself, he would return post-haste and with help! Ghayas ran back within the university walls. For you see, Ghayas had remembered, in his comings and goings around campus, one particular face. Ghayas had recalled meeting a Hindu boy. Surely, he would know what to do!

Luckily it did not take long for Ghayas to track down the Hindu boy he had met not long before this moment. He had even remembered his name, beckoning him. Ghunsham! My brother! There was a grave injustice happening, just outside that very university and Ghayas needed his help. Please, Ghunsham, Ghayas urged, having ignited a noble quest before the boy. Young people the world over waited in endless anticipation for a purpose. A call. This Muslim guy needed Ghunsham. Of course, he would follow.

Ghunsham hunched over, catching his breath from the quick sprint required to keep pace with a motivated Ghayas as he brought them before the sad woman, her sorrow at least in some way diminished by Ghayas's promise to return fulfilled. Quick, brother. This woman, she is a Hindu! Like you, Ghunsham. Her husband has died and she has no means of burying his body and releasing his soul to the peace of the hereafter! Ghunsham tripped over his words. Indeed, he was a Hindu boy, but he did not know all of the ritualistic particulars of a Hindu funeral. He was no priest, but Ghunsham could see Ghayas was missing some of the niceties between Hindu and Muslim custom. You see, for starters, her husband needed to be cremated, not buried, as was custom in Islam. Ah! shouted Ghayas, excellent point! So how would they arrange for the cremation of this poor woman's departed husband? Ghunsham reacted so as to not disappoint the man who called him to duty. They needed to see a Hindu priest and Ghunsham knew where one lived, not far from there.

A plan materialising inside of Ghayas's head, he headed away to bring this poor woman and her husband's body to the home of the Hindu priest. So Ghayas charged Ghunsham with comforting the woman while he gathered more help and saw to arranging transport for everyone. The sun now sank well below the horizon as twilight quickly turned for full night. Ghayas confronted a gang of his closest Muslim friends. They knew Ghayas and had been mobilised to demonstrate under his leadership in the past. When he said a grave injustice was afoot, they would come running, loyal to the end, no further question needed. A small battalion of Muslims at his side, Ghayas then made for the university administrative offices. The office knew Ghayas's face as readily as his reputation. This boy was a troublemaker and would stop at no level to pester and annoy until his way was had. The request for a university bus was peculiar but the registrar looked to the clock, which ticked ever closer to closing time, and knew that if Ghayas's request was fulfilled, he would leave him in peace. Ghayas would add a smile and a clamour of gratitude to the package.

Now in possession of university transport with a small army of Muslim students, Ghayas returned to the poor woman and Ghunsham. Quickly, they loaded up the husband's body and filed into the small bus. Ghunsham directed them through the streets of Jamshoro to the modest and quiet street upon which the Hindu holy man resided. Midnight close at hand, Ghayas galloped through the front garden and began rapping on the front door. After countless delayed moments, a half-dressed and mostly asleep Hindu priest answered the door.

Son, do you realise what hour it is? Yes, Ghayas responded, but a great injustice of religious significance has occurred. The Hindu priest looked at the Muslim student and then to his bus, followed by his gang of fellow Muslim students, a Hindu student, and a poor Hindu woman. Confusion abound, the Hindu priest thought to turn around and double lock the door if he knew what was good for him. Ghayas pleaded. He explained the situation. How he came across the woman in need and what befell her husband. The efforts of the admirable Ghunsham and his comrade students. An epic legend painted, our noble heroes stood before their final trial. A Hindu funeral would be needed to complete their quest and thus deliver a victorious tip for justice on the great scales of the universe. Before he could begin to contemplate what concern a Muslim boy had with a poor Hindu woman's misfortune, he looked into Ghayas's eyes. He knew what raw passion looked like. Based upon that look, this boy had a fire in his heart that bore a restless soul and if the priest didn't finish dressing and follow through on this man's requests, he would rouse the entirety of Jamshoro in pursuit of this 'justice'. The line between hooligan and hero nearly erased, this holy man was not a gambling man.

So, as the earliest hours which logic dictates as morning past, the university transport carried a determined Ghayas, his unlikely fellowship now made complete with the priest in full regalia towards the Hindu temple on the other side of town. Upon arriving at the temple, Ghayas's band of justice warriors unloaded the body as the priest readied the temple and the incinerator. After laying flowers around for ornamentation, the priest carried out the elaborate ritual of prayer, reciting hymns and mantras. He invited the gentlemen to join the poor woman in viewing the body before it was to be committed to the flames. Ghayas, surrounded by his fellow Muslim students, sat next to Ghunsham, giving him a classic look of satisfaction. He had done good. They all had. Meanwhile, the priest oversaw the cremation of the husband as the woman's tears turned from sorrow to relief and humble joy. Her beloved's spirit was now allowed to carry on, freed from the body. Following the funeral, Ghayas, Ghunsham, the Muslim brothers and the priest, stood along the banks of the Indus as the woman cast her love's ashes into the river's continuity. From the earth we all come, so to it we shall one day return. The woman

7

would be incapable of expressing her gratitude to the Muslim boys, the priest or Ghunsham. Burdens lifted and peace was allowed to return to this riverside town.

As Ghayas rode back in the university transport, dropping everyone off at their respective homes, he looked out before that eerie illumination morning provided just before the sun broke over the horizon. A smile appeared upon his face. Ghayas's smile was unique, stretching along the lower edge of his face, paralleling his jawline. A peculiar smile that conveyed complete joy and utter satisfaction with the beauty of life.

For that day at least, justice had been delivered.

Chapter One

RESTLESS SOUL

AN OFFICIAL BIRTH certificate will tell you that Ghayasuddin Siddiqui was born on 1 December, 1939. The truth though could have been anywhere from the addition or subtraction of a couple of days to the further side of a different month. It was said by his mother that it had been raining heavily that day. Time moved slower then, and prohibitive travel and red tape frequently offset the official registration of newborns. The world was on the brink of yet another great war and the British Raj had greater concerns at hand than the accuracy of some Indian boy's birth in some distant village.

Populism and fascist sentiment were taking the European continent by storm. The ageing established powers shook in their boots as change barrelled towards them at Mach speed. Colonialism had made the world a smaller place. Ancient trade roots had been co-opted to create an interconnected global economic bloodline fed by way of industrial development, thrust upon the edge of a blade, and upon the development of the twentieth century's war machinery, left to the submarine's mercy. Subjugation of the African and Asian continents resulted in a global wound that had been left to bleed, drop by drop, rebellion after rebellion, for generations. A shock to the system was inevitable.[1] Ready or not, the age of empires was at its twilight. Just as there seemed nothing left to conquer, the hearts and minds of humanity willingly chained themselves to the rule of ideology, nationalism, and the pursuit of dominance over all others. A European flag flying from every corner of the globe, it was time for the so-called

9

'civilised' continent to descend into the barbarism of world war. One last show of glory, for King and country, but not much else.[2]

The cost of this show, in both blood and gold, would leave the great empires unsustainable. Their hold on their colonies had, in the lead up to World War II, only been by the grace of a stubborn case of rigor-mortis. Both the riches of the "less than civilised world" and the strategic importance, for war and trade, were too tempting a price to be denied by even the least greedy of imperialists. War by war, the winner was allowed to keep this increasingly expensive trophy, yet the losers were to turn their colonies over to the victors. Each new colonial administration had to begin from scratch to develop a dominating system, complete with institutions, to run the machine. As the machine grew so did the output, and with it the effort required for maintenance and upkeep. As the colonies themselves suffered, their pain too was exported in the form of troublesome revolts and, essentially, a complete misunderstanding of reality, as decisions made from thousands of miles away over lands and people completely alien to the powers that be was reaching its limit.

World War II was less a direct cause as it was the final straw. Empires exhausted their machines and the will of the Other struck at the slightest hint of opportunity. By Victory in Europe Day, the atrophy would prove too much and the Other refused to remain under the feet of European rule any longer. This was especially the case for Great Britain. The empire which the sun never set upon would spend its first New Year after its glorious defeat of continental fascism in the dark. Huddled in bombed out ruins, enjoying rationed goods and resources, the British people could hardly afford the petrol to take a stroll down the free streets of London. The recovery would be slow, and require the efforts of a nation and considerable help from outside. But for a brief moment in time, the illustrious capital of the British Empire reflected the state of her distant subjects spread across the furthest reaches of the globe.[3]

Only the flaws of the Mughal Empire survived the two hundred years of British rule in the subcontinent. By technical rendering, British rule topped out at a clean one hundred and ninety years between Clive's victory at Plassey and Gandhi's independence, but the memory of two hundred years is etched upon the hearts of all of Mother India's children. It also has a nicer ring to it. In that time, the British did establish a highly sophisticated train system that spanned the subcontinent as well as implement an education system and a language that would allow the Indian people to climb the ladder of global society. There is also the groundwork by which the vast area of India could be unified. And cricket. Of course, these gifts were not necessarily provided out of the goodness of the Queen-Empress's heart. They were the unintended residuals of a very conscious strategy to dominate.

The trains, very cleverly, reoriented the ancient economic trade circles of Asia so that all roads might then lead to London. The English language and education only sought to perpetuate the greater glory and might of Britain. The harmony between peoples of different languages, religions and lands witnessed in the Asia of old—ruined by the British high command in India— only further revealed the sickly attempts at such unions as seen today in Europe and the West. Difference was the vital element to British rule. Ironically, this was also the key to Britain's ability to unify the subcontinent. 'Divide and conquer' was elementary level knowledge in the lesson of British imperialism and India was perhaps its most shining example. The harmony that Mughal India had attained between peoples of different ethnicities and faiths was deranged effectively through its being rooted in the very institutions Britain brought to the subcontinent. Emphasise these differences so that they will be too preoccupied with fighting each other to think of resisting the Raj. And as for cricket? Well, let it not be said that the British only exported misfortune.

The dark cloud that accompanied the arrival of the East India Company on the shores of Surat was not India's first bout of inclement weather. Delhi has been sacked numerous times, perhaps even beyond what history has taken account for. Control of the territory has passed between warlords and emperors alike, from the Persians and Ottomans of the West to the Chinese and Mongolians of the East. Alexander the Great even claimed the mystical land as a piece of his vast empire. But under the reign of the Mughal emperors, India flourished in a golden age it has not since seen. The Mughals did not interfere in local or ethnic affairs, preferring to cooperate with peoples of various backgrounds and belief structures. While Persian was the official language, the elites used an altered form of the language: Urdu. Urdu borrows vocabulary from the Persian, Turkic and Arabic languages. Hindi is essentially the same language, only using a different written form, drawing from Sanskrit.

Allowing local freedom in line with the rule of the central Mughal governance, India was allowed to be the crossroads of many languages, cultures, and religions. This resulted in some of the world's most beautiful art and architecture, which still reside throughout India, Pakistan and Bangladesh. The Mughals built the Taj Mahal as the flag bearer among a list of forts, tombs, and mosques that showcased their beauty to the modern world. Beautiful traditions of painting, calligraphy, and the highest achievements in poetry arose during this era. Science and technology also reached new ground under the Mughals. The Indian economy rose to global dominance. The Mughals built the cities from which the British Empire would extract its wealth. The Mughals established the industrial traditions of textiles and manufacturing that would be grossly capitalised upon by the West. Historians currently debate what led to the decline of the Mughals, having to correct some of the bias history forged when the first Britons arrived with the East India Company, and continued throughout the rule of the Raj. What is clear is that threads were laid bare and unravelled with great ease, strand by strand, at the hands of British colonialists.

Before the British, it is commonly said, there were no beggars on the streets. Division was not merely a tool of maths for the British. It was the tool by which India and numerous other colonies were controlled. While the caste system already existed in India, dating back to the times of the Aryans, the British system spared no pre-existing cultural flaws in their strategy. The caste system was duly absorbed into the divides which fuelled the capitalist mode of production. A way of life. Private property was a poison which once dissolved into the water basin of India could not be inoculated against. Whereas before the British, all was common, under the Raj there were landowners and subsequently, those without. The burgeoning economy of the Mughals was now being siphoned and extradited to the land and business owners. The British worked quickly to bring India under the fold of capitalism, turning the once beautiful country into another machine, the latest product of the industrial revolution, complete with its tendencies towards inequality and high levels of pollution.

The idea of Mughal India as the Golden Eagle slowly faded beneath thick soot pumped out by the British Raj. This memory only persisted through song and poetic verse passed down from elder to child. Once the centre of the world, India now resided at a distant corner of the British machine. This is the India Ghayasuddin Siddiqui was born into. Into a world ready to tear itself apart, and a deeply ill Mother India. These tectonic trifles swirled around in the clouds above the head of Ghayas, a restless boy. The city nearest his birthplace was Meerut, just east of Delhi, and home to the 1857 Mutiny, regarded by Muslims as the First War of Independence. This was when Hindu and Muslim soldiers from the British East India Company's army rebelled against their British superiors. The new subjects made clear their position on British changes to India.[2]

Ghayas's grandfather was a chief of his village near Meerut and owned a large farm, which improved upon his marrying

Ghayas's grandmother, a strategic move by way of social ladder ascension. This marriage was arranged, as was common at the time. This point is often misunderstood by those unfamiliar with the tradition. A difference needs to be noted here between arranged and forced marriages. Arranged marriages were not simply parents selecting a stranger for their child to dedicate their life to, based upon a criterion set to maintain, if not improve, the social standing of all parties involved. Arranged marriages were a diplomatic act in its most puritanical form. Parents essentially became third party negotiators, carefully weighing the considerations of the child, the potential spouse, and the potential spouse's family. The process was often drawn out over many years, sometimes even from conception. Delicate and elegant, the arrangement became an obsession for many a mother, auntie, and elder sister. Fundamentally the tradition is rooted in respect, security, stability, and love, especially for the others involved. Compatibility would foster a respectful and caring relationship, which would be the ideal environment in which to bring up the next generation. Forced marriages are a corruption of arranged marriages as the concern and opinion of the potential spouses is disregarded for the selfish motives of the parents or of one spouse over the other. Forced marriages are not proper contracts since both parties are not entering willingly, and one party being under duress is a fundamental contradiction of the tenets of Islam. Such marriage contracts, then, must be null and void.

The arranged marriage of Ghayas's grandparents proved fruitful, so much so that when Ghayas's father and his siblings came together, they realised that the division of the land for inheritance would leave the many with little. Since Ghayas's father, Saeeduddin, was not the oldest, he decided to leave the family farm and pursue a career working for the British Raj eager to give out jobs to the people of the subcontinent. Saeeduddin worked for the Customs and Excise Department, one of the first government structures established by the British in India. Their duty was to administer custom law and provide for the collection of import duties and land revenue. This post made politics a major concern for Ghayas's nuclear family. It also put them at the mercy of the Raj's needs. Thus, Ghayas would be born closer to Delhi where Saeeduddin was posted at the time.

Bullock cart would provide the proper Indian transport for a restless and rebellious young boy as he travelled between his home in Delhi and his grandparent's home in Meerut. From an early age, Ghayas had no time for authority or obedience, but he stood respectfully beside his father as other members of the department and politically active visitors passed through their home. Saeeduddin also received a healthy diet of political pamphlets and periodicals which once he had reviewed, often found their way to the attention of young Ghayas's eyes, between the sugar cane and rowdy boyhood adventures.

A sponge in his youth, Ghayas would, snapshot by snapshot, absorb the climate of the age. At times, without even realising it, he was growing in a bird's nest lined with the scraps of colonialism and bits and pieces of what would come next. Nationalism, religious identity, and the will for self-determination, are intoxicating for youth. This became fruit rapidly ripening as the British Empire's grip on India began to slack. Existential identity and enlightenment were the sparks that ignited the Second World War and their particulates travelled far once in the open air. Ghayas' father would have to relocate the family at the Raj's desire from one administrative centre to the next. One of these movements took the family to Incholi. This village would become famous as the selected venue for an early meeting between Jawaharlal Nehru, a pupil of Mahatma Gandhi, who would become the first Prime Minister of an India independent of Great Britain, and Muhammad Ali Jinnah, a lawyer who would become the first President of the new nation carved from British India, Pakistan. Both men had taken advantage of the opportunity of the education provided by the British, studying in the West, and used that essential tool to untether Mother India from the suffocating vines of empire and forge the two modern states we see on the map today. In the small village of Incholi, the independence movement developed. Meanwhile, young Ghayas was being developed into the young man who would, one day soon, fight for causes the young boy was unable to imagine, A boy at play in a crumbling British India, his father shaking hands with various government officials, introducing his young son, his head down, clinging to his father's side in the respectful gesture of that moment in history.

A tension subtly grew throughout the land. A snowballing disquiet reverberated in the air. The tools by which the British ruled India were beginning to backfire. India was, in alliance with Great Britain, at war with Germany. But the enemy in India wore a more familiar uniform and the fight was closer at hand than the battles fought on the African, the Middle Eastern and the European fronts. High tea was prepared using an increasingly bitter brew, left to steep beyond the point at which the cup goes cold. The policy of divide and rule was reaching a level of absurdity that stood to fracture the British Raj's fragile union.

In the city of Allahabad, the hometown of Nehru, Ghayas attended two years of school at the Islamic College. While the name may appear misleading, the Islamic College had no intention of forging the Maulana or Imam Siddiqui. In fact, the Islamic College only differed from the Hindu one in that there was a morning prayer at the beginning of the day. In fact, Ghayas does not recall seeing many Hindus or Sikhs in his childhood, largely because these identities were not at the forefront of the Indian citizen's consciousness. These various religions of the world flourished together in societal tolerance under the Mughals. Not just the major groups of Muslims, Hindus, and Sikhs, but the various subgroups within them as well. The harmony amongst different religious groups in Mughal India is well-illustrated in the tales of Anarkali. A dancer in the court of the Mughal emperor, Anarkali fell in love with the Crown Prince Jahangir. Their love transcended potential religious divides. Dismayed, the Emperor Akbar sentenced Anarkali to be entombed between two walls to prevent the affair. This action was not undertaken for her being of a different religion, but because her low class was not befitting a bride of a future emperor. There are many examples of the Mughal nobility marrying outside of the faith, such as to Hindu princesses. Numerous concessions were made to allow for a Muslim empire to rule over a predominantly Hindu population.

Just as the British brought such pervasive Western notions as capitalism and private property, which perverted the pre-existent class system of India to create a rich and poor class, the British introduction of power structures brought new value to the Indian's religious identity. In the two centuries of British rule, clashes between the religions, particularly the Hindus and Muslims, were constructed to keep the Indians fighting each other as opposed to their subjugators. Just as the pitted 'enemies' were beginning to find common ground for unison against British rule, the Raj introduced the Government of India Act of 1935. This legislative gesture had the innocuous appeal of the first steps towards independence, but something much more sinister lay within the details. While the Indian people were given more power to govern themselves, the legislative body created was to have designated seats for Hindus, Muslims and Sikhs based on population. Disaster struck after the first elections where Nehru and his party, The Indian National Congress, took a vast majority of the Hindu seats, yet the Muslims voted in favour of less nationalistic and smaller parties, giving control of the legislature to the Hindus. Jinnah, only a little over a decade before calling for a unified India free from Britain, now saw the potential horror of a post-British India becoming a Hindu state. The concept of a Muslim minority was born, and Jinnah equated the Muslims in post-British India to the next generation of slaves. Jinnah needed another option. If the Hindus were to have a state, then the Muslims would need a state of their own.

For various 'reasons' the British needed a swift exit out of India. One of the reasons they gave was that it was better to hand over the country quickly, rather than drawing out the process and creating further complications. After all, the negotiations required in brokering the end of a political relationship between two entities can easily be bogged down in endless debate and growing discontent on all sides. Back in Britain, the reality was much more dire. The Second World War had left the country devastated and the resources and time spent on the distant colony could be put to better use rebuilding the homefront. Although it should be noted that despite this desperate state, the British establishment still debated giving up India. Many demanded that India remaining under British control was important for the economic rebound needed following the war as well as for the continued perception of unity under the Empire. Britain had won, had they not? Why would they be required to relinquish their reward?

Yet the atrocities committed by the British and the detrimental effects of the Raj on society and culture proved a step too far for the Other. The Other chose to act and the snowball effect of revolution had proven ill-fated for the empire even at its strongest, which by the twentieth century's midpoint, Great Britain was very far from. The last Viceroy of India Lord Louis Mountbatten brokered a deal between Nehru and Jinnah. There would be two states: India and Pakistan. However, the task of drawing the partition of the new Indian world would be given to the Oxford alumni Cyril Radcliffe, a lawyer whose credentials included never having been to India. Using outdated maps and census material Radcliffe drew lines on paper, in a fashion perfected by the British, which would bleed for generations after the ink had dried.

The result was a central India, holding the territories with the highest Muslim populations as well as the three main centres of economic power, Delhi, Calcutta, and Bombay, between an East and West divided Pakistan. The borders would leave much to be desired in the engineering of the border near India's Punjab region and East Pakistan's denial of Calcutta. Last minute amendments and perhaps a sleight of hand resulted in the controversial gifting of Gurdaspur District to India, creating the Kashmir situation we see today. Pakistan was left at a considerable economic disadvantage and vast segments of the population found themselves on the 'wrong' side of Radcliffe's lines. A mass migration was launched. Hindus fled the East as the Muslims raced to the West, and the Bengalis were left to pray, tying their camels for the storms to come. The laws of physics demand that two opposing forces create friction. The movement of the Hindus one way and the Muslims in the opposite found its friction in a wave of clashes, riots, and massacres. Jinnah promised the garden of paradise in the new state for Muslims—if one could survive the journey, that is. The roads became dangerous microcosms of anarchy and the trains, those not set ablaze by one side or the other, constituted ideal bottlenecks for religious difference. Uncertainty fanned fear, the fear that you might be the minority in a new country subject to servitude before the new majority.[5] Everyone was a refugee.

Over one million people died as a result of the partition of India. Upwards of fifteen million were forced to flee their homes. Countless thousands of children vanished, never to be seen again, thousands of women raped, the horrors they faced left to our darkest imaginations. Not that they could be located, for in such chaos who remains to do such calculus, but to give exact numbers would allow for the mind to quickly write such totals off as insane or even impossible. Thus in noting these details, it is requested that the reader stops to think, not allowing such totals, numbers that represent people who suffered incomprehensible pains, to become a matter to brush off, or heaven forbid, perhaps even become impressed by. Words do not do the injustice its proper service. Although order needs constant reiteration and evolution, its tearing down and rebuilding is a most violent affair.

Even the slightest threat of anarchy and loss of control burns through the hearts and minds like an unquenchable forest fire.

This was not helped by the British departure plan. Some label this the first Brexit, having been moved up by 10 months, dashing any hope the people of the lost Mughal Empire had to plan for what was to come next. A hurricane of violence and polarisation dragged the once great world civilisation into a crazed person-against-person fight for survival, just as an earthquake often arrives quickly and with little warning. The fault lines in British Indian society were made physical, forcing all to question their identity and immediate survival. It was imperative for all of the Crown's former subjects to ensure that they found themselves on the right side before the dust settled, lest their rights and dignity be cast to the wind of whosoever was to fill the vacuum left.

We use words like 'genocide' and 'ethnic cleansing' to describe events of destruction on incomprehensible scales, yet what happened during this period demands a harsher term that puts these events in equal opposition and ubiquity, beyond the simplistic motives of two groups of people being different and thus in aggression against one another. The largest mass migration of human populations in contemporary times only gives the first page of a dark and twisted story. The conclusion is still being lived out even into the contemporary age of this book's writing. Two traumatised and injured nations looking across a line constructed by their former subjugators, through black and blue eyes with jaws clenched in never-ending hate, unable to transcend bitter grudges and broken brotherhood. Suspicion, fear, pain, and mistrust ride within the morning fog that roams over Kashmir, merely a microcosm for the tensions resident where once there had been one country of loosely interwoven peoples. This is the legacy of colonisation. While the wounds have grown and new scars have festered after the British left, the misery they cast Mughal India into cannot be forgotten or underscored.[6]

Yet the partition occurred in less than just times, at least from a global perspective. As those once labelled 'evil-doers' faced international tribunals for wrongs committed, it would again be the 'victors' who could escape the punishment of justice's cold balance. In his book, *Our Times*, A.N. Wilson would refer to the partition of India as a "gross mismanagement" which is a gross short-selling of the affair. Yet even he equated the accidental viceroy, Lord Mountbatten, to a mass murderer. Skilled in negotiation to the highest level, Mountbatten managed to walk his way through one of history's greatest retreats leaving Britain's reputation untarnished.[7] The historian Andrew Roberts argued that he should have been court-martialled upon returning to London, where he was instead hailed a national hero.[8] Yet Trafalgar Square still stands proud and the Foreign Office regales in images of a story, both inaccurate and insensitive, that disregarded the golden egg laying goose that India was, giving Britannia her wealth and global dominance. Even today, justice is a time-sensitive matter what with statutes of limitations and justice having no interest in the concerns of the Other in the twentieth century and, unfortunately, beyond. If this was to change in the new millennium, would it have the integrity to admit fault? Could it make right what it left so wrong?

The Siddiqui family found themselves on the Indian side of India. This contradiction is emphasised by the fact that the Siddiqui flight was less of a migration than it was an exodus. The Siddiquis, just like countless other Muslim families in Nehru's India, knew it as home. That quintessential safety. The rock that does not move in spite of all of life's tumultuous storms. On the 14th of August 1947, Lord Mountbatten would administer the oath of independence to Jinnah at midnight. It would be Friday, signalling the end of the week and British India.

The utterance of those words had moved the rock. Home was now over there, but home does not move so easily. Families were torn asunder choosing between what they had and what they could have. Saeeduddin needed to follow his government, the source of his pay cheque. For if the rhetoric floating about was true, he may not have a job in Hindu India and would he risk potentially subjecting his family to slavery? It was decided that the family would travel by train to the city of Sukkur along the shores of the Indus River. There, an old friend of Saeeduddin's would help the Siddiquis settle in. So, lost in the chaos which the subcontinent had been thrown into, Ghayas's mother, Batool, saw the trip as a long holiday. After all, this whole thing would soon resolve itself and they could return to their home, with the rest of their family. The Siddiquis would return to Meerut and Incholi to say their goodbyes to family and begin their arduous journey to Jinnah's paradise.

The summer of partition gave way to the winter's migration. It was well known that the railways, though set to their potential destinations, provided no guarantee of making it there intact or unharmed. In fact, the track record of such train journeys would have the odds stacked against Ghayas, his parents, his four sisters and three brothers.[9] From Meerut the first leg of the journey was rather routine, a quick trip to Delhi. It constituted the last breath taken before the dive into the darkness of a new sea. This train was not your ordinary transport to Delhi. It was a special train that would not stop, but continue on to transverse the volatile Punjab region, delivering its passengers to Lahore. The lack of punctuality in arrivals and departures could be forgiven, as long as said arrivals actually arrived.

Only a couple of months after the founding of Pakistan, on the precipice of Ghayas's eighth birthday, the train departed from India by cover of night. Fear ruled this exodus by way of thick chains of tension. Every loud bump along the track, exhaust spout, or shake of the car was a death blow to the system. Un-certainty beyond the vulnerable hide of the rail-car left the imag-ination to concoct what monsters were possibly laying out there. An unexpected stop could mean the end of the line. Would they be consumed in flames, forced into a catastrophic derailment, suffer bombs or kidnapping, or another punishment worse than death? The family rode through the night, huddled in prayer. For it would be by the grace of God that the Siddiquis would be delivered to the newly minted paradise in the West.

After the partition, like the sweetest of dreams upon waking, the idea that was India would wither, memory unable to recapture the essence as the lack of detail gives way to a collapse. With each passing moment, the sweet dream of India fades before the reverse evolution that constitutes a vanishing. As the imagination tries to construct with what scraps it can cling to, the pieces only become more abstract. Only a restless hunger remains, knowing that what was is no longer. The struggle has lasted for so long that there is no recollection as to why the fighting is occurring in the first place. The conscious is so racked with retrieving the sweet dream of India, that it is unable to sleep again and dream anew.

The fate of the Siddiquis now rested in the train's deliverance to a new paradise and a new dream. On the train, drudged down a less than certain track into the darkness of what lay ahead.

Chapter Two

PAKISTANI SPRING

BORDERS ARE INDEED a strange phenomenon. The belief that upon one step is the 'here' and another is the 'there' involves a remarkable level of intelligence. Fundamentally, borders simply demarcate change. For the human mind this is not enough. Categorisation needs logic and, with the assistance of the imagination, meaning. When land becomes water or a forest becomes a field, becomes a mountain. These are geological, but it is humans who take this to another level. Mine from yours, ours from theirs, home from foreign. Some borders you would not know but for a sign, such as the border between Austria and Hungary. Some are natural like the Mediterranean's separation of Europe from Africa. Others are gross hyperbole such as the DMZ between North and South Korea or Trump's dream wall between Mexico and the United States. What pre-dates the lines we have drawn in the sand and the maps we have come to accept as our world is the notion that when going from one place to another, not only our location has changed. Instead something more fundamental to our being is transformed when passing from the here to the there.

There is an old nautical tradition that when a mariner crosses the international dateline for the first time, travelling between two distinct days in the matter of a few metres, that they have developed a new maturity and wisdom of the seas. Similarly, when a person leaves their homeland, they are quickly labelled a world traveller, bequeathed with a certain wisdom therein acquired. As we leave our homeland, we suddenly are referred to by that identity, which is not always clear when we are submerged within

25

our homes, but suddenly a dazzling banner follows us as we fill our passports with new stamps. Cross enough borders and you begin to lose track of the meaning behind the identity that you share with your homeland. For some of us our surname ties us to a certain identity often arising from an ancestral homeland or profession. It should be remembered that these are all artificial and only exude the power that we give them.

The drawing of Radcliffe's line presented the human brain with an interesting opportunity. When the first wave of immigrants flocked to the United States around the turn of the eighteenth into the nineteenth century, many of their surnames were altered by the officials at Ellis Island. Some even changed their first names to acclimate better to other 'Americans'. Most interestingly, many of these new monikers stuck, passing down through the generations to their offspring. Other immigrants have had comparable experiences. The children—Ghayas and his brothers and sisters, collectively a part of those fleeing one way or the other during partition—felt a certain level of metamorphosis within themselves. But, as in other such stories, where the new name is imposed, Ghayas and his siblings decided to take that power for themselves. They would determine, for themselves, what the future had in store. All of this began with something so innocent as taking on a new family name. Ghayas had always had a fascination with the surname Siddiqui, but that was not his original surname. Rather, huddled in prayer as their train rattled along the tracks towards either a new beginning, or a quick ending to a brief story, Ghayas and his siblings agreed that from their deliverance, they would be children of India no more. As their train pulled into the platform in Lahore, into the new nation of Pakistan, they would disembark as Siddiquis.

Yet, the utterance of a new name is easier proclaimed than bestowed meaning. For the meaning would come in survival. The power entailed within the surname Siddiqui lay not in some child's game to pass the loud yet, in retrospect, rather harmless storm. The power of the Siddiqui name lay in its testament to childhood's end, both for this particular clan of four girls and four boys, but also for a nation, an identity, and a society torn asunder in the aftermath of empire. The train tickets were as good as pennies dropped into wishing wells, for the steel car barrelling through the Punjab had been famous for ending its trips in numerous locations, the least of which being their intended destination. For the British Raj had departed the subcontinent, taking with them the chains that kept at bay the dogs of war. Yet, for generations they had starved these dogs. Divide and rule instilled an artificial, yet all the more intoxicating hate between the Muslims, Hindus and Sikhs. The Punjab, being one of many epicentres for this new war, had housed all three peoples once upon a time in harmony. But the orchestration of the British exit from India opened the flood gates with utter disregard for what would happen when oil and water were free to run together. Intended or not, partition was the logical conclusion, and hate never dies quickly or quietly. Civil war, genocide, anarchy, nationalism, racism; this is the vocabulary the political scientist used to standardise and, try as they might, even dehumanise the horrors humans are capable of committing.

The Punjab had descended into chaotic madness. All were innocent, yet none were free from punishment. In the fray, families were torn in directions a compass would be useless to decipher. Trains ran west and trains ran east as though, with the setting sun, the border between Pakistan and India was solidifying in the cool night air. Best not to be found on the wrong side come morning! The common fate for these trains of deliverance was to be set ablaze, roasting their fleeing families within. A bomb might be the best-case scenario, making it quick yet no less messy, though the darkest destinations arrived with the quiet that accompanies a train's screeching halt. A locomotion no more, as it would likely never move again. As for the families within, there was the slaughter of the Other's blade painting the countryside red. Rape

27

was not only common, but well-documented, a conscious fear on the mind of those risking the trip. Worst yet, Jinnah's fears were often made reality as the survivors of these stalled trains would be sold into slavery to fulfil unnameable deeds of terror. In the Punjab, there were no heroes or villains. All sides—Muslims, Hindus, and Sikhs—did equally appalling acts, at times appearing to compete in their despicability. No one will ever know the true number of victims from this anarchic horror show. The distinguishing of these evils from all the others that accompanied the partition is no small task. For as the clunking steel box that carried the Siddiquis-to-be through the hell that was came to a meticulous and heart-wrenching stop, the family within held their breath in anticipation of what hand they had been dealt beyond the tracks.

Ghayas's eldest uncle sighted the relief, hands raised in grateful prayer, of a new nation, standing upon the platform in Lahore. The Siddiquis' special train had made it. Later it would be found out that this was the first such migratory train to have actually completed the journey without incident to what they now called Pakistan. A state of their own. Desperate prayer was traded for exultant jubilation as the welcoming embrace between Saeeduddin and his brother sealed what could only be the beginning of a better future. Ghayas and his family would stay in Lahore for a day or two in the ancient splendour of the Mughals. Distinctly Punjab in a now divided region, here was where Indian independence was made official less than two decades before the Siddiqui's arrival. Eleven years after Nehru hoisted the first independent Indian flag in Lahore, the Muslim League and A.K. Fazlul Huq, the first Prime Minister of Bengal, presented the Lahore Resolution. In that spring of 1940, Jinnah metamorphosed from champion of Hindu-Muslim unity into the leader of the Pakistani independence movement. Before the Siddiquis could get comfortable, they were to hop on a Pakistani train, aimed due south, to the new capital: Karachi. Karachi was the one colonial port that Radcliffe had so generously left to the new Pakistani state. In the birthplace of Jinnah, the future of the infant nation would be moulded. The mountain stronghold of Islamabad was still a remote plateau amongst lush forests bridging India and Afghanistan; a postcolonial idea for another day. The pulse of new Pakistan was in the Asian city of lights. Karachi would be the hotbed upon which many a young activist, including Ghayas-uddin, would cut their teeth upon.

A small and insignificant village in a vulnerable location was transformed into a major seaport after the British arrival in the eighteenth century. Ghayas, with his three brothers, four sisters, Batool, and Saeeduddin, entered Karachi with over a million other Muslim refugees from India. The population boom would accompany the growing internationalisation of the city as a hub of many languages, cultures and peoples. Karachi was named as the capital of the new state and would become the centre of commerce and the new Pakistani economy. Distinctly colonial at Pakistan's founding, the city itself would transform, developing its own distinct identity. In Karachi, hopes and dreams were born. A canvas lain stretched out to have ideas and preferences splattered upon it, mixed and refined until modern Pakistan emerged, rising above the other colours. Here a new struggle materialised. A fight for the heart and soul of the Pakistani people. Ghayas in the metamorphosis of adolescence found himself being formed alongside a brand-new nation. A renaissance swirled like a hurricane over Karachi, the gale force winds of ideas tore across the coastal city. Democracy, Islam, law, the state, and the future of the colonial structures left by the British vied for their positioning aside many interpretations and philosophies in this new order.

Jinnah's fear of nationalism would lead him to push for the independent state of Pakistan. He knew the cultivation of paradise would be no easy task and would require continuous work and upkeep. The state was to be a safe place for the Muslim Indians, and in forming a safe place for one group, the hope was

29

to make a safe place for all of God's children. Speaking for the first time to an independent nation, he stated, "You are free, free to go to your temples, free to go to your mosques or to any place of worship in this state of Pakistan."[10] The comparison between Jinnah and George Washington of the United States speaks not only to the love that each man garnered from their country, but the hope and love they trusted their country would bring to its people. "You may belong to any religion or caste or creed—that has nothing to do with the affairs of the state," spoke Jinnah.[11] Perhaps the Mughal zenith was not so distant after all. As Nehru worked to build a secular state, so too did Jinnah on the far side of Radcliffe's line.

History's unfinished business has a way of disregarding intentions, but despite the religious motives of Pakistani's independence movement, Jinnah's dream ought not to be denied its due consideration. Washington, Nehru and Jinnah, driven by the situation of their place and time, saw the possibility of a world that provided for the common good of all people, equal before the state. The spectre of nationalism and the forces of enmity and hate take their toll on paradisical gardens left unattended. Behind the movement, Jinnah suffered from tuberculosis made no better by his indulgence of the frequent cigarette. Jinnah would succumb to broken lungs on 11 September 1948, barely one year into the building of his garden. A great test then stood before Jinnah's successors: a clever act of tight rope to construct a Pakistan that could be equal parts postcolonial success story, free and democratic, as well as a homeland for the bountiful return of an Islamic golden age.

After a couple of days staying with Ghayas's uncle in Karachi, Saeeduddin would settle the family to the north in Sukkur. It was in Sukkur where Saeeduddin would find a new post working at the Customs and Excise Department, no longer of the British Raj, but now, rather, of Pakistan. Many a bustling metropolis has planted the idea of fortune and glory in the minds of the suggestive youth. Ghayas would leave Karachi for the time being, but the city lights would dance within his head as boyhood met its end upon the platform's edge. Ghayas would return soon enough to Karachi, the cradle of a nation and many a young man converting a restless spirit into directed activism.

Sukkur would constitute the end of the relatively nomadic lifestyle Saeeduddin's family abided by in old India. The dust of independence settling, Ghayas and his siblings would receive their schooling from the railway school, originally set up to educate the children of parents working for the robust railroad system of British India. While the adult Ghayas saw education as one of the top resources a society is required to provide for its people, the same cannot be said of the student Ghayas Siddiqui. Having an eager young mind and being a meticulous hard worker are traits that lose their focus against the backdrop of general disregard for authoritative figures and the revelation for many a student that a world spun fast outside the school house walls. While reading and accumulating knowledge was always dear to Ghayas, the implementation of the theoretical into the realm of practice was a primal urge. Although it can be said that it is fair to note Ghayas as a philosopher, he would not think twice of trading the armchair for the opportunity to be out in the streets, shouting for justice. Ghayas's education was of the British system, one of the last and strongest remnants of the colonial system. It was his gateway to a better life. Much of the old colonial system was essential to the Siddiqui family's post-partition life, from the education the children would all receive to their father's employment, the means by which food was put on the table.

A major question for all of former British India was how each community and state would embrace postcolonialism. The situation behind the partition was highly complicated. Reducing the new state of Pakistan down to the will of Jinnah underscores the fervent debates going on throughout all the newly constituted borders. A prime absurdity of revolutionary thought is that the old way must be cast out, burned to the ground, started afresh.

It is especially the case in former members of the British Empire to find that their entire society has not only been penetrated by the empire, but irrevocably bound to it. Transportation, the economy, even the political structures, were all husks left over by the British, and like hermit crabs, made their own in postcolonial Pakistan. Jinnah and much of the political elite of young Pakistan were educated abroad in Britain. As their education had dictated, they wanted to make democracy work. The more conservative elements of society wanted something different; not a tool used by the oppressors but something more 'Islamic'. An entire spectrum of thought developed, ranging from a desire for Pakistan, the theocratic Caliphate, to Pakistan, the secular utopia, and everything in between including the concept of an Islamised democracy. Add to this non-religious political parties and those of religions other than Islam, and with the world itself swirling towards its next global conflict, ideas of communism and socialism had their place upon the stage also.

A divide in Indian Muslim thought dates back to the Mughal Empire. One side, largely observant of a purist Islam, saw the world in black and white. Us and them, them being the *kuffar* (non-believers). They believed the Other sought to dissuade the good Muslim away from their religious obedience, and thus it was the job of this faction of the Mughals to defend, with blood and sword, India as an Islamic land built upon its commandments. The other side of the Muslim Mughals understood and valued the importance of India as a truly multicultural country. They valued the translation of Hindu and other works into Persian (the state language of the Mughal Empire) and Muslim works into other tongues. They believed that a great abidance to higher spirituality could result in a united India, one in which Muslims, Hindus, and anybody else could live together in harmony. This is not to be confused with later, and more Western, concepts of secularism. The sides on this fight were by no means clearly defined and it was not faith versus the faithless; rather, a more sophisticated difference between strict definitions of state religious identity and the belief that a government could exist both outside of and in cooperation with various ideas on the matter of religion. All sides fought tooth and nail for the prominence of their ideas. Once India was sliced between its Hindus and Muslims, the debate was reignited. Before the ink had dried on Radcliffe's lines, the wielders of power in Pakistan knew that the conservative devout would need to be appeased. This was seen with the reconstitution of Pakistan as an Islamic Republic in 1956, following the adoption of a constitution that took many of its cues from the religious right. Matters were made almost incomprehensible with the realisation that the military was also a source of political power as much as popular opinion.

In the midst of Pakistan's ontological gestation, the greater Muslim world longed for a return similar to India's romantic dream of the Mughals. Scholars and the extremist alike longed for a locus of power for the *ummah*. The power recognised and feared by the enemies of Islam had found its constitution in the Western notion of empire and state. Thus, it was the dream of Muslim thinkers to find or build an Islamic political entity to both tilt the geopolitical axis towards the Muslim world and to defend the ummah from annihilation at the hands of the West or other such bogeymen.

Perhaps taken for granted at the time, the demise of the Caliphate in the Ottoman Empire spelled Islam's last great hope of a Muslim powerhouse. Only three hundred years after the peace at Westphalia would Europe accept that the key to global dominance lay not in empire, but in the state. The Western-educated scholars of the post-World War II Muslim world luckily did not require three centuries to incubate the idea. A state for Islam was the key to everything; the solution to the theory of everything. Some declared the Islamic state would be born out of a careful study of the *sharia* to distil the purest Islamocracy. Others felt the quicker path would be through building a strong army. The cool prevailing heads of the day knew that a state, by the definition of the West, needed two things: a set of boundaries and a people bound to a common goal, secured through identity. It would be education that would bring about the Islamic state, not a flag or sword. Students were the key to the future sustainability of the dream Islamic state. Ghayas was growing up and developing just the set of skills that the Muslim scholars of the time needed to sow the seeds of revolution. And a set of borders, made independent specifically for the protection of the ummah, landed squarely in these scholars' laps. The old boys would stop singing the lamenting song of the Ottomans to take up a new ballad, one set to a more upbeat melody, a song for Pakistan, the Islamic State.[12]

The secular and less-than-desirable postcolonial sentiment of the founders of Pakistan demanded a voice from and for the ummah. The puritanical conservatives had their opportunity to see out their idea of an Islamic India in Pakistan. Abul A'la Maududi wasted no effort in taking the opportunity offered to him, be it by circumstance, history, or the will of God. Maududi was born into the decline of the Muslim civilisation, which he had seen being strongly related to the lack of a unifying authority. Muslims had no sultan, no *khalif*, to stand behind or be inspired by. The Ottomans passed their glory long before the Great War shuffled off their sovereign coil. Atatürk's secularisation of Turkey drove the final nail into the coffin of a Caliphate in Anatolia. The Levant and Mesopotamia were now protectorates of the British and the French, a fun new label since 'colony' was now out of vogue.

Maududi saw the Muslim world as in dire need of revival. The Qur'an and sharia needed to be brought back into focus in the modern world. Islam again needed to take its post as one of the great global civilisations, if not *the* true global civilisation. He stringently opposed British rule in India, but understood that for Islam to survive, it would need to take advantage of and acclimate the tools of the West to allow Muslims to flourish. He noted how those educated in the Islamic schools of the time had nothing to contribute beyond the mosque, yet those who went abroad to study hardly seemed to return to assist the community. Thus, the Islamification of education needed to bridge these two extremes. Likewise, the concept of democracy itself could benefit the ummah, if given some Islamic revisions.

The independence of India movements tore Maududi from his beloved theological study and thrust him into the world of politics. After all, according to Maududi, Islam permeated all elements of the Muslim's life, including politics. Thus, a politics of Islam needed a champion. Originally, Maududi stood against Jinnah and the Muslim League's cry for a separate state for the Muslims. Maududi would only be pleased by one India, united under Islam and sharia, despite the Hindus greatly outnumbering Muslims in the former colony. After partition, Maududi changed his strategy, instead championing the idea of 'theo-democracy'. Sharia compliant democracy would allow the ummah to run the affairs of the state. Maududi's compromise with the Muslim League would provide for a society similar to his earlier ideas of an Islamic State with the abolition of interest-bearing banks, the requirement of women to be veiled and the implementation of punishments that included public lashing, stoning, amputation, and execution, depending on the crimes committed and their degree of affront to God.[13]

Maududi had two major tools that allowed him to rise to influence and then prominence in Pakistan. First was his organisation, Jamaat-e-Islami. Maududi launched the Jamaat in 1941 with its twin organisation in Egypt, the Muslim Brotherhood, founded in 1928. Together these two organisations would spread the message of Islamism the world over. Jamaat-e-Islami originally was founded for the sole purpose of turning India into an Islamic State. They embodied the us-vs-them realism of the

Salafists of old and saw themselves as warriors defending Islam from the infidel by whatever means available. Compromise after the partition being a done deal, the Jamaat shifted towards the 'Shariafication' of modern Pakistan. The Jamaat would spread far and almost reverse conquer the former British Empire—that is, in the former colonies that did not outlaw the organisation. The strategy was profoundly simple: the only battle worth winning is that over the hearts and minds of the *Ulama*. Propaganda and infiltration of the education system were the most sure-fire methods, and the channels the Jamaat capitalised on ran from Hyderabad to London.[14]

Maulana Maududi's second tool was his command of the Urdu language. He was an impressive writer from a young age and, despite reports of his reclusive working nature, was an incredibly charismatic speaker. At the age of seventeen Maududi was editing his first Urdu newspaper, *Taj*. Throughout the 1920s, Maududi edited and wrote for various Pakistani news sources. On top of this he was an avid student of religion and philosophy, even learning English and German so he could determine how Europe rose to power. It was a great failing of past Islamic scholars and the ulama themselves that they never asked the simple question: how did Europe come to dominate the globe, instead of the Muslims? This would be a key question for the young minds looking for direction in this new age. It was Maududi's mission to equip those minds with the questions and framing needed to bring the Muslim world back to its former glory. Armed with a fiery pen and his army of students à la the Jamaat, Maududi became an ideologue and a people's champion. Ghayas and his generation, having been ripped from their normality and most likely their homes, lived under enough of empire to acquire its bad taste. They were primed for someone to tell them that the future could and would be theirs. Ghayas being a diligent, yet read, hard worker with activist tendencies would appear an attractive instrument to Maududi and the Jamaat-e-Islami.[15]

Ghayas can still remember reading one of Maududi's titles, *Banao aur Bighar (Making and Unmaking)*. The first books Maududi wrote pertained to a more theological interpretation of Islam, but as the empire waned and partition dawned, his writings quickly fell into the realm of the political. Ghayas admired what one man could do with language. His approach to history was of particular appeal to Ghayas. Muslims had been doing it wrong. They dreamed of a romantic ancient civilisation and ignored those who rose to power. The greatest sin of the old teachers of Islam is that they never asked how the West rose to win the day. Maududi studied the Western philosophers and much like Plato's enlightened one, developed the ability to see the shadows on the wall. But how was he to convince the others?

The answer had a great deal to do with educational reform, and even more to do with asking the right questions.[16] These fundamental drives existed at the heart of Islamic intellectual discourse that still continues, although a bit more reformed and refined, to this very day. For the teenage Ghayas, every question his curious young mind was asking, the works of Maududi seemed to either have the answer or give explicit directions to seeking out that answer for himself. Already a young activist, the cause shrouded in anti-colonialist sentiment, Ghayas knew that this was what he would spend the rest of his days doing. It was a romanticised notion; after all, he had to figure out how to get to that far away goal. Although how better to find out the magician's tricks, than to meet the man with the top hat himself?

In 1953, Maududi was sentenced to death for his involvement in stirring up anti-Ahmadi sentiment that launched disastrous rioting in Lahore. Maududi called for the Ahmadiyya community of Pakistan to be officially labelled 'non-Muslim' for his belief that they did not consider Muhammad as the last Prophet. The riots resulted in the deaths of over two hundred Ahmadis and the declaration of martial law. Due to the popularity of the anti-Ahmadi movement and Maududi himself, the sentence was reduced to a life sentence, before being eventually thrown out entirely after two years. At the age of fourteen, Ghayas learned that Maududi was entertaining visitors during his stay in Multan Prison in the north of Pakistan. So, the ever resourceful Ghayas managed to club together the funds for the train ticket and found himself poised and eager upon a multiple hour train ride to Multan, ready to meet his hero.

It is often noted that one should never meet their heroes. This advice did not need to be heeded by the fourteen-year-old Ghayas. For meeting Maududi did anything but diminish the grandiose image of the man. Ghayas was struck with awe before the imam. His height would be lost in his presence. He looked a great deal older than he was, but imprisonment tends to have that effect on one's aesthetic. His dark eyebrows and bushy beard going snow-white with each passing day sealed the image of a wise and charismatic man. The thick round glasses through which he examined and judged the world instilled his authority. He was not a thinker removed from society, up in his high tower of knowledge. He was as much a theoretician as he was a teacher, and had been known to hold discussions in his own home daily where all speakers were given their due—especially a young and eager mind travelling from the far corners of Pakistan to the desolation of Multan Prison.

Now, here the fourteen-year-old Ghayas sat before a man he had idolised for many years as he listened and exchanged words. For that moment both men were equal in the eyes of God, and a tremendous respect was mutual. This was essential. Maududi placed the importance of the student and reverence for their potential power so high, that he would quickly push aside decorated heroes and heads of state to hear what the inquisitive mind had to say. It was Maududi's view that in the command of language, Urdu in this case, that Muslims would allow themselves to be free of the impediments of the West and the often oppressive English language. Everything done must be done in service of the community, whether it is lifting it out of one form of poverty or another, or correcting its false assumptions. Liberation is not something accomplished individually, but may require proceeding alone where others will not follow.

The details of this dialogue have faded to the fog of memory, but as per Maududi's style, a mutual exchange was had. Ghayas would listen in humble respect, absorbing all that he could. A new vision being built. Meanwhile, Maududi would demand questions, ideas, and wisdom from the young student, for education is a mutual transaction, not a dictation. Perhaps at first timid, Ghayas would speak his mind and Maududi would express joy in his ever so subtle way. A sparkle in the eye, hidden beneath thick glasses. As will happen with each person Ghayas comes to admire in his life, aspects of their being are plucked and nourished within Ghayas's own mind, so as to be incorporated into his own. Both men still had a great deal left to accomplish in their respective lives, but that need not be a deterrent for a warm conversation. Maududi the journalist, the devout follower, the political activist, and the dedicated intellectual would provide a template for the young student to fill with his own life.

First things first; Ghayas needed an education and was dedicated to finishing school and obtaining his degrees. But a commitment is often easier vowed than followed through. The cries of rally and standing up for injustice easily distracted the young Ghayas from his classwork. This balancing act created a man of patience with a willingness to change, adaptive to failures, and persistent in all his endeavours, even if they must be undertaken alone. A path was materialising before the young man.

When Ghayas was preparing for his FSc (Pakistan's national level exams equivalent to A-levels) his father asked him what he wanted to do with his life. Ghayas's earliest interest was in politics. Perhaps he could have become a solicitor and then worked his way up the political ladder from there? It only seemed the natural progression. This was, after all, the creature his father had created. The political magazines left around the house for him to read, the continuous talk amongst the local Muslim community of political developments afoot in India, meeting and shaking of hands with the various who's who of political and intellectual life, the instillation of a keen sense of moral justice, and having raised a boy in a place ripe with political potential.

Ghayas's father retorted that his intentions were noble, but he asked, where would that get him? Everyone wanted to be the next Jinnah. As a result, Pakistan was a country saturated with unemployed lawyers. Choose a more profitable career, perhaps one that was profitable to begin with, his father pleaded, one with a future. Develop a skill that Pakistan needed, or better yet, that the West needed. That was how you would be able to support yourself, a home, and a family. Activism did not make for stable career. His father's words spoken, the pendulum had been forced from the liberal arts to the hard sciences. It was determined that Ghayasuddin Siddiqui would pursue his university studies in chemical engineering. Though he need not have been perturbed. His dream of becoming a lawyer temporarily shelved was to be fulfilled by his younger daughter Uzma, who qualified as a lawyer in London half a century later. But even then, in the back of Ghayas's mind remained the germ of an idea, that perhaps his activist spirit could more easily be continued, if supported by a decent salary.

Upon completing his FSc, Ghayas returned to the city of lights for his undergraduate studies. Karachi being both the capital city as well as the frontline of fierce political debate in 1950s Pakistan, Ghayas was easily drawn from his studies to attend a rally, protest, or demonstration on the other side of town. While he had been aware of Jamaat-e-Islami from his schooling in Sukkur, it is hard to say when they took an interest in Ghayas. Had his face become a recurrent one from protest to protest? Had this short, moustached man piqued an interest as he started not only winning a spot for himself in the Student Union but campaigning on behalf of other students? Ghayas was not your run-of-the-mill, hooligan rebel rouser. He was grounded in fundamental morality too often lacking in the politically active. For you see, Ghayas had a rule. He was good at mobilising the masses in support of the causes he took on. His rule was that he would support any individual if their position was logical and just. At times this has failed Ghayas, as sometimes logic and justice hide more sinister intentions. But, in accordance with his rule, he will still work tirelessly for the cause, until he no longer agrees with it and then he will simply walk away. No harm. No foul. No grudges. It was more than politics; it was justice. This was the deal for those on whose behalf he campaigned and likely was the terms given when he met the university representative of the Jamaat, who he noted was a gentle, good-natured man. He was interested in promoting young activists and it is not hard to imagine the potential he saw in young Ghayas. For Ghayas would, in an instant, drop his school work to run towards an instance of injustice.

The Jamaat became a refuge for Ghayas. While his heart was never in chemistry, the Jamaat gave him purpose, a cause to believe in and the fight of any young Indian turned Pakistani. The chance to succeed where past generations had failed. The chance to overthrow the tyranny of empire and build something purer in its place. This was the shot to lift Muslims out of their dogmatic slumber and become leaders in all elements of civilisation the world over. His education needed to expand beyond the classroom. The stakes were too high to squander over experimental precision; the real experiments were out there in the world. In the laboratory, these were just the mundane steps to deliver one to the true examination over which futures would be taken on or surrendered.

Quickly, Ghayas worked his way up the ranks of the student wing of Jamaat-e-Islami, the Islami Jamiat-e-Talaba. IJT was the embodiment of Maududi's strategy for building up the young generation, lighting the fire to then watch it rise from the ground up.

The IJT shaped Ghayas, giving his determination a goal down the road and feeding his restless spirit with what looked like a change to save the world. He was made a professional activist in their image. Their mission was the pleasure of Allah, to build humans in the exact parameters laid out by God and in turn, to build a society based upon the tenets of Islam and sharia. *Dawah*, the call to Allah, started amongst the students, and through training and organising the students to fix the problems within their own lives, educational structures would fix society so as to be better in line with the will of God. A very attractive proposition to all young, eager and easily persuaded youth looking for meaning.

Ghayas did take a few stances to maintain his in-favour opinion of the IJT in accordance with his one condition of membership. Thus, he also developed another rule. Historically, the IJT was well known for its destructive tendency. Ghayas would not be so easily tempted to towards what, to him, was senseless hooliganism. The destruction carried out by IJT, in Ghayas's mind, was as logical as destroying one's own home in order to convince one's self to tidy up. The IJT that Ghayas ran out of Karachi University would respect the property of their brothers and sisters. Their movements would be more sophisticated than blind rage and mindless destruction. A great majority of Ghayas's body weight was contributed to his loving heart and ever-expanding mind. As his studies continued, all it took was one of his mates running to find him in the library or the laboratory, saying "Brother Ghayas, we need you to stand for Pakistan." Without question or word, Ghayas would take to the street with his fellow activists.

This reached a zenith when two members of the Jamaat-e-Islami showed up at Saeeduddin's front door.

"*As-salamu alaykum* Uncle," they would politely introduce themselves. "We are in search of Ghayas. You know the famous activist. The Ghayas who failed his BSc!"

When confronting Ghayas, his father's tone did not as much express disappointment in his failure due to the distraction of his activism, as much as confusion as to why his son was famous for failing. The bright lights of Karachi, it had appeared, made an Icarus of the budding activist. In fulfilling his commitment to his father and to his own future, Ghayas would leave Karachi behind, choosing instead a quieter place away from the cacophony of big city politics, to focus on his BSc. Ironically, life had brought Ghayas to the birthplace of the Jamaat, Hyderabad, in his attempt to avoid the temptations of his activist tendencies. More specifically he was to obtain his BSc in chemistry from Sindh University in Jamshoro, on the other side of the river from Hyderabad. So, it would appear at least, that the Indus River was the only force on earth that could keep Ghayas from distraction.

But only for a time. In Jamshoro, the activist Ghayas never took a break. The man was who he was and nothing would change that. The restless soul had been tamed behind a mission, the justice and fairness of the community; however, that would evolve over his life. The story of the Hindu funeral that opened this book nicely illustrates who Ghayas is and what he is all about. He hunkered down, completing his BSc without delay, for an activist who lacked the discipline to finish his education was bordering on his oh-so-loathsome potential for being another ruffian hooligan. Although he still found time to attend demonstrations and manage campaigns for the student union as well as organise events. Becoming a nuisance to the administration but also receiving both his BSc and MSc degrees, Ghayas had learned how to play the game. By this point he had led students, defended the less fortunate, and proven himself as a force of great potential not to be reckoned with. However, one event would push his gaze beyond Radcliffe's borders.

While serving on the university student union, Ghayas organised a special delegation to travel to Dhaka University in East Pakistan for an exchange visit. Travelling by air, since it was the only way to get from Jamshoro to Dhaka without 'leaving the country', the delegation arrived after a short journey. Ghayas packed his university books to read whilst out there to keep on top of his studies. The books would all return unopened. Good intentions of studying again trumped by his greater passion. Ghayas was beside himself, learning that his Bengali counterparts were so similar. The students of Dhaka seemed even more curious and rifer with activism than his fellow students back in the West. The common stereotypes of East Pakistanis being backward or uncivilised were quickly squelched. Mutual learning was shared between the representatives of both student bodies. There was a growing animosity in the East as the students Ghayas spoke with expressed fears that East Pakistan was simply held as a training ground for the Pakistani army. Disgust was voiced over making Urdu the official language when Bengali was more widely spoken in this area. The cultural milieu of East Pakistan also made it nearly impossible to separate the Hindu from the Muslim influences. The Jamaat's efforts in East Pakistan were a mess. Their call was to prevent the Hindu 'invasion of Bengal' and to protect the land for the Muslims. The confusion appeared to be similar to the Salafists upholding order in a society married to the multiculturalist sentiment.

Ghayas's delegation travelled to a number of other universities throughout East Pakistan. A picture of this place developed clearly in the mind of Ghayas. A question flashed before his mind. Could the union of Pakistan last? And more importantly, was this in the best interest of the people? Was the Islamic way not the most beneficial for all? The confusions confounded Ghayas as he began questioning things taken for granted by way of ignorance. The world was indeed a larger place and the answers, wherever they might be, could only be found by getting out there. Friendships were forged and a greater perspective of the Muslim community began to gradually take shape. The sense of change, still familiar from partition, was again in the air, although this time, Ghayas felt he had an upper hand in what was to come. For this change might be more radical, or at least could come about quicker and in more frequent intervals, all throughout the world.

Upon returning from Dhaka, the world out there was now on Ghayas's mind. He had learned what he could from Pakistan and perhaps his abilities would come to greater service for a greater community out there. There was no more room to grow in Pakistan. It was time to meet the West, that which had been cast as the penultimate villain in the collective narrative thus far. Time to meet the West on its own terms and continue the education that Ghayas had only just started reading into. The next step was a PhD, the cause of justice for all still focused. The question remained: where would he make the port of entry into the great world beyond?

Chapter Three

INTO THE WEST, IN THE DARK

ONCE SET INTO his mind that he would be leaving Pakistan, Ghayas took to writing a series of letters that flew out into the larger world, asking for admittance into a chemistry programme where he could obtain his PhD: a status higher than any lordship or knighthood to a young Pakistani man looking to build a new world order. While waiting for a response, Ghayas continued to teach chemistry in Karachi, a post he had taken up after graduating from Sindh University in 1962. As 1963 succumbed to the metamorphosis of autumn, a healthy stock of universities would respond to Ghayas' letters, but none would make a better deal than the University of Sheffield. Sheffield was not only one of the first to reply, but also one with a most generous scholarship based on Ghayas's good MSc grades. Ghayas had no money and would need all the funding he could muster. So, to Sheffield it was for the young Ghayas—fitting as the University of Sheffield prides itself on being one of Britain's civic universities.

As the industrial revolution raged in the nineteenth century, the community of Sheffield—a city known largely for its factories, coal mines and steel mills—desired better, modern training facilities for its workers. At the turn of the century, the community brought three major educational institutions (the medical school, the technical school and the city college) together to form a university. The drive of this community movement was to make higher education not merely the luxury of the upper class, but an essential societal right for everyone, including the poor and working classes. The community's commitment to this undertaking is seen in how the founders raised funds for the initial endowment for the university. They went out into the city and asked labourers to donate one penny of their wages to the new university. This strategy was a resounding success. It would appear that yet another university was planned out only a few years before Ghayas would need it. It would bring him to the West and provide him with a nearly ideal place to transition between Pakistani and British life, not to mention the friendships he would forge, and the further prodding of an old restless spirit that the political atmosphere of the United Kingdom provided, tax and duty free.

A future seat secured for Ghayas, he now had to figure out how to get to Sheffield and claim said seat. Again, he had no money, but he had many friends. One friend informed him that a local charity was accepting applications to assist with travel expenses for Pakistanis wishing to study abroad. The friend noted that the charity, if it was to be becoming of such a title, would have to give the famous young Ghayas this particular donation. After all, he was the local hero, renowned for having failed his BSc. The charity covered the cost of Ghayas's plane ticket to London as the summer heat gave way to a cool breath of change in 1964.

To take those first steps out into the larger world requires a rare form of bravery. Yet, this was not Ghayas's first time leaving home and it would not be his last. Ghayas was a man for whom home was something greater than what could be so easily confined to geographical constraint or a limited cast of characters. It was necessary for Ghayas to leave home, not only to advance himself, but to truly reach out and take power for his community. The West could only be won in the West. So, not only was Ghayas stepping out of the familiar, he was going in due course for the lion's den of the enemy. Where better to confront the former colonial master than at its heart: London, capital of the old British Empire. London, and the rest of Britain for that matter, had taken its place in the minds of many foreigners as a distant metropolis dreamed up into a fantastical fairytale land. A land that powerful monarchs called home, where masters of the English language forged their classic works, and flourished as one of the major hubs of Western culture. London must have been a sight; a mosaic distinctly modern, cast in powerful industry, yet rooted in a deep history pieced together into a unique style and culture. The history, the people who had walked its streets, and the power the country commanded, must have created a beautiful city of light and prosperity, leaving first time onlookers crippled by its majesty. The pain of reality would waste no time sinking into Ghayas as he arrived in the city along the Thames.

His long flight might as well have taken him to the moon than to London. Instead of finding a cinematic alien wonderland upon arrival, he would find something more aptly labelled a hazard to one's health. It was bitterly cold and the worst of winter had not yet shown itself. The whole place seemed to be covered in a fog that never dissipated. Perhaps this is where London obtained its 'dreamlike' status, in the clarity-distorting blur. The days were unbelievably short, as if they hadn't even occurred in the first place. As he continued on, walking through the air, he noticed the distortion was not simply fog but pollution—and in ample quantities. The jet-lag only made matters worse as Ghayas tried to adapt.

Overall, his first walk around London must have felt like discovering a lost world or walking upon a foreign planet, and no doubt he felt he was under prepared, lacking essential equipment for biological acclimation. The shops closed at five o'clock sharp, so the milk would often have to wait until the morning. Ghayas's exploration was not a sightseeing holiday; he had business at hand. After all, London was only a pitstop. Sheffield was the destination and it was not Ghayas's way to lolly-gag at pitstops. Yet he was in no state to jump right into his studies, let alone decolonise the Muslim world. In Knightsbridge, Ghayas would find rest and refuge within a Pakistani government-owned hostel for students near the embassy. A couple of nights' rest revealed that London was no Karachi. The gleam of empire as reflective as fog and soot.

Ghayas was directed by his university lecturers to meet another Sindh University lecturer, Aijaz Ahmed, who was also pursuing a PhD in chemistry from the University of London. Aijaz would recall Ghayas as a university activist from his days in Jamshoro. Aijaz would later take Ghayas to London's King's Cross station for his departure to Sheffield.

Ghayas noted that the people were especially nice in Sheffield. He was subject to the warm neighbourly British welcome given to new strangers. Ghayas was a rare sight for Brits of the time. His arrival preceded the wave of Asian immigrants that would flood uninhibited into the Isles, in response to a labour shortage in the mid to late 1960s. Few would have foreseen such an event coming, so to them, Ghayas was a curious fellow, but deserving as any stranger of a warm cup of tea and a tip of the hat. This was all prior to the influx from the distant Commonwealth, which would trigger the resistance that fuelled a lockdown on immigration policy in the 1980s, and led to the raising of the flags of British nationalism and racial tensions. The short, moustached man was given the benefit of the doubt and welcomed in with all the respect and dignity any human being could expect from a modern society. Ghayas also noted that the British seemed especially bright and cheery, even though a major portion of their small talk involved discussing the dismal state of the weather or the government.

What nigh-absurd jolliness from the people and composite smoky atmosphere Ghayas experienced in London would be magnified tenfold upon arriving in Sheffield, despite being a relatively small town in comparison to that mega-city. And, as if the factories weren't doing a sufficient job, everyone seemed to be a smoker in Sheffield. It was the fashionable thing to do at the time.

It was also one of the only things to do as much of contemporary luxury, such as motorcars and televisions, were rare gems at this time. Sheffield itself was revelling in the luxury of an economic boom as the war effort carved an economic niche for the town's steel industry.[17] At this time, the superiority of British steel and its asking price on the market might well have solved the mystery of the people's irrational bliss.

The only person in town who appeared not to be drinking from the well of optimism was Ghayas's first landlady. Arrangements had been made for Ghayas to live in the flat above her residence. What Ghayas would learn upon ascending the stairway to his new home was that the landlady, typical of many property owners, could not be without a sadistic streak and obedience to frugal corner cutting. This particular landlady had control of the lights. So upon arriving home late in the day, as Ghayas reached for the door atop the stairs of his new home, the lights were switched off. This was something Ghayas did not agree with, so as per his policy, when he no longer agreed with the opinions of his colleagues, it was time to end the collaboration. So, it would seem, it was time to go. Ghayas grabbed his bags and descended the stairway outside the darkened flat. He handed the landlady her rent and wished her good day, making it clear he would not be returning. Utility control did not seem an overbearing requirement for Ghayas's lodgings, since for the few hours a day he would use a flat it would be to sleep, but his rule was his rule. The majority of his next six years would be spent on campus or in the community.

Indeed, the university was the hub of activity in Sheffield. This was where Sheffield made its port to the rest of the world. Speakers would be invited in from all over the world to lecture to the young minds congregated in the small middle England town. Sheffield was also conveniently located in a triangulated midpoint between Manchester and Leeds from London, where more and more students of Asian descent would grow their communities in the coming decades. When Ghayas arrived upon the scene there was no British Muslim community per se, at least not as it is known and continues to take shape in the contemporary consciousness. What Sheffield and other cities and towns throughout Britain did have was a highly motivated class of students from South Asia and North Africa eager to obtain the highest education available on the globe, either to take it back home to advance the situation there, or to start a new life here and thus carve a niche for themselves, the seeds that would give rise to British Muslims.

For the world was changing. For some, going home would not be an option, or at least not a preference. Much of South Asia and North Africa was marching in retrograde fashion in terms of human rights and political liberty. Thus, the work these hopeful students sought delivered greater power for them in the United Kingdom, or at least, the UK would allow its visiting scholars a platform on which to stand. In the wake of this blossoming of diversity came an array of ideas, worldviews and personalities. Great Britain at this moment was a sandbox for Muslims to play at developing their ideologies, philosophies, and eventually movements, free from the prejudices and racist sentiments seen elsewhere, and which would eventually plague Britain in the 1980s to give rise to the rough waters of contemporary Islamophobia.[18]

Ghayas's PhD research aptly focused on pollution, the unfortunate by-product of Sheffield's industrial affluence. As the effects of sulphuric oxide had already been well-studied, Ghayas decided to investigate the effects of nitric oxide in the air. Being one of the first to take on this field of inquiry, a great deal of work was required to paint the full picture. The weight of the multiple hundred-page dissertation entitled 'The Formation of Nitric Oxide in Flames' by Ghayas would give one the impression of deep complexity. In truth, as Ghayas stated, the concept was rather simple; it just required a great effort in experimentation to reveal the simplicity. A massive furnace needed to be constructed to contain the flammable testing. Other complicated experimental designs contributed to the age-old cliché of scientific research—that is, the 'hurry up and wait' methodology. Most of a given day would be spent setting up the experimental apparatus and only then could data be collected for analysis. This required a great deal of planning and if one measurement or calculation was off, it would mean a day scrapped and the return to square one the following morning. Patience was more than a virtue; it was a survival tactic. Ghayas being Ghayas, would spend an entire morning setting up a complicated experiment only to get a call from a friend or fellow student that he was needed to oppose this or that grave injustice that was afoot. Thus, without so much as a thought, Ghayas would run off to save the day and a whole day of academic experimentation would be wasted. It was no wonder that it would take Ghayas six years (1964–1970) to finish his PhD work. Ghayas was the first doctoral student his supervisor Dr. Eric Rothwell had taken on, and Ghayas felt himself a certain disappointment to his mentor. That being said, he did stick with it until the bitter end, even if he would occasionally find himself on a day trip to London for a quick demonstration or rally or to engage the community.

Again, the temptations before Ghayas in both situation and the brilliant and diverse minds he was surrounded by were of an irresistible blend. But Ghayas had learned from his past mistakes in Pakistan. This lesson was not how to resist the distraction of activism, but rather how to balance his time between research and the community. Not required to teach, Ghayas set out upon his studies while wasting no time in finding himself elected as Secretary General of Sheffield's Islamic Society. It would appear Ghayas did more than just casually attend the events and lectures put on by the society. Even in accordance with definitions of 'active membership' Ghayas set the bar high. High enough to be seen by the newly formed Federation of Student Islamic Societies

(FOSIS), of which he was made Assistant Secretary. Ghayas was always proud of the causes he championed and to say he stuck out in a crowd is quite an understatement, because he was probably leading that crowd. Much as the Jamaat-e-Islami saw the raw potential within Ghayas, so too did FOSIS, who could channel his abilities to make the organisation influential amongst not just students, but anyone and everyone passing through England worth a shilling to the Muslim world. His study office was a laboratory, but under certain lighting, it looked more like a campaign headquarters with students flowing in and out, not to ask his opinion in stoichiometric balancing of an oxidation reaction, but to discuss the topic of balancing Islam in a postcolonial world.

One day in 1966, while working on one of his complicated experimental set-ups, he caught wind that Cassius Clay, *the* Muhammad Ali, Heavyweight Boxing Champion of the World, would be in London for a rematch with an old rival, Sir Henry Cooper. During their last fight a few years before, Ali noted that Cooper had hit him so hard that his ancestors in Africa felt it. Physically, he was beating down the Western oppressors in the ring, but he also rallied the cause outside the ring through his dedication to non-violence and becoming a conscientious objector during the Vietnam War. In America, he was a hero of the civil rights era, fighting for the black man, but in Britain and elsewhere he was the closest thing the Muslims had to a superhero. Later on, he literally would take on the mighty Superman in a 1978 special DC comic book. Ghayas was not particularly a fan of boxing but would not skimp on the opportunity to meet a fellow Muslim fighting for the cause, in a world that was not particularly amused by a Muslim wielding power, even of the celebrity variety.

Naturally, the experiment was abandoned to inevitably be restarted the next day as Ghayas rushed off to the train station for London. Learning that Muhammad Ali was staying at the Capital Hotel, Ghayas made his way towards the centre of town.

He walked to the concierge and asked simply if the boxing legend would have a conversation with a student activist and a 'fan' from Sheffield. Brother Ali kindly met him at the restaurant in the lobby of the hotel and they spoke. It was the simple back and forth that would likely just as well come about from two old friends catching up after spending some time apart. After a short conversation, Ghayas bid Muhammad Ali adieu and hopped back on the train, returning just in time for bed. The next day the experiment would be meticulously set up and hours sacrificed to the research progressing data he desperately needed. London became Ghayas's new Karachi, making occasional jaunts to meet a whole gallery of individuals, themselves just passing through the old imperial capital. Just as quickly as he would arrive in London, he would be back off to Sheffield, to return to his studies in a somewhat less distracting environment.

Ghayas wasted no time in establishing a system of work both tending to his studies and the needs of the people. It was apparent from the start that Ghayas had a talent for effecting change. The various groups of Muslim students at Sheffield saw Ghayas as a leader, not bent upon personal accumulation of achievement, but dedicated to a sense of justice that transcended his singular existence. This garnered the attention of Ebrahimsa Mohamed, then General Secretary of FOSIS.

Ebrahimsa had come to London in 1962 from Malaysia to study Law. In London he became involved in a variety of Muslim organisations before helping to found and become one of the first heads of FOSIS. Ebrahimsa was instrumental in organising numerous individuals of import on their travels through Britain and giving talks at various universities, especially beyond London. As his Assistant Secretary, Ghayas worked closely with Ebrahimsa to assist with events and occasionally, direct some of these individuals back to Sheffield for a talk during their travels to Manchester and Leeds. In 1964, Ebrahimsa came to Ghayas with news of his next event. He told Ghayas that he would be organising and accompanying Abdul Malik Shabbaz, aka Malcolm X, on his visit of the United Kingdom. Following his pilgrimage to Mecca, Malcolm X decided to embark on a world tour to see the wider Muslim world. Ebrahimsa personally guided Malcolm through most of his British travels in 1964, as well as when he returned in 1965 to speak out against anti-black sentiment in Smethwick, a fortnight before his assassination. Along with the FOSIS treasurer, Hoosain Rajah, a Mauritian based in Manchester, Ebrahimsa worked with Ghayas to organise Malcolm X's speaking engagements at universities throughout England, from London to Manchester, including, at the behest of Ghayas, a stop at Sheffield University.[19]

The December of 1964 brought a remarkable degree of endless cold. Ghayas hopped on the bus to Sheffield train station, where he met the tall and slender Malcolm X. Ghayas shook his hand, welcoming the man to Sheffield and Britain with warmth that could conquer the winter. Malcolm's dominant presence was underscored by his humble demeanour. A quick joke was Malcolm's preferred way to ensure awkward extended silence did not spoil a pleasant greeting. The crass and direct nature of American comedy is often lost on the British and their international students, but no matter, for the jaw-aligning smile of Ghayas reassured that their good humours were harmonised. Ghayas would accompany Malcolm back to Sheffield University. Upon arriving on campus, they would go straight to the student union, where that night he would give his lecture. In the union were also prayer facilities, and so Ghayas and Malcolm prayed in the day's silence that would be thought unconscionable in the energetic roars of this particular night.

The chilly day gave way to a bone-deep cold night, that 4th of December. Malcolm stood over the podium, small enough to be likened to a child's replica toy, before a lecture hall devoid of much space to stand, let alone a vacant seat. The room was overflowing, but this was neither new nor even a problem to

Malcolm. Sporting a newly minted goatee, his classic clean-cut, refined dress was on display with his trademark horn-rimmed glasses. The audience ranged the visible spectrum of skin shades. Those critical of Malcolm X would describe the scene as an unstable mass of chaos, rowdy and ready to surrender to entropy and clash upon the right, or perhaps wrong, words uttered. *The Sheffield Telegraph* painted the scene of unruly rebel rousing and yet another of the rapidly proliferating instances of corruption of the youth. The reality was something much more elegant, cool, and never outside the control of the lecturer. Malcolm stood before them all, the conductor of this train, wherever it was destined to go. Chaos, violence, anger; all bowed before the might of Malcolm X, channelled through his rhetoric and penchant for the inspiration of others. The anticipation was a provocative speech on the racial tensions of America through the eyes of a black man living across the pond. Malcolm was no less controversial in that moment in time than he would be after his untimely death within the next year.

But Malcolm himself was undergoing a metamorphosis of sorts. Men like Malcolm X are often stereotyped into the collective emotional memory of history. The world knew him as the sword of the American Civil Rights movement, the militant, hate-stirring agitator whose fiery tongue led him to the same gruesome end that like-minded revolutionaries seemed destined towards. Malcolm the man is often disregarded, veiled in historical events and the quotes pulled from his grand opus of collected words.

Malcolm, however, was a simple and humane individual, and when he stood in Sheffield, he was on the precipice of unprecedented personal change, just as the globe too was about to fall to the mercy of the turning wheel of time. A few weeks before, he may or may not have told an eager white college student that she had no place in the affairs of fixing the race problem in America. His decision to take part in the *Hajj*, a holy pilgrimage to the ancient capital of Islam in Mecca, came at the dawn of a new stage in the complicated life of Malcolm X. He had just announced the severance of his ties with Elijah Muhammad's Nation of Islam. When he returned to the United States his entire life would be subject to a radical change. But before he was to return, an even greater force stood to transform the man, as those who have partaken can attest. Hajj changes people. Malcolm prayed with blonde haired and blue-eyed Muslims as well as black, brown, and yellow-toned individuals. His notion of ally and enemy was cast into disarray. The black struggle indeed was not solely a historical fight for the freed American slaves; it was much more complex. It included a cast of others not yet encountered or even imagined within the limiting aperture of America's race struggles.[20] Entire world histories of ideas and philosophies were converging upon battles that would be undertaken across the world throughout the 1960s and 1970s.

Malcolm X would leave the United Kingdom, remembered for his statement of taking this fight from simple rebellion to a war, conducted by 'any means necessary'. The volatile language of Malcolm X is something that even the most profound religious experience could not take away. Though his tone was now more sophisticated, his language seemed to have taken on a more metaphorical style. It was to be left to the interpretation of historians what Malcolm's addresses conveyed. He was invited to speak at Oxford and Sheffield on the theme of extremism, where his speeches echoed that extremism was not something brought about by the disenfranchised, for instance, the Muslims or the black supremacists. Malcolm noted that they found themselves in radical times dictated by radical men on all sides, so to take a non-radical stance was itself a radical notion to the new normal. Thus, radical was the only way to be.

Interestingly, Malcolm made note of items that would read different to British and American audiences. The notion of 'blackness' itself was different between the two worlds. In America, black referred to the Negro, descendants of the slaves taken from Africa. Islam was not yet a concern of the American consciousness, for they had just recovered from the hauntings of the fascist Nazis and were turning their nightmares to the themes of communism and social debauchery. Islam was largely ignored in the American consciousness, only valuable in being labelled as anti-Christian to hurt the momentum of such challengers as Malcolm X. Despite his efforts to preach Islam as a religion of acceptance of others and a resistance to injustice, American audiences generally only saw a black man, a foil to Martin Luther King Jr.'s pacifist side of the Civil Rights movement. Britain along with the rest of the world watched the goliath battle for civil rights occurring in the streets of America. The fight in America was not simply a domestic affair, try as the FBI did to snuff it out. It was a global historic battle and the results coming out of the United States bore stakes upon which the global disenfranchised could crawl out from the feet they found themselves beneath.

Blackness in Britain carried a more diverse otherness in its meaning. For the Caribbean Brits were just as black as the Pakistanis or foreigners with other skin shades imported from the former colonies. Even the working-class of Britain looked up to the messages coming from across the pond. The struggle was greater than the American's narrow view and Malcolm was only on the cusp of seeing the larger picture before his life was violently taken away.

Malcolm X's transformation to seeing the global struggle inherent in the black struggle allied brilliantly with the differing definitions in blackness between the United States and Great Britain. His allusions to Patrick Henry, a radical of the 'give me liberty or give me death' variety, garnered tension-relieving chuckles from the assembled crowd, for the once romanticised American rebellion against the British imperialists was itself losing credence, as America itself dawned the hate of imperialism and globalisation. Too often the hero of the little man finds himself using that badge of duty to represent his own debt of tyranny which he enacts on others, either out of revenge or to root out some fancied notion of evil. America itself engaged in foreign affairs that undermined the revolutions of other former colonies. Malcolm's wit also shined through as he mentioned hearing of a writer by the name of Shakespeare, who wrote the tragedy of *Hamlet*. Hamlet reflected on his uncertainties between waiting and actively and violently pursuing a justice he desired. Malcolm X spoke of power never being something that the powerful voluntarily surrender. In his call for the vanquishing of power from the white man, he spoke of a new type of unity amongst blacks and, particularly to this crowd and its organisers, Muslims. This carried a metaphorical weight that transcended the violent cries heard by the passive listener.[21]

Malcolm's performance before the mass at Sheffield was a magical blend of political rally, motivational speech, a call to prayer, and a mastery of the rhetorical art on display. Ghayas saw the power of the spoken word to start spiritual fires within those who heard Malcolm X speak. He was also in awe that this man spoke to a greater unity in the cause. In the days leading up to Malcolm's talk at Sheffield the controversy was almost unbearable; a man who was known for condoning violence and famed for fighting hate speech with equal and opposite vitriol lacked the class and dignity of a prestigious educational institution. It also coincided with a Sheffield university student magazine publishing an article in support of voters in the West Midlands constituency of Smethwick, who in the General Election of October 1964, had said "black immigrants were inferior and should get home". On 3 December, outraged students held a large demonstration against the magazine for what they saw as 'racialist tendencies'. The following day Malcolm arrived on campus. Ghayas was the secretary of the Sheffield Islamic Society that hosted Malcolm and was frustrated by the "unfortunate coincidence that he is coming when the racialist question is in the Union. His visit has nothing to do with it", Ghayas was quoted as saying at the time to *The Sheffield Telegraph*. Ghayas invited the white student union secretary, Neil Rackham, to introduce Malcolm X to counter suspicions that he had been invited to stir up racial tensions.[22]

Yet Malcolm did not come to Britain to raise an army or convert the masses. He came with shades of reconciliation and seemed to lay it all down; the whole history of the struggle, allowing bygones to be bygones so that all of the hated and oppressed brothers and sisters of the globe could unite to seek out their own justice. As the rest of the world began seeing themselves in the individualising practice of compartmentalisation that results from patriotism, nationalism, and other such identity crises, Malcolm X not only demanded a universal struggle, but lifted that struggle to begin the paramount war of this generation. Unfortunately, the 'us and them' rhetoric of the age would continue for several more decades, but Malcolm had shaken things up by saying that the distinction between us and them may not be such a simple empirical assumption as was once thought. Finally, Malcolm X demonstrated for Ghayas that the battle was to be fought here in the West. Such ideas and struggles bore more weight in the US and the UK. The avenues were greater and the structures were freer, to allow for more obscure figures to rise up and be heard. In Pakistan, such voices would quickly be taken care of and a victory in Pakistan would only be Pakistani, the greater world of the oppressed unaffected by such small waves upon the beach.[23]

The following morning, Ghayas would travel with Malcolm via taxi to the train station. Malcolm's words still echoing through the halls of Britain's most prestigious educational centres, it was time for the giant to return to the States, where he would shortly meet his ultimate fate. Ghayas and Malcolm shared a few brief words on the trip to the station; his fascination was with Malcolm X the icon and also with this new message of unity against a global struggle. Certainly, more great thoughts would have been formed by this luminary, had his life not been cut so tragically short. Ghayas and Malcolm exchanged salaams with a hand-shake, before the conclusion of which, Malcolm pulled in the much shorter Ghayas for a hug. Keep fighting the great fight for them all. The image of Malcolm waving as his train departed, destined for oblivion, is etched upon the mind of Ghayas. Malcolm X would be gunned down while speaking before a crowd at Manhattan's Audubon Ballroom in less than a year.

Throughout the 1960s, Ghayas's continued work with FO-SIS, whilst toiling away at his PhD research, provided the fore-ground for a transformation within himself. Ghayas, already a relatively globally minded individual, was thrust into the issues facing the various corners of the Muslim world as a reflection of the strangely diverse community he found himself a leader of in Sheffield. To grapple with the current affairs of the day, Ghayas along with his FOSIS colleagues launched and ran a small month-ly periodical with a title that spared no mincing of words: *The Muslim*. Ghayas's study now a frankensteinian common space amalgamated from laboratory equipment, the comings and go-ings of various parties and event planning apparatuses, now made space for the editing and publication of a magazine. The idea of taking global power from the West to Muslims rode on the back burner as the more specific political motives of various parties came and went. Even his boyhood influence and support for the Jamaat-e-Islami was waning as Pakistan's potential for becom-ing the Islamic state that the Muslims desired drifted off into the 'what could have been' shores of history, cast away as military proliferation and dictatorial systems of governance flourished in former British India. Despite the prohibitive hurdles that stood before Ghayas' return home, it is a wonder if he actually longed for it. Nevertheless, this strangely historically specific community Ghayas found himself within saw his leadership tendencies and exploited them to their fullest extent.

Sheffield of the mid-1960s found itself home to a large popu-lation of students from Sudan and Egypt. The Egyptians were the most well-established Muslim population in Britain at the time. While the readings of Maududi were largely restricted to Urdu-speaking populations, his sentiments from the Jamaat aligned well with the Muslim Brotherhood. The Egyptians of Sheffield quickly came to know Ghayas as the man who got things done. He soon became their leader and, though perhaps not totally conscious of the fact, the organiser and mouthpiece for the Muslim Brotherhood. The Muslim community of the time simply exported their political sentiments along with their students, so the issue of Nasser's taking of Egypt became an issue for the students of Sheffield also. The Sudanese students would similarly flock to Ghayas to seek his help in organising events, demonstrations and speakers on their behalf. Ghayas was at the forefront of the issues facing North African Muslims and their grappling with political change in which the role of the faith, military power, and the voice of democracy made their battlefield in the war for the future, a war still being waged today after all this time and tumult.

In this capacity Ghayas bumped into several prominent figures from across the world, bringing them to Sheffield as they made their tour of Britain to reach out to eager, young Muslim minds. Said Ramadan, the activist, humanitarian, and son-in-law of the founder of the Muslim Brotherhood in Egypt; Malik bin Nabi, the Algerian writer and philosopher educated in the West and dedicated to tracing the fall of the Muslim civilisation; and Anwar Ibrahim, the leader of the Reformasi movement and parliamentary leader in Malaysia, highlighted the dossier of Ghayas's guests during this period. Their issues, much as the issues of his fellow students, became his issues, so long as they abided his one rule of being just.

Although his dedication never wavered for a second, he could not keep up the act of being a political activist and a student forever. Funding alone was a more precious resource than oil. Ghayas was fortunate enough to receive a scholarship provided by BP through the university that amounted to £26 per month. In

1960s Sheffield, this was enough to get by, but a bit of padding was something that no student could refuse, especially if they were prone to making frequent trips to London. It was common for students to spend their holidays taking employment for spare spending cash or to advance their career aspects. Ghayas, ever open to a new experience, took one holiday break to try out this student cultural trend. He went out into the Sheffield community to work as a sorter in one of its many factories. Ghayas's experience in the factory would contrast Adam Smith's notion of the pin maker finding his 'being' in his labour. In fact, one day in the factory helped Ghayas come to the realisation that he, in fact, did not need additional cash. So, at day's end, Ghayas punched out on the time clock, received his daily wage and politely expressed to his employer that he would not be returning in the morning, thank you and good day. It would appear that Ghayas's opinions no longer aligned with his employer's and, as per his policy, it was time to go.

Ghayas's own life was in flux in conjunction with the rest of the globe, and Pakistan was no exception. Ghayas's parents were hard at work in search of the perfect bride for their son. A storm of letters passed through the postal offices of Sheffield and Sukkur. Much as Ghayas was quick to put off his school work for the cause of social justice, it would appear he was not as eager as his parents to find a wife. An arrangement was established between his own and another family of good standing, but Ghayas used the excuse of school work to avoid returning to Pakistan to meet his bride-to-be. There was no callousness here as Ghayas would make it up to his failed father-in-law-to-be by way of writing him a heartfelt letter that was deeply apologetic for the troubles caused by his prolonging and eventual smothering of the intended marriage.

To his family, Ghayas was rapidly becoming another of the *kalapani*, a stereotypical title given to those who left Pakistani never to return, eventually leading to radio silence and a presumed vanishing from the face of the earth. This was possible at the dawn of the 1970s before the interconnected age of wifi, mobile phones and social media. Kalapani derives from the colonial 'cellular prison' in which those sentenced to service there might well have been forgotten for their chances of return from that degree of imprisonment was unlikely. The time it would take to see out the ritual and the expense of travel kept Ghayas's heart and mind at work in the UK. But, after six years of successful evasion, Ghayas's feet could be dragged no further.

In the winter of 1970, a letter arrived in Sheffield explaining that Ghayas's mother, Batool, was ill and begged him to come home. Now, Ghayas is a trusting individual, but not such a fool as to be duped by a textbook case of parental entrapment. It was common in these times for mothers to play sick to get their sons to come home, especially when the matter of marriage needed to be taken care of. Ghayas, wise to her ruse, would not be dragged halfway across the world for a minor cough and to be wed off, especially with his PhD near at hand and the affairs of the Muslim world only becoming all the more draining.

However, the arrival of this letter corresponded with an old friend taking a holiday in London. Zubeir Siddiqui was an old friend of Ghayas's from Sukkur. He now worked in Saudi Arabia, but had recently visited Pakistan as he frequently travelled to Karachi and, as a close family friend, would visit Ghayas's parents. Zubeir confirmed that Ghayas's mother was indeed truly ill and while ulterior motives may be at play, it was his advice that Ghayas return back home to see her. Ghayas thanked Zubeir for this news, but it would be of no use as Ghayas had only enough money to pay for his room and board in Sheffield. He could not afford the exorbitant price of a ticket to Karachi. Zubeir smiled and shook his head so as to relieve Ghayas's worries. Zubeir would buy his ticket for him. So, as winter passed for spring, Ghayas would travel back to Pakistan in 1970 for the first time since leaving for his conquest of the West six years prior. To be clear, Ghayas's travel was strictly business; he wanted to see to his sick mother Batool, not to meddle in other trivial affairs such as marriage.

Upon touching down again in Jinnah's garden, Ghayas could not help but notice a whole age of change had swept through the land. Not only had the once richly optimistic new nation fallen into disarray over constitutional kerfuffle and the looming crisis in East Pakistan, but it was also under the control of a military man in the early stages of the executive's fall from Jinnah's grace to dictatorial malice. Home never sustains the glamour and shine of memories romanticised and the tides of age were most apparent in Ghayas's parents. Five decades and a slew of kidney issues confirmed Zubeir's bad tidings concerning his mother. But no matter. Batool may have had a ticking clock set against her, but her determination never wavered. She would see Ghayas married before the final curtain call. Batool then dropped a list before Ghayas and Saeeduddin, researched and scrutinised, a work that would put the whole of Ghayas' dissertation to shame. They had work to do, and one did not dare think to deny a Pakistani mother.

One by one Saeeduddin and his son Ghayas went through the list. One by one they eliminated each potential candidate. If a spark was not had in that initial meeting or if they lacked an education necessary to comply with Ghayas's intellectual fortitude, the match would be doomed to fail on launch. The list exhausted, Ghayas, Saeeduddin, and Batool sat about the family home as the sun set on the eve of defeat. But Batool had an idea, something she had not thought of before and now kicked herself for not having considered earlier. She asked Saeeduddin if he remembered Anis Ahmad. Anis was the elder brother of Idrees, who had married Ghayas's sister, Azra, back in 1965. Since Idrees and Anis's father had died in 1960, Anis, being the eldest son, was charged with organising his brother's wedding. Ghayas had just arrived in Sheffield so he missed the wedding, but Batool recalled that her new son-in-law's brother had a daughter. She too was at university and a strong personality in her own right, as was re-called from the wedding. A perfect match for Ghayas if only the spark he desired could be ignited. Batool collected a photograph from the wedding for Ghayas to look at.

Anis Ahmad, yes. He was not only a character from Batool's memory, but also from Ghayas's own history! To think that Ghayas sat upon his hands for two years, simply teaching chemistry in Karachi between receiving his MSc and casting off for the UK (1962–1964) only shows a lack of having paid attention to the story thus far. On his lunch breaks, Ghayas's stomach sought satiation alongside his restless spirit. This was done through live-ly political discussions with his friend Israr, who worked as a member of the atomic energy commission in an office near Kara-chi University. During his lunchtime visits, Ghayas would enter Israr's office to find a civil engineer, who worked nearby, also present and who would become a frequent voice in their political discussions. That civil engineer was none other than Anis Ah-mad. Ghayas remembered the man as an honest and simple man whose political sentiments and ideas on Pakistan and the world very much fell in line with his own. Little did Ghayas know he would be spending his off-year lunch breaks talking shop and discussing politics with his future father-in-law.

His signature smile dominating his face as he gazed at the wedding photograph, Ghayas agreed to the match. Her name was Talat. The woman who would become the love of his life and constantly at his side, defending his ideas, pushing him to his potential, and often holding him up when nothing else could. Talat, the independent, readily outspoken, and highly educat-ed woman might appear a strange match for the quiet and re-served Ghayas, but love at first sight is often only a fantasy for the tales of children. True love is an ongoing project, a contract that can often take many lifetimes to fulfil. A greater example of what love can transpire from an arranged marriage and mutual commitment, loyalty, and evolution is hard to find beyond the union of Ghayasuddin and Talat Siddiqui.

But first, the match had to go through the ritualistic red tape. Talat had moved north in 1965 as the capital was soon to switch from Karachi to Islamabad. Similar to the Siddiqui flight from India to Pakistan, Talat and her family journeyed north to meet their father just as a war was breaking out between India and Pakistan for the second time since partition. What normally was a one-day train ride from Karachi to Islamabad became two days filled with black outs and the screech of air raid sirens. As Anis's new home resided within the ever-tumultuous Punjab region, the journey was long and ill-advised. In fact, most traffic was flowing the other way. Yet, the family would be reunited and settle in Rawalpindi despite it being one of the most dangerous cities in Pakistan at the time. Seventeen days after Indian forces crossed into Pakistan, aiming for Lahore, the war would end and Talat and her family would settle into Islamabad's twin city to the southeast, to stay until Batool was to make an offer for a match.

Rawalpindi was over a thousand miles away from the room where Ghayas and his parents sat. But there was no need to fret, for Batool had been waiting Ghayas's whole life to initiate the match. Batool didn't need to hop on the next train north, but instead initiated the proposal through Talat's maternal aunt, Shamim Fatima, who also lived in Karachi. Shamim would then meet Ghayas and his parents on behalf of Talat. The ball was then in Aunt Shamim's court. She was quite impressed with Ghayas and rapidly approved of the match, sending word back to Anis and Talat's mother Sardar Fatima.

Due to Batool's poor health, she would be unable to attend the wedding if it were to be held as per tradition near the home of the bride, in this case, far north in Rawalpindi. Shamim assisted in getting the wedding to take place in Karachi, so that Batool would get her wish and witness the wedding of Ghayas and Talat in the June heat of 1970. As the festivities came to a close, the match made, both Ghayas and Talat being students, agreed that they would need to finish their respective studies before deciding upon where to start their life together. Talat would fly back to Rawalpindi to finish her last year of university before Ghayas's late July flight back to Sheffield. In a highly irregular move, Ghayas himself entered the plane to see his bride off after she had boarded, sealing his commitment and dismissing any notion that he might become just another kalapani upon his return to Britain. Ghayas now had a new motivation to hunker down and finish his dissertation, for soon Talat herself would finish her studies and be on her way to join him.

Indeed, 1970 was a big year for Ghayas. Not only would he add husband to his long list of titles, but that of Dr., for he would defend his dissertation and be granted the rank of PhD, and thus depart from Sheffield much to the delight of an administration rid of another one of those pesky student activists. Dr. Rothwell too could flash a proud smile that his first PhD direction ended a success. The date printed on that dissertation, 3 August 1970, bore more sentiment than a monumental achievement. It would also be the day Ghayas's mother, Batool, would pass away. To her, the dissertation would be dedicated. Ghayas had also fulfilled his promise to his father, who would pass away a decade later, to successfully complete his education. Upon finishing his oral defence, Ghayas confined his dissertation to the library, never to look back. What career may have awaited the fresh PhD held no bearing on Ghayas's mission. With his formal education complete, the need for a quiet retreat from the distracting cries of justice was no longer required. Out of the frying pan and into the fire, Ghayas moved to London. It was time to launch that seemingly requisite phase of life for future Muslim leaders both in the past and continuing to this date, the journalist years.

Ghayas would have his brush with journalism when he went to work with Hashir Faruqi to set up *Impact International,* a news magazine. The taste Ghayas would receive was not the sweetness of honey he had hoped it would be. The periodical started under a tent near a hospital in central London, but would quickly grow through round-the-clock effort. The office would develop on Seven Sisters Road off Finsbury Park. It was a new decade and Ghayas had a job to support his new wife.

Following the death of Batool, Talat would suspend her studies to travel to Karachi for the funeral to mourn in Ghayas's stead for a month afterwards. By 1971, Talat had finished her studies as well. Communication had been difficult for the first year of marriage, having to rely on the time taken to both write and deliver letters. Phones were around, but of a much different fashion than what rides in the contemporary individual's pocket. They were large and, in Pakistan, an item of luxury. Communication as an instant message or simple text was beyond the realm of fantasy, truly unthinkable. One had to 'book a call' which involved a calculus that would easily confound a postgraduate student of maths. Arranging for a time to use a neighbour's phone, accounting for time zone difference, and a prayer that the operator could connect your line and that the intended receiver would be present to pick up the line all made telecommunication an act highly dependent on the will of God. This doesn't even account for the expense of hearing a loved one's voice. And after all that effort, the conversation would barely be allowed to extend beyond the necessary exchange of accounting for how the weather was in your particular corner of the world. The art of the act was in being concise, hardly a virtue to anyone hoping to maintain a long-term relationship. Despite this, Ghayas and Talat would get on just fine regularly writing letters back and forth. In this distant age, the postman was a lifeline; now most of what post remains in circulation is discarded without even being opened. It was no surprise that upon finishing her studies, Talat would quickly make the arrangements for a move to London.

If Ghayas's journey to Britain could be compared to a trip to the moon, then Talat's was a journey to Mars or some equivalent celestial body at a greater distance. The trip was long, being Talat's first major embarkment via airplane. The weather was terrible upon her arrival and did not seem to improve much throughout the year. The cold was just the beginning. The most shocking thing for a woman raised in Asia's city of lights, Karachi, was how shortly after the sun going down, the whole place would go quiet and everything would close, save the pub, just as supper was being enjoyed. Karachi lived well into the first hours of dawn. What respectable, civilised place would close its shops at the first signs of evening? The whole day-to-day strategy would have to be amended. Groceries and other shopping had to be taken care of during the restrictive window of daylight hours. As more immigrants moved in from her former colonies, slowly, Britain learned how to have a night life, one of the numerous cultural sophistications the former colonists would import into Great Britain.

The worst thing about Talat's new home was her inability to find people with whom to speak in Urdu. Having received a British education, Talat had no trouble speaking English, but even a mastered understanding of a second or third language cannot remove from the heart the comforting instinctual drive to speak one's native tongue. Every daily conversation required English and the only access Talat had to Urdu came from the occasional run-ins with another Pakistani or Indian family. These special moments would kindle Talat's equivalent of a 'Christmas level of celebration', or perhaps more appropriately expressed, an 'Eid level of celebration,' every time.

The first year in London for the Siddiquis would not be the fairytale ending in the fairytale city one might expect. It was a difficult year of uncertainty and adjustment. Their first home was in Tottenham, a two-room flat above another family in which they all shared one bathroom. A budding journalist, Ghayas found himself reporting as back home appeared to be falling apart. Indeed, the civil war erupting in East Pakistan ignited a great fire in

71

Ghayas's heart even on the day of his PhD dissertation defence. As a journalist though, Ghayas would not falter in the tenets of truth and fairness inherent in the worthy profession. The Fourth Estate must not fall victim to any of the others. Ghayas was present at the first pro-Bangladeshi protest, a massive affair at Hyde Park. He recalled the questions and fears that his friends had made during his tour to Dhaka University a decade earlier. The imposition of Pakistan upon the Bangladeshis was reaching the tipping point and looking no better than what the British had done to Mughal India. A genocide was occurring, but the event was turned into a political dispute. The affair, legally, was civil war as the infinite wisdom of the Geneva Convention left political dissonance out of the definition of genocide. Thus the great postcolonial disputes of the 1970s, 80s and 90s would go without such a moniker and be deprived of international justice, so Ghayas reported, for all sides need their fair due.

Upon the conclusion of Ghayas's descent into the sea of people at Hyde Park, with banners and masses toting the soon-to-become-famous Joy Bangla slogan, Ghayas sent word back to Faruqi that something was happening in Hyde Park that *Impact International* ought to be covering. Ghayas's reports were denied and eventually Ghayas worked out that his editor was being given notes from another source telling him what was to be reported and how. Funding and influence were being handed down from Jamaat-e-Islami and *Impact International* was rapidly becoming the mouthpiece through which the ideology of political parties was being funnelled out to the people. And to them, the rebels in East Pakistan were the enemy, not just to Pakistan's stability and future, but to the whole of Islam.

This stood in the face of the very push that drove Ghayas to join Hashir Faruqi and Abdul Waheed Hamid in forming the monthly periodical. *Impact International* was to be independent. Let the community decide what they do, but their duty was to present all the facts they could find. Hashir Faruqi relented, but when unable to accommodate Ghayas's opinion, without hesitation, Ghayas tendered his resignation. His condition had been broken and it was clear that his opinion stood in opposition to that of the new editorial line at *Impact International*. The time had come for Ghayas to go his separate way. A testament to the civility of Ghayas's departures, after concluding his tenure with *Impact International*, Ghayas and Hashir stayed close and on good terms despite the disappointments of the past, and are still friends to this day.

The mess with *Impact International* and the memories of Dhaka emboldened Ghayas's heart for the East Pakistanis: the Bangladeshis. In 1972, following a brief stint in a West Pakistani jail, Sheikh Mujibur Rahman, recently proclaimed the first president of the newly independent Bangladesh, made a visit to London. He would be dubbed by the Bangladeshi people *Bangabandhu*, 'friend of Bengal'. On a cold January day, he would be greeted in the lobby of the Claridge's Hotel by the man famous for his hotel meetings with the heroes of Britain's former colonies: Dr. Ghayas himself.

The situation in East Pakistan greatly disturbed Ghayas the more he looked into it. Pakistan, the dream of his childhood, to be a free place where Islam could be realised without the persecution of others, had now joined the rest of the globe, concerned more with power than the good of its people. Their ideas and motives had been corrupted, making room for justified violence and killing. Ghayas would learn that Jamaat-e-Islami was backing the Pakistani military and that their student wings were twisted into militant training corps. The organisation, Islami Jamiat-e-Talaba, that had made Ghayas into the organiser and activist he became, were now training the youth of Pakistan to go out and kill the kuffar. His own experience with having to tame the hooligan tendencies which the IJT fed upon made the leap in logic easier to swallow. They conducted horrifying atrocities in Bangladesh. The original, intellectual schism of Islam in Mughal

India had been resolved, or more appropriately, forgotten. One side did not so much as win out over the other, as Pakistan simply descended from being a Muslim paradise into another military dictatorship, veiled in the holy crescent.

Ghayas's heart was broken for a second time; the dream of Mughal India was dead, now too went the dream of Pakistan. A handshake and another friend made, Ghayas departed from Claridge's. Bangabandhu would go on to serve as President and then Prime Minister of Bangladesh until his assassination in 1975 at the hands of his close friends and colleagues, under the likely patronage of more powerful, West Pakistani backing.

Since Ghayas's academic performance during his PhD was somewhat less than of the highest quality, his degree would offer him little assistance in finding a career. Despite this, because of the degree he held and with his background in the field, he was able to seek out employment as a chemistry teacher. The Siddiquis would move to Corby where Ghayas would teach chemistry at the local schools. Talat's own education also gave her the experience necessary to teach, so she too took up employment as a chemistry and biology teacher at Corby Technical College. Corby took Ghayas out again from the volatile life of an activist in London, though it seemed an unfit fall into conformity for one who seemed propelled towards the top of political activity. Here was where he would establish his family and turn his motivations towards their wellbeing.

This, of course, did not mean the occasional jaunt to London was an extravagance. Ghayas and Talat still stayed quite active in the community, attending various meetings and demonstrations. Just because the Siddiquis had found day jobs did not mean the world ceased to spin or lack the need for defenders of justice. North Africa and South Asia were alive with change and political turmoil and grave injustices were still being committed in the early 1970s. Actions were being taken to set in motion a struggle that would take three decades to become a headline worthy of the concern of the West. Ghayas and Talat would come across many like-minded and motivated individuals looking to find a way to cope with the growing hold of a new generation of autocratic rulers in the Muslim world and do their part for the ummah. There they were, in the streets of Britain, the leaders of what would come to be known as the British Muslim community, each with their own unique trajectory, marching for justice, looking for the catalyst to propel their potential into action. It helped that they began to recognise each other from event to event and find solace in speaking their native tongue with each other.

One man in particular stuck out as a reoccurring presence, busy at work on something throughout all of these activities. He had just had his journalist phase abruptly ended by his first heart attack, although you'd have never guessed the man had a single biological incongruency when you heard him speak. At the University of London Union, Ghayas would find that jaw-aligning smile eagerly grow upon his face as a speech took place. Stroking his beard, Ghayas found himself blown away by the man's rhetorical talent. He too was a child of India, trapped within the limitation of Pakistan after the partition. He understood the problems of the ummah in a way that Ghayas had not felt since first reading Maududi all those years ago. And suddenly, the stage presence he had seen in Malcolm X was alive again here in London. This man could be the voice of an entire people. After all, charisma and rhetoric had driven many movements in the past. Yes, many of those movements ended in catastrophe, but this man had Islam and justice behind him. His command of the English language belonged alongside the others within history's pantheon of famed orators. His speech was a mosaic of words, gestures, and the constant adjustment, removal and replacement of his glasses. This man, Ghayas thought, I need to work with.

After finishing his talk, Ghayas rushed to meet the man, the first of his contemporaries who could speak like the great men before them. Ghayas shook the man's hand, expressing how their ideas aligned and an agreement that it was time for the Muslims to return to the Golden Age they had left in antiquity. Ghayas had spent his whole life up to this point chasing down every giant who came through London, just to hear them speak. Now he had a potential friend at his side. Someone who could do more than speak with him, someone who could take all the rhetoric and actions committed in the past and bring it to life in this new age. Ghayas, the action man, this chap, the voice and spirit. Together they could change the world. The hand Ghayas eagerly shook belonged to a man named Kalim Siddiqui. Another Dr. Siddiqui, of no relation biologically, but tethered in a historical calling.

Kalim smiled as he returned Ghayas' energy. "Please come to my house and be my guest. You must try my wife's cooking. There, we will discuss the future of the ummah."

For as much sizing up as Ghayas had done, little did he know, Kalim too was looking for a man to help him change the course of history.

Chapter Four

THE MAN FROM SLOUGH

THE NEARLY TWO-HOUR car ride from Corby to Slough was of little to no trouble for Ghayas. Behind the wheel, Ghayas found a new freedom to go where and when he desired. No more coordinating trains, transfers, or less than trusting bus schedules, not to mention the often dubious trek from station to final destination. Now residing beyond the fold of London, he needed better accommodation for travel and one that allowed him to make his way down to the capital for the occasional lecture or demonstration. Slough still remains in what could be considered the Greater London area, served by the Great Western Railway operating from London Paddington, but allowed for a comfortable escape from the hubbub of the city. It was a quiet place, ideal for deep thought, but not the symbolic locale where one would want to position a seat of power.

By this point Ghayas had grown used to the bitter winters of London. On this December day, the long winter between 1973 and 1974 was only just beginning. Ghayas parked his car on the street, ready for whatever the future had in store for him. The house in Slough had nothing terribly distinguishing about it. A modest home for a modest individual, Ghayas noted. A block similar to many other rows of chimneyed houses squirming about and branching in a seemingly arbitrary pattern. The map of England as we know it today. At the door Ghayas was greeted by the warm salaam of Kalim, his wife shouting her welcome from the kitchen where she was putting the finishing touches to their meal. It was commonplace in this home as it is in many homes that a guest's right is honoured in the most pleasant of all fashions: through a person's stomach. For Kalim's wife as well as Ghayas's and many of the first generation of Indian women that came to London, captured that one beautiful cultural relic. Not simply a recipe, but an entire ritual that produced the finest cuisine India had to offer, and some of the finest the world was ever blessed with. This is not to be confused with what was found in London eateries, the dulling down of flavour found in equal parts between fragrance and taste, to deliver something palatable to the stereotypical English, like chicken tikka masala. These were the dishes that not only brought about a sense of serenity, but ones that were responsible for many great thoughts and dialogues too.

As usual it tended to be a case of putting the cart before the horse, and with the meal finished, it was time for the first meeting. But first, tea would be had. The common option was Earl Grey or PG Tips, which Kalim would quip was utter rubbish. Nevertheless, both their cups would be filled with a steamy British cup of PG Tips and warmed milk. As would become their custom, Ghayas would lean forward to listen as Kalim twisted around in his chair, acting the words he spoke, flinging his glasses about for accent and punctuation.

Kalim was not impressed. Yes, the world was changing, but the future laid out was not the future that Muslims longed for, had dreamed of, had bled for at the twilight of Empire. The supposed revolutions stretching from Tripoli to Jakarta did nothing for Kalim. There was no pride to be stirred and the fires of minor squabbles did little to illuminate the greater cave they found themselves in. The engineered nation-state, the haunting ghosts of Empire that carried on into the present day, tripped just as the trap layer had planned and ensured the Muslims would not return to their golden age any time soon. The ancient capitals of Damascus and Baghdad were to be in the hands of the new Ba'athist, military tyrants disguised as socialists. Turkey was a long lost cause by this point, now working on its fifth clone of the Atatürk, each one seeming to be getting more militant than the last copy, in both credentials and practice. The Israeli government played the victim, but became the bully with the assistance of their big brothers in the West. Western influence and money sprinkled all around, the lifesaving oasis, delivering sustenance to the states in which Muslim brothers and sisters found themselves. In Egypt, Anwar Sedat, the hand-picked successor of Nasser, kept business as usual, applying the thumb to those who still dreamed of the Islamic State. Likewise, in Pakistan, yet another disappointment as it became yet another military dictatorship, forgetting its Islamic origins. He had never thought highly of Jinnah, for as a boy, Kalim had seen him riding about in a horse-drawn carriage. Another colonial viceroy, he would think to himself. After all, his education and plans were built with the same tools the empires of old had left lying around, used to ensnare Muslims around the world in the concept of the nation-state.[24]

Kalim had just returned from the International Islamic Youth Conference in Tripoli where the not quite thirty-year-old, newly made leader of Libya, Colonel Muammar Gaddafi, launched his new political theory. He called it the Third International Theory, a way by which the third world countries of Africa and Asia could pull themselves up from the hangovers of colonialism. The theory focused on providing an answer to three questions. First, the resolution of the oppression brought on by capitalism, an interesting take on socialism that mixed Leninist theory and Islam. Second, resolving the oppressive nature of democracy, that being the tyranny of the majority. This was accomplished by a complexification of a congress that provided for popular rule above any chance of oligarchy. The last was an answer to the denigration of society, an answer to which he turned back to Islam and provided a less than progressive social engineering to order culture and thus provide for the people to be better, in a sense. The conference overwhelmingly rejected Gaddafi's ideas. Again Kalim was not impressed, but what he saw here animated the gears of his mind, twisting about, manufacturing grand ideas. A vision.

The root problem was nationalism and all of these various dichotomous modes of thinking that pit man against man. The Muslim is left in a battlefield armed with identity as a weapon. What are they expected to do? Islam needed a caliphate. It needed a central authority to direct, lead and reignite the true revolution. Now, Kalim knew this was grandiose. Something he would never see in his lifetime, but the groundwork needed to be laid. It was incumbent upon him and his peers at that moment to begin a great exercise in critical thought. Books and articles beckoned to be written. A new examination of journalism, science, and theology needed to be launched. Great dialogues needed organising so that the rich ideas swirling around the minds of global Muslims could meet, discuss, and reason out future opportunities. Kalim had a master plan in his head for a great project and he needed manpower—and of course, funding.

This is my office, he stated. This house and the one next door could be where it all begins. It was quiet enough to think and write and edit. Kalim's gestures and words raised in volume. We need to start with the youth, he proclaimed. Find young chaps at university, help them along in their schooling and give them a platform to change this world. We can create something great, right here in Slough, Kalim closed, with a sip of tea.

Kalim's heart had not fared well with the lifestyle he had lived up to that point in Slough. The failures of his heart would define the rest of his life, but his mind was sharp and knew what it wanted. Where his heart was failing, a man sat across from him who was the embodiment of a pure heart. Often the heart and the mind differ slightly, at least in priority, but unified, they keep the body alive. Back and forth these two men sized each other up. Whether or not they realised it, they had formed a seal of friendship, a necessary ingredient for the realisation of dreams, or rather, a brotherhood. Unbeknownst to both men, they were interviewing each other. Kalim needed a right-hand man, someone behind the scenes, for revolution is not a solitary movement. Ghayas longed to bring his organisation skills back from their untimely retirement, to be an activist again. Kalim spoke with conviction and truly believed each word he carefully uttered. This man was going to change the world and would be just the person Ghayas needed to help him along his lifelong mission towards justice and fairness for all.

I have one condition, Kalim bhai. Ghayas looked beyond his teacup into Kalim's eyes. I will support you for so long as I agree with you. Should we disagree, we will part company. No harm, no foul, no misgivings. Leaning over, Ghayas looked up at the mighty Kalim.

Kalim smiled, a jovial laugh followed. He agreed.

All parties referred to the work that followed at the house in Slough as 'part-time' work. Though what pay cheques read of part-time work often are the causes to which one gives their full-time effort. A job is a mode by which one makes their sustenance. A career is the full optimisation of a particular skill to carry out one's livelihood. Often these two can blend, but there is a mysticism where passion can take a position within such a social role. For passion is the lifeblood of one's existence. The reason to get out of bed in the morning. Kalim wrote for *The Guardian* and taught international relations at the University of South California's West Germany campus. Ghayas still held his post, teaching chemistry in Corby. But their true work happened in Slough. They would be joined by an all-star cast of young college students, a paradise-seeking science journalist, Ziauddin Sardar, a student of political science, Ajmal Ahmad, and a Canadian Imam-to-be studying at University College London, Zafar Bangash, amongst their ranks.

The routine was analogous to the garage start-ups of Silicon Valley, except at a cooler temperature and with an indisputably Islamic style. Kalim's wife would work magic in the kitchen, in quantities fit for small armies, which could not be denied as an essential element of the meeting's programme. Following the meal would proceed Kalim's Socratic questioning and energetic debate amongst the young students and the Siddiquis. From the house next door to Kalim's an office would materialise, constantly growing its amount of business as winter turned to spring and so forth. Kalim was building his anti-empire complete with new ideas and an anti-army that would help him reconquer the world. Ghayas's being was enriched as he was back in the game. The activist had gone pro. He also found solace in being able to help young students. Not removed enough from his own university days, he recalled the hardships of studying in a foreign place, with new people and ideas, often in contrast to one's own, and the constant looming threats entailed with the issue of funding. If he could be the support and lamp bearer for these budding youngsters, well, nothing put a smile upon Ghayas's face so easily. Together, Kalim and Ghayas were revealing their greatest potentials.

Since Tripoli, Kalim had been cooking up a grand idea. After adding in the inputs from the few meetings the group had in his home, a document had come forth. Kalim presented to the group what he would call 'The Draft Prospectus' for the Muslim Institute. There are a great many accounts of monumental documents being presented throughout the history of humanity. Not too many of them are immediately proceeded by one of the primary authors having his first heart attack.

The heart attack was a great blow to the mighty Kalim Siddiqui. The doctor's orders were to cease all work and to kindly go into the world of retirement. Kalim acquiesced the doctor's orders, or at least his interpretation of them. After all, even the wisest Imams tend to differ on the final details of the *batin* (inner meaning) and *zahir (*outer meaning) of the sacred text. He resigned from his role as sub-editor at *The Guardian* and the USC's West Germany campus. He would later recall walking into

The Guardian editor's room handing in his notice. Why are you resigning, Kalim? You have such a promising career here, asked the astonished editor. Kalim, never one to miss an opportunity to mince his words, "Given my background, you would never have considered appointing me as the next editor when you retire." And with that he walked out, leaving his ex-boss speechless.

In his mind, he must have thought himself rather clever, for just as the doctors had ordered, he was to take it easy at home. It wasn't important that they knew he had simply turned his home into his office. It is not like they could stop him from thinking and, in his mind, he perhaps saw no correlation between intellectual effort and coronary exertion. Similarly, in 1978, Ghayas also resigned his teaching post in Corby to become a full-time member of the Institute. The house in Slough transformed into the first base of operations for the Muslim Institute for Research and Planning. The group had elected Kalim their Director and Ghayas the Assistant Director. Out of the house next door to Kalim they ran the Open Press, where the first major works of the Institute were published. Kalim's recovery was marked by a highly robust and productive grand entrance for the Institute.

Ghayas would wake early each day just as the sun made its first peaks over the horizon, take his tea and breakfast, and then be off on the commute to Slough, where the day began around ten in the morning and would run until the day's work was finished. At times, this would align with normal work day hours; often it would result in the burning of midnight oil. The hours were not set, for passion does not abide with the human appreciation of time and space. Of course, the commute was quite the trek for Ghayas, so it was time to move closer to London.

Kalim noted with a chuckle that his 'distant relative' Maqsood Siddiqui would travel with Ghayas to the village of Chesham. It was the end of the line for the Metropolitan Line; the small village was developing a new neighbourhood after the sale of a plot of farmland. Up the hill from the high street, Ghayas arrived with

Maqsood at the first stop, a house still being constructed. Over-looking the village off to the east and the gorgeous moors to the south and west, the house-to-be would have a wonderful view of the setting sun from the living room. The grammar schools would be wonderful places for the next generation of Siddiquis to gain their education. It was perfect. Right there, Ghayas bought the house which he and his family would occupy to this day.

At around the same time, an idea consumed Kalim's work. He felt that the Institute needed an office in London to gain rec-ognition. The addition of an official London address to the flurry of paper snowflakes flying from the Institute would only serve to advance the cause. And imagine what that cause could do with an address in London's famous Bloomsbury area!

The late 1970s were just the rocket ship launch that the Mus-lim Institute needed to solidify its place in the recovery of the ummah. Kalim and Ziauddin set out writing work after work. At the same time the two travelled to Saudi Arabia to secure what funding they could from old contacts. The funds they raised were partly used by the Institute to purchase London properties as in-vestments. At the same time their works and names were getting bounced around at conferences. Day by day, Ghayas would ar-rive in Slough to think, write and edit. Perfection was demanded; it was the least they could all do for the ummah. The stars had aligned and for a flutter of a moment, this interesting group of in-dividuals became one, dedicated to what they would each spend the rest of their lives doing in their own unique way: securing power for the Muslim people.

The Western style had foiled the possibility of prosperity in the Muslim world, so a new system was needed. Perhaps a large pan-Islamic system could be founded, or perhaps it would need to be a country by country, community by community pursuit. Either way, the Institute was on the case. It needed to create both the framework for taking power and provide a platform for gen-eration after generation to continue the project that was, from the start, understood as a multi-generational journey. Kalim and Ghayas began making trips around the world, consulting old contacts and securing more funding. South Africa became a sort of second home for Kalim. By 1978, the Institute had secured the funding it needed to give Kalim his dream: an office in Bloomsbury, the intellectual capital of England, perhaps even the world. The heart of Britain's publishing empire, it was in the power to define, in words, that the realm would exert its power beyond waning territorial claims. Bloomsbury also housed the University of London, its campuses and colleges. An address here surely demanded respect and was certain to impress. At No. 6 Endsleigh Street the Muslim Institute would find its new home. Now the director could breathe a sigh of relief. Kalim could rest assured that they were now in the big leagues. They had an office, a healthy stock of publications, funding, a dedicated and hard-working assistant, and a superior class of young Muslim intellectuals to progress the Muslim world to dominance.

As Kalim sipped his tea, self-assured in the future before them, his noble assistant Ghayas sat nearby, reading a newspaper. A shockwave ran through him as he flipped through the sheets.

"Kalim bhai, I think something is happening in Iran."

Chapter Five

THE GLORIOUS IRANIAN DECADE

THINGS WERE INDEED happening. Kalim and Ghayas stood, mesmerised before the television's glow. The images projected showed a tall man cloaked in robes, with a bushy snow-white beard and thick dark eyebrows, descending the stairs from the door of Air France Flight 4721 onto the tarmac. Imam Ruhollah Mūsavi Khomeini was stepping foot back into Iran for the first time after 14 years of exile spent between Iraq and France. As he announced the new Islamic Republic in a comprehensible rhetorical Farsi, Kalim and Ghayas witnessed something different. To Kalim, this was not some Western educated puppet establishing a dummy regime nor another military brat who confuses obedience at gunpoint for religious devotion, a clever veil for a half-cocked attempt at Islamising the Western system of dominance. No, Imam Khomeini was the real deal. To Ghayas this man sounded the part of the last Mughal emperors; the glory of what could have been was, rather, being actualised between the news broadcasts. The Islamic State they once thought was decades down the road was now staring them directly in the face.

There are a variety of views on the 1979 revolution in Iran and what came in the years following the revolution only sought to further distort the truths, already subject to the bending of the corners of reality that results from the emotional bias of memory and political propaganda. The revolution itself was relatively bloodless, at least by the hands of the revolutionaries. The Shah did not share this regard of human life in his actions. Kalim believed that the American and British intelligence organisations would pay for their crimes of deposing Mohammad Mosaddegh in 1953, but he could not have fathomed it would turn out in the way that it did. The Shah, after all, was the worst of Western puppets, both secular in sentiment and Western in education as well as with the power of the military heavily on his side, the trifecta that was damning the Muslim world in one clean-cut devil of a man. Reza Shah and his family's luxurious lifestyle not only turned the public against them but strengthened the resolve of the other side of the pendulum, awaiting the balance of an overdue recoil.

Almost following the calendar year of 1979 to the day, the fall of the Shah and the rise of the new Islamic Republic played out. Beginning with the winter of anger that ended 1977, the following year became the year of student protest and civil disobedience. The unrest reached a head during the autumn where 1979 was rung in, each demonstration growing in intensity with every peaceful protester gunned down by the military or the Shah's secret police, SAVAK. By New Year's Day 1979, Iran was seized by strikes and demonstrations. On January 16, the last Shah of Iran, Mohammad Reza, riddled with cancer and the side effects of his medication, left Iran for asylum in Egypt, giving the country to his long-time opponent, Prime Minister Shapour Bakhtiar. Within a fortnight SAVAK was dismantled, thousands of political prisoners freed, and Imam Khomeini invited back to take up residence in the holy, scholarly city of Qom.

On 1 February 1979, Ayatollah Khomeini arrived in Tehran on a plane with an entourage of international journalists to ensure no mid-air foul play. Millions of Iranians greeted the Imam as he stoically made his grand entrance, assuring the loving people that the government would soon be theirs. Fighting in the streets continued between the Shah's departure and the eighth of February when the heads of the Iranian Air Force arrived at Imam Khomeini's home to pledge their allegiance to him. On the eleventh of February, the combined guerrilla and rebel troops overwhelmed the forces keeping Bakhtiar's government in power. The rest of the Iranian military declared themselves neutral in the conflict. By the first of April, spring at last, a national referendum was held and Iran would become an Islamic Republic under a theo-republican constitution. By December, Imam Khomeini would become the Supreme Ayatollah, the leader of the first truly Islamic state.[25]

The revolution not only signalled a moment of hope for the future of Iran and the Iranians, but a moment of jubilation for the great Muslim community. Finally, a postcolonial state that had cast away the chains of Western domination. This was the definitive moment in the lives of those who had been living the great struggle since the end of empire. Those intellectuals who sought to provide the groundwork for a new world order had one presented right before them, and with no spared expense.

While Saudi Arabia had provided a fruitful ground for funding and thought, its Western bias and influence would only reveal itself more and more as Iran rose to prominence. No longer were the *Wahabis* the sole authority over the Muslim world. The *Sunni-Shia* divide is often compared to the schisms within Christianity, but the rivalry within was largely peaceful until only very recently. Sunni and Shia lived together quite harmoniously for most of the history of Islam.[26] Ghayas himself had not thought himself to have known any Shia before the revolution, or at least you'd have never known whether someone he'd known was or was not. Imam Khomeini being a Shia leader of Islam was not as big a deal as it would become during the cold war between Saudi Arabia and Iran in more recent years. He was Muslim and that was all that mattered. In fact, his stoic mannerisms would have made him seem even less Shia had Kalim and Ghayas been as familiar with the ways and culture of Shia Muslims.

Kalim must have taken a particular delight in what Imam Khomeini had accomplished in the tumultuous year of 1979. Khomeini was an Islamic scholar, but he had also studied the philosophies of the West, applying himself to Plato and *The Republic* in particular. In the first days of the Muslim Institute, the key was to find a way to take the Western or any other system of governance and make it work in the specific framework (or frameworks in some cases) of the Muslim community. Khomeini becoming the Supreme Ayatollah was actually an accurate representation of Plato's Philosopher King, parodied and perfected under the auspices of Islam. Meanwhile, the ideal republic worked by rule of the popular majority and separation of powers endemic to democracy, under the leadership of the wisest men of the society. The Islamic State that Kalim and Ghayas thought a distant hope beyond their lifetimes had arrived. There was no time to spare.

The Muslim Institute shifted gears as No. 6 Endsleigh Street transformed into the Iranian embassy to the world, bound to the mission of exporting Imam Khomeini's revolution to the rest of the Muslim world. With each passing day, Kalim consumed more and more of the revolution from its rhetoric to the controversy that was taking the region and the Muslim world by storm. Kalim became an Iranophile of the highest order, his writing turning to praise and defence of the Imam's revolution and a call for all Muslim brothers and sisters to join the revolution. This was the avenue, through a toll road, that would bring the ummah to power. The question remained: at what price would this express lane be maintained?

A great debate broke out over the Iranian revolution between government officials, the media sources, and amongst students and intellectuals. Revolutions by their nature are volatile and revolutionaries are bent upon overthrowing. A problem always arises when the revolutionaries take control; the role of rebels is no longer needed, yet when one fights for such a long period of time, the reasons for fighting fade as the fight itself becomes a way of life. Iran cannot be toted as a pure revolution. It bears many of the flaws of other revolutions. A great purging would occur, throwing out many of the original revolutionary leaders, as power and paranoia tends to poison logical thought processes. The hostage crisis at the old American embassy left a permanent dark mark on the Iranian revolution. For Kalim, such instances were the necessary evil of revolution. The West was, after all, the great enemy bound to the responsibility for their actions. War demands a price, and liberation comes at one of the greatest costs— Ghayas understood this. As long as the revolution itself did not go the way of the other military dictatorships of the Middle East, the hope and good the revolution could bring to the Muslim community outweighed these minor indiscretions.

Not all of the original Muslim Institute would hold such a position. In the past, the Institute would come by its decisions following deliberation and only when complete consensus was reached. The Iranian question would not be left by Kalim to the fate of democracy. Kalim would abide no compromise. Iran was the future of the Institute, full stop. Naturally, the Institute grew ill with hostility. One of the most vocal about the issue was Ziauddin Sardar. Following an intellectual battle with Kalim over the merits of revolutionaries, Ziauddin would storm off from Slough, not to return. The backers of the Saudis also left the Institute over the growing enmity between Khomeini and the King of Riyadh. Kalim did not enjoy the bitter taste that welcomed the 1980s, but he had the stomach for it. Ghayas's heart was in the students and their wellbeing. But his dedication must remain for the greater education at hand and the community they sought to serve and lift up. Kalim would assure Ghayas, any great historical revolution must suffer such disloyalties. The work for the ummah was greater than any one individual. Thus, the revolution was greater than him or Kalim, greater than any of them. Those who stood against them had to be cut loose; this was where the stand against the West was to be made. As the many fights against the West had driven brother against brother in the past, how could this be any different?

The transition would be marked not only by a change in ideas and the tune of their writings, but hiring new staff who were supporters of the new Iran. Kalim had long felt the movement needed a microphone and like all major movements, a newspaper was requisite. Since 1972, Lateef Owaisi and his wife, Zahida, ran a local community paper in Canada called *Crescent*. Zafar Bangash had moved to Toronto in 1974 after completing his studies and a year later began writing for the paper. Lateef was a warm-hearted, gentle and softly spoken man who took young Zafar under his wing.

However, Zafar had his eye on the editor's chair. Soon after the revolution, Zafar would write in praise of it. This caught the eye of Kalim and in 1980, he invited Zafar to London to discuss the future of the paper with himself and Ghayas. After follow up meetings in London and with Kalim and Ghayas travelling to Toronto several times, it was agreed that the paper would be rebranded as *Crescent International* with ownership transferring to the Muslim Institute's publishing wing, the Open Press. Zafar was made editor in name only and editorial content was provided by Kalim and Ghayas. Zafar would later joke that if he was assassinated for what was published in *Crescent International* they would have killed the wrong man.

Ghayas became executive editor and for the first few months Ghayas would prepare the content of the paper and post it by DHL from Endsleigh Street to Toronto, where it would be typed up and typeset for copy. This was an age before fax machines were commonly used, let alone email. Meanwhile, Zafar had managed to sideline and push out Lateef and Zahida from the paper they founded, as he travelled across North America as the paper's glorified salesman and editor-in-chief.

Kalim would reward his loyal friends as those on the edge would be quickly brushed out of the way. The revolution needed the momentum of progress and would not be held up by minor squabbles. The Institute would quickly reconstitute itself as something very different from the hopeful ragtag garage band of young students looking to change the world that it was less than a decade before.

Kalim's blood boiling from the trauma the Institute had suffered, now embarked on a greater cardiac strain as he and Ghayas began their many trips to the new Islamic Republic. No matter, for the heart Ghayas bore could carry them both along through this new decade. Kalim and Ghayas, two Siddiquis, must have looked quite the sight. Two bespectacled men attending conferences clad in plaid blazer jackets and the casual professionalism of Western business attire, surrounded by men in long tunics, vests and robes, their heads topped with wool caps or turbans. The works of Kalim and the Institute quickly rose to prominence amongst the Iranian intellectuals and the two men would be hailed with similar affinity afforded celebrities, at least as close as two academics could find to rock star status on this globe. Hailing themselves the representatives of the rest of the world, the Sunni Muslims, and the ummah to whom they would deliver Iran's beautiful revolution, they were ranked among the most honoured guests in the Islamic Republic.

Kalim and Ghayas made good company with one of their reoccurring contacts, Mir-Hossein Mousavi, one of the ground troops of the revolution who would become Foreign Minister before being appointed Prime Minister of Iran. Ghayas and Mousavi hit it off like old friends as both Mousavi and his wife were famous activists like Ghayas himself. As revolutions go, many of its warriors are eventually eaten up by the machine of change. Mousavi would experience this when the post of Prime Minister was eliminated in 1989 and his invitation to be a part of a new government was rejected. He would remain disenchanted and retired from politics until beckoned back at the turn of the millennium to be a grand reformer of what now stands as contemporary Iran.

Many times, Kalim and Ghayas would be met at the airport by Mohammad Khatami, the then Minister of Culture and Islamic Guidance. To Khatami, these men were a great asset to the exportation of the revolution, which was one of Iran's key strategies throughout the 1980s. Khatami would once ask Kalim and Ghayas's opinion on whether or not he should run for the presidency in the early 1990s, but Ghayas had insisted that their role was restricted to affairs outside of Iran. The domestic affairs of the Islamic Republic were just those and the influence of Ghayas or Kalim would be highly inappropriate. Khatami would eventually seek and win the Presidency of Iran in 1997. A common note Ghayas had of all the early revolutionary leaders of Iran was their modesty. They would wear tattered clothing and shoes worn down and full of holes.[27] These were true believers and their morality only stood to embolden the idea of the revolution which, as Kalim had pointed out, was greater than all of them.

One of Ghayas's most honoured meetings came when he was granted an audience with the Supreme Leader in the early days of the revolution. Due to protocol, Kalim was not able to meet Imam Khomeini, but Ghayas was able to meet him as a member of the public. Far from one of London's many illustrious hotel lobby cafés, the Imam was seated on a simple chair in his small garden. Ghayas was impressed by his modesty and simplicity. Such an old man had brought down the king of kings. His simplicity was similar to that of Maududi when he had met him in jail. Despite being tall, his presence was not the Hollywood grandeur that his layers of cloaks gave him during his press conferences. He had a caring nature that extended to you in a comforting warmth. Yes, the Philosopher King of Persia he might well have been, but there he was, an equal amongst all of Allah's creation.

Age and travel had left him thinner than the robust plump of other world leaders, but all the more a truly wise man. His dark eyebrows so easily demonised by the media expressed a considerate and perhaps less stoic than he'd prefer to have known, simple man. He spoke Farsi and immediately felt bad that an interpreter had not been prepared for Ghayas. Ghayas told him in Urdu not to worry, and the Ayatollah was blown back. He understood. The Farsi Imam Khomeini spoke was a common vernacular that was simple and easy for all of Iran's people to understand. His speech therefore had enough in common with Urdu that these two men, born a great distance apart, could be joined together by their greater history of Mughal emperors, who would allow them to make sense of each other's words. Much of the details of the conversation are lost to memories that may never be tapped into, but one important lesson stayed with Ghayas all these years later. The community, the Ayatollah said, is above all else. What community? The Iranians? Our local community? The ummah? The world? Our family? All of these? None? The community was the ummah of Shias and Sunnis together. The Supreme Leader gave the smile of a childlike sense of curiosity and wonder only befitting a true philosopher. A Philosopher King at that.

With Kalim and Ghayas making the conference circuits, moving between Tehran and London, and with Zafar publishing their words out of Toronto, a nice global network was making good on the promise to export the revolution's ideas and sentiments. The Muslim Institute would design and run an annual 8-week intensive Arabic course over the summer at City University popular with local students bringing in teachers from top Arab universities. The course would help students understand the language of the Qur'an. In 1981, *Muslimedia* was launched by the Muslim Institute as a news service of articles sent as a portfolio to Muslim media outlets across the world in the hope that they would get published. Its editor was Zafarul Islam Khan, an Indian-born graduate from Cairo University who had worked at the Libyan Foreign Ministry as an editor-translator. He was the son of the great Muslim scholar and peace activist, Maulana Wahiduddin Khan, who was critical of overly politicised interpretations of Islam. But in the 1980s his son was a promoter of Kalim's cause.

In 1987, Zafarul Islam Khan got a PhD in Islamic studies from Manchester University and would return to India, setting up the *Milli Gazette* in 2000, an influential fortnightly for Indian Muslims. He would also be elected president of the All India Muslim Majlis-e-Mushawarat, an umbrella body for Indian Muslims, in 2008.

In 1987, an Arabic version of *Crescent International* began publication under the name of *Al-Hilal al-Dawli*. This was produced by Dr. Basheer Nafi, a Palestinian-born historian living in England, Dr. Shihab al-Sarraf and Dr. Adel Abdel Mehdi. The latter two were Iraqis—one Sunni, one Shia—who would one day be on opposing sides after the fall of Saddam in 2003, with Shihab becoming a representative of the political wing of the Sunni insurgency and Adel becoming the Prime Minister of Iraq and a member of the Supreme Council for the Islamic Revolution in Iraq (Sciri) that founded the Badr Brigades. But back in the 1970s they were all on the same side as exiled members of the Iraqi Communist Party and would share a flat in Poitiers in France. By the 1980s they would ditch communism for Islamism and become supporters of Khomeini. Soon after the launch of *Al-Hilal*, Ghayas travelled to Rouen in France where Adel had a small flat. Ghayas caught the train from London to Paris and from there a train to Rouen to discuss the matters of the day with Adel. The flat was so small that Ghayas would spend a night in France, sleeping on the floor.

Between the tiresome travels, normalcy returned to 6 Endsleigh Street where Ghayas, after his breakfast, tea and newspaper would, by a routine system of train hopping, arrive in Bloomsbury to crack on until the work was done, sometimes not returning home until well past sunset. Think, write, edit, repeat. Meanwhile, the burgeoning population of immigrants and the swirling of international affairs throughout the Muslim world raged, and racism and white nationalist sentiment experienced a pendulum swing in response. Thatcher's Britain was revving up at full speed. Naturally, Kalim and the Institute began to more directly butt heads with the Conservative government of the era. The 1980s spelled the age of fear: fear of disease, rebellion, and whatever shadows the imagination could manage to stretch into monsters.

The 1980s also bore witness to the heady days of the revolution and the emergence of what Kalim would coin 'the global Islamic movement' with Iran at its centre. He hypothesised and promoted the idea of an overarching framework that joined up local and national Islamic movements into a global movement calling for Islamic revolutions across the Muslim world and a convergence of Muslim political thought. Logan Hall at the Institute of Education would be hired out by the Muslim Institute to host annual world seminars on the political goals of an Islamic civilisation. Major figures and activists from the Islamic movement in the Arab world, the Indian subcontinent, the Far East and Africa would come together to connect, network, share their experiences and discuss their futures. Papers would be presented at the seminars that would later be published and circulated globally, not least through the *Crescent International* and *Muslimedia* outlets. London would soon become the most high profile centre of the Islamic movement with more freedom in the 1980s to gather and debate than existed in most of the Muslim world. Logan Hall would soon be so associated with these seminars that some thought that the very building was owned by the Institute, rather than the small offices at 6 Endsleigh Street.

As the 1980s wore on, so did a war between Khomeini's Iran and Saddam Hussein's Iraq, who had been given resources from the Saudi crown.[28] Because of this, Ghayas's visit to Iran would involve less and less meetings with the leaders. Even his now good friend and fellow professional activist Mousavi was increasingly hard to find, let alone see in person. One day at the Tehran airport, Mousavi, still wearing shoes with holes in them, ran up to Ghayas, apologising profusely for his perceived evasion. The war with Iraq had taken its toll on the young state. Mousavi implored Ghayas to come with him. They walked along the tarmac, not to a plane, but instead to a (at the time) state-of-the-art military helicopter. Mousavi and Ghayas strapped in. Where they were going exactly was classified.

As Ghayas looked out of the side of the helicopter, the violent whipping of the rudder and aggravated wind deafened him, but the sights stained pictures in his memory. Devastation filled the shoreline of the Shattal-Arab, the Persian Gulf flowed into the clashes of blue that formed the horizon. Old tanks and trenches speckled about, smoke still rising from recent carnage. Hundreds of thousands lost their lives on both sides and accurate numbers may never be known. Hundreds of billions of US dollars spent on destruction. The helicopter they rode in demonstrated the class of power that a state had, capable of taking ideology to new levels. The might of a military, weapons acquisition, the capacity to declare war, the money, a budget. The state had something that the individual dreamer could never imagine. Mousavi wanted Ghayas to see the horrors of war. Blood and gold. These were the real stakes of the revolution. Did they have to be though?

The 1980s also served as the explicit assurance that Kalim and Ghayas were no longer the young men they were at the beginning of this journey. 1981 was the year of Kalim's second heart attack, resulting in bypass surgery. The excitement and work of exporting a revolution was proven not to be the retirement the doctors had in mind. The bypass worked as a sort of new lease of life for Kalim. Bypasses were expected to last for at least ten years. Thus, a new timetable stood before Kalim. His greatest work still remained to be written. It was time to write his magnum opus, the words that would usher in the Islamic Revolution. Not the one from 1979, as he would note, but the next one. The one that would demand global recognition and respect for the Muslim people, a grand authority to bring new voices to the table of international affairs and stand against the oppressive nature of Western dominance. So Kalim, Ghayas at his side, embarked again on the last great ride. Conference by conference he would present his ideas and draft new papers. His ideas would be dedicated to Imam Khomeini and his hope to read them to him. Unfortunately, Khomeini would pass from this world before he could deliver the paper, but he would be allowed to read it to his successor, Ali Khamenei. Eventually it would become the groundwork for his last book published in 1996, *Stages of Islamic Revolution.*[29]

As the sun set on the 1980s, Ghayas found himself hearing about the latest book from Salman Rushdie. He had never been terribly impressed with any of Rushdie's prior books; he was more of a fan of non-fiction, lacking a proper appreciation of the subtleties of fiction. This book in particular, *The Satanic Verses*, came with small whispers of controversy. Only a small part of the book, Rushdie's characterisation of the Prophet Muhammad, was beyond offence, greater even than personal insult. Ghayas and Kalim discussed the book, aware of what Rushdie had done to the image of the Prophet, but Rushdie was not the first—adding to the great tradition that spans back to Dante—and would certainly not be the last. The two agreed that they didn't have the time or resources to make such a big deal out of a madman's ramblings. Plus, as Kalim knew from his *Guardian* days, no press is bad press, so an attempt to speak out against this book or even get it banned would only lend favour to his coffers. Nothing increases book sales like controversy! They agreed to let the mediocre attempt at social commentary under the sheepskin of ill-contrived mystical realism fade into the obscurity of dusty library stacks.

The revolution in Iran suffered the fate of all major revolutions. The burnout set in. Paranoia and power-wielding would corrupt as it corrupts all indiscriminately. The expense of a decade of war with Iraq and the parting of ways with Western powers left a decimated economy. The fate of the Islamic Republic seemed to be diminishing with each sunset. It was looking like the glorious revolution would meet its end with the passing of its first Supreme leader.[30] The world at large was also moving on. Changing. The spectres of communism revealed naked emperors as the Berlin Wall fell. The secular militants had grown deep roots in the skeletal remains of empire, comprising the nation-states of the contemporary Middle East. Economic rollercoasters and the evolution of social trends left the world in a collective hangover at the end of the 1980s. Worst of all, the ummah was tired. The thinkers and fighters of the postcolonial world watched on as what hair remained ran grey, and the updating of prescriptions replaced updated appraisals of their worldview. The revolution was exhausted and the bright eyes of hope had been weighed down by the bruised bags that follow age and stress. The hope of the ummah appeared to have gone the way of Kalim's heart. Even Ghayas found age creeping up on him in Chesham. His children were now reaching the age when he began the great fight: what did they have to look up to, what hope would define their generation?

In February 1989, Ghayas and Kalim were visiting Tehran for yet another amongst the gallery of unremarkable conferences they would attend. In the early morning of 14 February, tired, they left the Laleh International Hotel in Tehran where they would often stay and made their way to Mehrabad airport, hoping for a quick and painless flight home. But it would appear Allah had other plans for these two. A heavy snow descended upon Tehran and as they stood amongst the crowds of other would-be passengers, they watched as flight after flight was cancelled. Ghayas needed to begin making arrangements to return to the hotel for the night. Just as he was about to do so, out of the corner of his eye, Mohammad Khatami, the Minister of Culture and Islamic Guidance, appeared, dropping off another dignitary. Khatami spotted Kalim and approached the gentlemen.

Brother Kalim, Khatami hearkened. He wished to have a word, for there was a matter of Imam Khomeini's highest priority he wished to discuss with Kalim.

Very well, an exhaustion-made-agreeable Kalim proceeded, following Khatami off to a distant corner in the airport terminal.

Ghayas stood back with their bags. Perhaps their old friend Khatami could still get them a flight out of Tehran?

Chapter Six

THE WAR OF WORDS

TIME MOVES DIFFERENTLY in airports. Rather, time seems to tread towards absolute zero—that is, until it is time to go and then truly it is time to go! How long exactly did Ghayas stand with the luggage as Kalim and Khatami spoke? Well, it was, in airport terms, the exact amount of time that a small conversation had to take. Once that time was spent, Kalim skipped back to Ghayas. Khatami, a busy man no doubt, gave a quick salutation for he had to make haste to his next meeting with Imam Khomeini. Ghayas saw him off with a wave. He waited patiently as Kalim caught his breath. The assistant listened as Kalim held back a smile and his voice grounded itself in excitement. Kalim took a deep breath. First, the bad news. They would not be spending Valentine's Day in London, but would be on the next flight after the storm cleared. The good news? Well, there was going to be a lot of that to go around. Kalim's boyish smile had lost its ability to humour Ghayas by this point, so he grabbed the luggage and carried on, for there was no point lamenting in the airport when they could be seeing to arrangements for the night.

Khatami's words with Kalim were part and parcel of the trips he and Ghayas would make to Iran. There would often be these unscheduled, abrupt and impromptu meetings where Khatami or Mousavi or one of the other ministers or government workers would approach the two Siddiquis, asking for their opinion on the hot topic of that particular week. This week, as the buzz would have it, it appeared that Salman Rushdie's book had wound up on the desk of Ayatollah Khomeini and being the leader of the Islamic state, it was incumbent upon him to act.

The Siddiquis, meanwhile, returned to their hotel to rest off the inclement weather responsible for their delayed exit. As they sat in the lobby a young man spotted these well-known personalities and ran up to them excitedly. The young man asked, "Have you heard the radio?" We don't understand Farsi and we're tired, came the reply. There was an announcement. The book is banned. Death to Rushdie. The radio sang of the announcement heralding their Supreme Leader in flawless Farsi. The Imam had issued a *fatwa* against Salman Rushdie.

Kalim was elated. Popular mythology maintains Kalim as the grand master of the fatwa, but this is simply not the case. While Kalim and Khatami spoke for a while about Rushdie, it is not clear whether Khatami had raised Kalim's opinion on Rushdie with Khomeini or whether it would have made the slightest bit of difference to him. Ghayas and Kalim had always made clear their stance on domestic affairs and political acts of the Iranian government. They would support, but never influence. And while some would argue that such imprudence may be needed in dire affairs, Kalim would have been one of the last to say that Rushdie was any threat to the ummah. After all, as Kalim stated to Ghayas, he knew how popular opinion worked; he understood the press. His jubilation arose out of the fact that this could have wider implications on the respect and dignity of the Muslim world. Kalim's support of the idea came not as a preconceived master conspiracy, but a reflective opportunistic measure.

Khatami's crossing paths with Kalim in the airport was more the subject of chance than anything else. He was merely passing on the news. To think a proclamation that had been carefully debated and reasoned by religious scholars had any influence from a foreign cheerleader in the few hours before its official release is nothing short of ridiculous. Kalim had rejected doing anything on the matter of *The Satanic Verses* when Ghayas first spoke to him about it earlier that year. What changed is that now a figure of political leverage could launch a fight that would take power back for the Muslim people.

A fatwa was simply a legal opinion in accordance with Islamic law, sharia, handed down by a qualified Muslim jurist. Countless fatwas on issues ranging from waging wars to domestic disputes have been handed out over the centuries. They are not legally binding in accordance with state judicial systems, but often are presented as an answer to a question. Imam Khomeini's fatwa stands out for multiple reasons. One, it calls for the punishment of death to Salman Rushdie for his grave offence to Muslims, the Prophet, and the Holy Qur'an. It was also the ruling of the leader of the first Islamic State. A decade before, Muslims finally had a locus for global political power in the new Islamic Republic of Iran. Now the only political leader out there to speak for the Muslim people, regardless of his Shia background, had called upon all true believers to carry out justice. This justice carried historic weight for the entire history of Islam; Muslims have been the butt of the joke, often recklessly demonised in the great works of Western literature and art. This was central to the revolution. Muslims standing up for themselves and ending the era of ridicule the West had imposed upon them for so long.

The flight between Tehran and London had become routine for Ghayas and so denied this particular flight any significance. However, this flight was the first out of Tehran after the fatwa and the aircraft was parked up separately at Heathrow until security checks had been complete. The British government was on high alert fearing that the Iranians may have sent a hit squad on the first flight out of Iran. There were no assassins. As they departed the plane, Kalim turned to Ghayas with a smile. The Imam has rewarded us for our support of the revolution, Kalim beamed.

Ghayas found himself in deep confusion in the early days of the Rushdie controversy. He knew Kalim's long career with *The*

Guardian taught him all too well how to get headlines. Wouldn't this whole thing just result in a boost in sales of the damn book? And Kalim knew well how the elite intellectual talking heads of Britain worked. What was to stop them turning Rushdie into a martyr for secular liberalism? Yet Kalim understood this risk well. These were all definite possibilities, but he had faith in the questions this whole ordeal would unearth. Also, Kalim loved Khomeini. It was his duty to defend this fatwa but to remain within the laws of the land. This flirtation was a skill Kalim had nearly perfected in his career. It would require a well-choreographed dance, politically and rhetorically, through the media. The roar Islam was capable of voicing needed to be felt and understood.

Yet the stakes were very real. A man was being condemned to death before the mercy of a group of what would become very offended people. Would the Muslim Institute support the killing of a man? Was this the penultimate conclusion of all those lively, progressive discussions in Slough? Ghayas's questions pulled at the thread between honourable and well minded, and blind loyalty. Ghayas's conditions ran through his mind. Kalim was the unabashed revolutionary. He was not afraid to call this what it was: war. And war would carry with it the natural by-product of casualties and martyrs, certainly. And was it not about time that the West suffered a loss or two on behalf of a history of transgressions and insults? But no; Kalim, in all his fire, knew the game at hand would require playing by the rules of a gentlemen's game. The war needed to be more sophisticated than discharged anger. Kalim leaned in towards Ghayas. They, as global ambassadors of the revolution, would support the fatwa of Imam Khomeini, just as any devout Muslim ought to. But, remember, devout Muslims are also bound by the Word of God to follow the laws of the lands in which they make their residence. In the United Kingdom, murder was illegal. So, as the devout Muslims they were, they would both support the fatwa, but as British citizens they were not allowed to carry it out; a comfortable contradiction that Kalim would take full advantage of.

Kalim knew how to make Salman Rushdie's life very uncomfortable while also being a law-abiding citizen. The man knew headlines and knew just the words to say to provoke without incriminating. This was Thatcher's Britain though, and fear was the name of the game. Both sides knew how to dig it up, but the art was in being able to play in it without actually getting one's hands dirty. The glorious accomplishment in Iran was wearing out its edge; the revolution was not only yesterday's news but the war with Iraq and for global popular attention was proving, regardless of outcome, a costly affair. But this was just the bombshell event needed to reignite the revolution. Kalim's second revolution was the global revolution that would finally leave the West to recognise and demand the respect of the Muslim people. It was a message as sweet as wine and equally as intoxicating, and, of course, one Kalim himself would never imbibe.

The truly bizarre reality was that, prior to September 1988, Iran adored Salman Rushdie. While *Midnight's Children* gave him grief in India, most notably a lawsuit from Indira Gandhi, it identified with the postcolonial diaspora and the so-called 'third world'.[31] *Shame* in the same vein was so loved that the Persian translation was given an award by a special council appointed by the ministry of the new Islamic Republic itself.[32] *The Satanic Verses* was a slap in the face to some of his greatest global fans. Perhaps Rushdie was the reason it has been said one ought never to meet their heroes!

By the fourteenth of February 1989, a flurry of death threats had already rolled into both Rushdie and his publisher's office following the book's release in September of 1988. Indian media had called for a ban of the book and it was already banned in South Africa, Pakistan, Saudi Arabia, Egypt, Somalia, Bangladesh, Sudan, Qatar, Malaysia, and Indonesia. Demonstrations had occurred throughout the Muslim world and in the UK, and there were already cases being made that the book ought to be banned as a violation of the blasphemy law. In fact, the world took little notice of the UK's first major book burning demonstration of *The Satanic Verses* that took place in Bolton on the second of December. Over seven thousand Muslims attended this rally. Better covered was the Bradford book burnings of January that were attended by both Muslims and non-Muslims. A handful of people had died in demonstrations against the book in Islamabad, Jammu and Kashmir. All of this, even before the Imam's proclamation. The Muslim world and its allies were already unified against Rushdie's book. Khomeini simply made it official and offered an 'Islamic' solution to an offence against the ummah. The announcement of the fatwa reminded the world, already on the verge of chaotic violence over words written, that a war was already at hand. In response, it appeared that all sides picked up arms and the troops were to be mobilised to the new battlefields of the contemporary warfare of the time: the television. Now the world was plunged into war from the comfort of their living room couches, armed with tea and biscuits.

The news cameras and the periodicals ate up everything they could get and Kalim gave them everything they could ask for. Like Oliver on the stage, Kalim's inner performer was in full blossom. The words got messy. Confusion racked the British Muslim community as they attempted to put all the pieces together. The lefty liberals fell into line just as Kalim had anticipated and in some cases, better than was expected. The racism and ignorance built up over the Thatcher decade was just waiting to overflow in hate and fear mongering. Respectable intellectuals showed how much they truly did not understand about their Muslim neighbours. Writers such as Christopher Hitchens flew to the defence of Rushdie,[33] but their appeal to the sanctity of freedom of speech in the civilised West was riddled with flaws. Indeed, the world today still has trouble understanding the fact that freedom of speech also means having a responsibility to the consequences of one's words. Charlie Hebdo in France, the Danish Jyllands-Posten's cartoons. The contemporary world is never short of hate speech and no doubt, the consequences of such spilt bile will continue to be felt for years to come.

The UK's hate speech bans were not here to rally behind—those would not come until the new millennium. There was a hope in the blasphemy laws; after all, under these very laws, not much more than a decade earlier Denis Lemon, the editor of *Gay News*, was ordered to pay a fine and, although he did not end up serving the time, was sentenced to jail time over his publication of James Kirkup's poem *The Love that Dares to Speak its Name* in which Jesus Christ and his disciplines are portrayed as homosexuals who share more than just bread. Although the West would again prove its lack of concern for the Muslims, the blasphemy laws specifically stood to protect the public from the defamation of the Anglican Church. British common law had no term for xenophobia and Parliament had not even adopted a definition for anti-Semitism, let alone Islamophobia.[34] The resolution to this dilemma could not rely on the Western system; it relied upon a new way, a distinctly Muslim style of handling the matter, as well as a bit of creativity.

Kalim and Ghayas toured the English countryside, travelling to the universities they had spoken at numerous times over the past decades. Manchester, Birmingham and Leeds were just some of the stops on the Muslim Institute's Anti-Rushdie UK tour. There was a ferocious energy in the students they came across on this tour. This was the moment that would shape the new generation just as the Iranian Revolution had inspired the generation before them. A pent-up rage of youth and rebellion, waiting most patiently throughout Thatcher's reign for the blue touch paper that would light the powder keg. The tired, worn and beaten survivors of the nightmare that was the 1980s found a second wind that would not be under-appreciated. Students had their postcolonial struggle, their chance to stick it to the West. Young

Muslims all over England clapped and cheered when Kalim and Ghayas came to town. The fatwa was echoed in every corner of Britain and it was readily clear that Rushdie's home was becoming a dangerous place for him. By way of *Crescent International*, the movement had crossed the pond and Canadian Muslims showed equal levels of vitriol over Rushdie's words. Margaret Thatcher and her Conservative government were pressured to step in, providing Rushdie with round the clock protection. Ironically, the woman Rushdie himself had dubbed 'Margaret Torture', giving her about as kind a description as he did the Prophet in *The Satanic Verses*, was his defender through his darkest hour.

A common defence of Rushdie's words comes in the excuse that few actually read the book, for if they had, then they would understand his metaphorical language was actually not directed at denouncing Islam. The ring of this tune is still heard thirty years on. This sentiment reflects the unfortunate state of ignorance reigning supreme in our supposedly advanced civilisation. The matter of *The Satanic Verses* was not simply a misinterpretation blown out of proportion. Throughout the book, Rushdie, and perhaps it is debatable as to whether he was aware or not, makes very directed inflammatory comments about the Prophet and towards Islam.

Yet, Rushdie's reputation is for being a clever wordsmith. After all, a subsequent book written by him, *Two Years Eight Months and Twenty-Eight Nights* does not take a degree in maths to reveal a clear reference to 1,001 Arabian Nights. It is hard to believe that Rushdie was not aware of what he had done with the novel. It would have been respectable if he simply would have come out and been honest; instead, he was a coward of the highest order, hiding behind the bias of the state and the Islamophobia woven into the fabric of society. He rallied the banners of free speech when he himself could not admit to what he was, in fact, saying. All of his works are less metaphorical than they are allegorical. This begins with his first book *Grimus*, where he anchored his characters in a specific reality. He was clearly discussing India and Britain and numerous historical characters throughout. Then when he was called out on it, as in the case of Indira Gandhi, he thought he could simply apologise and move on to spew whatever filth he could dream up next. It would be very hard to make the argument that Rushdie was not aware that his use of the title Mahound for the obvious allusion to the Prophet did not elicit the medieval Christian use of the term as a caricature to mock and demonise the man, and by association, the people of the book. In fact, he perhaps thought himself rather clever. It holds that the clever man and the intelligent man are not always one and the same! It takes profound idiocy to think that this point alone would not offend. Yet, he continues on.

The titular 'satanic verses' are in fact, direct verses from the Holy Qur'an. If giving a racist caricature of Muhammad was not enough, he was made a bumbling fool who stumbles upon revelation and shares his bed with prostitutes, who just so happen to bear the names of Muhammad's wives. The whole book then appears to channel all of the hate and fear of the West by stating that Gabriel's revelation to the Prophet was the revelation not of God, but of Satan. He then claimed the inherently authoritative nature of Islam had spread the message too far to be revoked. He further touches on various historical instances in the history of the Prophet and of the followers of Islam, through the lens of the less than sympathetic writers of Western history, perverting them with the worst aspects of human nature so as to make it all seem not simply misguided, but evil.

To rub salt into the wound, his two main characters are a horrendous anthropomorphic portrayal of the archangel Gabriel and a man bearing the name Saladin, the name given to the ultimate devil of the crusades in the Western worldview, a man who might as well not have existed but was a nice symbol as the usurper of the holy land. Rushdie's greatest offence was in purporting that this tale was the struggle of all postcolonial Indians.

It is a grave insult to the community when one member has the talent for words yet uses them to demonise his brothers and sisters, hiding his bullying within the sympathies of the other.[35] At its heart, the affair revealed the new level of treason afoot in *The Satanic Verses*.

Rushdie said in numerous interviews that this was his least political book.[36] Maybe, in fact, he can be given that. Rushdie's first mistake was thinking he could muck about, throwing egg on the face of Islam and that there was nothing anyone could do about it. Sure, well done Mr. Rushdie, you perpetuated the great tome of orientalist sentiment and reached a level of literary progress in line with the monks of medieval Europe. His second mistake and the one that his ignoramus army of followers that defend the book staked their play on, was that the war his words launched was political. The act of war that is *The Satanic Verses* is not a political fight, but a spiritual and religious one. Political battles are a daily occurrence and these wars have proper means and venues for their play. Political battles can end by convincing one of their opinion and even by the shedding of one's own ideology entirely. A fight with one's religion, a key element of their identity and being, is not something won by clever rhetoric and logical games. To pick at another's sense of being as one would a political identity is like thinking one simply peels the skin of an apple to get to the seeds.

The confusion between political and spiritual war made the Rushdie Affair all the messier. A hand was forced and countless died as a result of protests and would-be assassinations against Rushdie or linked to his book and eventual knighting. It resulted in the fatal stabbing of translator Hitoshi Igarashi and the mortal violence against publishers, translators and others involved in the propagation of blatant hate. The belief that this is just a political issue has led to countless other instances of violence across the globe and shows no signs of easing anytime soon. And to think he thought a public apology could make it all go away? Rushdie equally unified the Muslim community against him as he fractioned the community within itself on what to do about it. The Muslim community, particularly in Britain where Ghayas found himself, was united in suffering a spiritual and religious assault. What would divide them was the politics by which they would choose to oppose the novel.

Unfortunately, the popular media of the time conflated this grand existential crisis into a simple dichotomy: either you are offended and thus support death to Rushdie or you see the book as yet another collection of harmless words and support freedom of speech and art. The true complexity of the issue at hand was seen at the demonstrations before the great home of the Mother of Parliaments at Westminster Palace. To the casual onlooker, a demonstration in Parliament Square is not a strange or uncommon occurrence. The assembled masses on the 27 May 1989 must have just appeared to the bystander as a rather big band of Muslims upset about something. Unfortunately, the lack of clarity gave the portrait of a volatile group rife with violent intentions, unhinged and anarchic. This was not the truth. The 80,000 Muslims and their allies assembled represented a community brought together for the first time with the mosaic of beliefs, backgrounds and ideas that one would expect out of any such microcosm. The danger was that the police, bound to maintain order, could not fathom the diverse collection of opinions within the demonstration. Their job was not simply to keep the demonstrators safe from the general public, but to also keep the demonstrators safe from each other's radical different ideas on what to do with Rushdie. Kalim would not be in attendance for this demonstration and Ghayas was in Tehran.

Yet, the two Siddiquis' presence was felt through their supporters. His skills mastered from his days as a student activist in Karachi, Ghayas mobilised Barelvi and Shia mosques in support of the fatwa and arranged to have hundreds of Khomeini banners to accompany the demonstrators as they marched. He knew how to take over demonstrations and gatherings to assure the assembled were equally as much seen as heard. On one side of the demonstration stood Kalim's supporters and the various leaders of the tribe-like mosques that were developing throughout Britain, their key differences being as to what degree Rushdie should be killed. In the middle stood those who opposed the book for its offence, calling for the publishers, Viking Penguin, to take the book off the printing floor, but generally they disagreed with the fatwa, Imam Khomeini's position as the grand *mufti* of the Muslim world, or a combination of the two. And on the far side of the spectrum stood such groups as the Southhall Black Sisters (a group Ghayas would become friends with later in life) who opposed both the fatwa and the banning of Rushdie's book.

The rally began in Hyde Park where the banners calling for 'Rushdie Must Die' were hoisted mere metres from other banners calling for Freedom of Speech. From Hyde Park the mass moved to pay their respects to the Madame Prime Minister at 10 Downing Street. As particles set in motion tend to do, interactions occurred. By the time the group made it to the Prime Minister's residence, riot police were already dispatched and clashes ensued, not merely between the people and the police, but amongst the people themselves. The group made it at last to its final stop: Parliament Square. The old statue of Winston Churchill, cane bound and cloaked, must have looked especially haggard that day surrounded by the 80,000 demonstrators wielding all varieties of banners, national flags, messages of death and peace, nooses, and vandalised copies of *The Satanic Verses* as well as a burning effigy of Rushdie.[37] The chaos played out with the final result being over eighty arrests and numerous injuries. It could be forgivable if the onlooking leaders of the UK were unable to figure out what exactly it was the demonstrators wanted. Clearly, they were angry about something.

Kalim took note of the chaos, but he as well as those who actually gathered quickly realised that the Mother of Parliaments would have little, if any at all, by way of sympathy to hand out to the mass assembled. Kalim also disapproved of any chaos or rioting on the streets of London. Although he felt the demonstration was a huge success and emboldened support for the Imam's fatwa, and dampened attempts made by Saudi funded-organisations to turn UK Muslims away from the fatwa, he saw the limits of protests. That evening watching the coverage of the demonstration on the news at home with his children and Ghayas's children, who had all been at the demonstration earlier that day, Kalim was unhappy when some younger demonstrators were seen attacking the police and even burning a small British flag. This sentiment was shared with Ghayas's anti-hooligan beliefs towards destruction of property that he held since his days in Pakistan. Kalim felt he needed to think about how this energy could now be harnessed into something positive. His brain took on the duty of redirecting this potential that he knew could be easily as creative as it had been shown to be destructive. The structures in place in Britain were always going to be biased against any not of the ilk of Anglican Britannia. The affair would only be able to find its solution in something fashioned by the Muslim community itself. For Kalim, his masterpiece lay in wait for him to merely say the word and bring it into existence.

The potential for the unity of the British Muslim community was clearly imaginable at this point in history with the response to Rushdie's *The Satanic Verses*. Numerous groups sought to capitalise on this new entity to both bring its voice to the greater discourse as well as manage it day to day. The most basic structure of the Muslim community is the family. Through both the Qur'an and the cultural history of Muslims, this structure has remained the strongest and purest of structures underpinning the wider community, and what brought families together were the mosques. Unfortunately, and especially in Britain, the mosques would be prone to befall the corruption of politics. The funds which built the mega-mosques throughout Britain often came with the price tag of allegiance to various factions and sects. This is a common problem amongst organised religions and the unfortunate tribalism that resulted between nearby houses of worship was one of the pains that unified the Muslims with other religions, especially in the UK. Bringing the mosques together would be on par with herding cats. Undoubtedly a dubious task.

Other organisational attempts at bringing the British Muslims together were based on the importation of political parties from abroad and dedication to sects and their representation in the UK. The unity found within these groups, similar to the effect of political parties, were almost as much forces for division within the larger whole. Trends would be seen within the Muslim community that, for better or worse, were capitalised on in trying to bring them together. These trends included obedience to elderly wisdom and often masculine authoritative heads, despite the fact that behind the curtain, the women made sure the show went on, despite their demand to have more involvement in the decision-making at the mosques. Common language and the sense of unity in being 'the Other' also worked to create the earliest bonds of the British Muslim community.[38]

One school of thought was to work through the structures of British society to bring the voice of the British Muslims to the wielders of power, the shakers and the movers. Notably, at the rally on 27 May was an individual named Iqbal Sacranie. He distinguished himself above the assembled chaos with his quote that for Rushdie, "death, perhaps, is a bit too easy for him". It was a clever phrasing that would appease the constituency of the crowd calling for the blood of Salman Rushdie, yet kept him firmly against the carrying out of the fatwa's death sentence, despite the sadistic interpretations that rippled through the grapevine. Sacranie, like Kalim, saw the need for a voice amongst the British Muslim people. He was a founder of the United Kingdom Action Committee on Islamic Affairs at the time of the Rushdie demonstration. A need for something more concrete drove Sacranie to attempt to herd the cats. Fearing the rise of Kalim and the establishment of a separate parliament for British Muslims in 1992, the then Conservative Home Secretary, Michael Howard, suggested to Sacranie in 1994 that he set up a moderate alternative body that could represent British Muslims to government. This support continued with Tony Blair's New Labour Party. Diving deep into his list of contacts to members of the Muslim community in such areas as Manchester, Leicester and London, his friends bearing past associations with UK affiliates of the Muslim Brotherhood and Jamaat-e-Islami, Sacranie set out to make a governmental line between the British Muslim population and the UK establishment.

In 1997, Sacranie would take his place as the Secretary General of the new Muslim Council of Britain (MCB), a noble effort that earned Sacranie a knighthood. Although, it is hard to measure the impact this body has had since falling from grace with the Labour Party who later had a change of heart towards the contemporary platform. Just as it is difficult to say how much the MCB provided a mouthpiece for the British Muslim community as it did for its backer's interests abroad. The MCB, so determined to be an avenue to the establishment, has come to resemble the establishment itself, bogged down in never-ending campaigning and the gridlock of contemporary democratic bodies. It also fell victim to the very trends that have played a major role in holding back a second Islamic golden age, those being the respected authority of elders and their inability to either set up a stage or hand over power to the next generation, that has resulted in a resistance to change and a deficit of new, fresh input and ideas.

Kalim knew that not only would the British Parliament not hear out the opinions and cries of the Muslim population, but that the very Western modes of liberal, secular democracy and hierarchy layered in orientalist sentiment and the pursuit of dominance would not be the same modes through which the Muslim

117

people would find their justice. Kalim's ambitions and reach would exceed what was once apparently the limit of mortal beings. The sum of Kalim's life work would aim to the point where he would go next. To Kalim, this was a matter of survival. The Rushdie affair taught him that there would be no mercy for 'the Other' that he himself did not demand. Therefore, the British Muslim community needed an independent system of power to run alongside the British system, demanding it be respected. The bullet from the British soldier that killed the boy behind him, only just missing Kalim during his youth in India. The bearing witness to the failed opportunities in postcolonial Pakistan and much of the Muslim world. The cries of the educated youth. The Ayatollah's return to Tehran. The heart attacks. The fatwa. All of it swirling about and refined through the vast intellect of Kalim Siddiqui. He wished to launch a new Muslim world order within Britain. And so, the revolution would launch in London in July of 1990, at the famed Logan Hall of The Institute of Education. The inaugural event was a conference on 'The Future of Muslims in Britain' and the proclamation was a small booklet, the Muslim Manifesto.

Subtitled 'a strategy for survival', the Muslim Manifesto was no doubt a radical document. In fact, it bore a lot in common with other manifestos. It carried a tone of zero compromise and sought to rewrite a world in which Muslims in Britain stood equal in power and influence with any other population in the UK, thus shedding the label of the 'oppressed minority'. Similar to other manifestos, the objectives of the piece would not be realised in his lifetime, although in a way he could have never imagined, the groundwork would be done thanks to the efforts of his successor Ghayas and the community. Their accomplishment came in breaking away from Kalim's 1990 trajectory. The institutions he hoped to establish could and would be established in the next few decades: a women's council, a youth organisation, a charity, a society. They all exist, but in a less centralised and less radical form that is more acclimatised with the greater human society.

Kalim's manifesto calls for all Muslims to abide by British laws and even the minor cultural backsteps, but this is only a temporary measure until they can be corrected through the influence of a power-wielding British Muslim society. Kalim's manifesto failed in that he desired the changing of the hearts and minds of the British people as well as the elimination of the flaws existent within the present Muslim community. To ask this is a flirtation with absurdity. The solution could not be simply Muslim or British Muslim; it had to be a solution for all, achieved through the efforts of all. This is the global project of humanity. Though, perhaps to see this, Kalim's vision needed to be seen out to the best ability available to the limits and potentials it was born within, so that a lesson could be learned and growth harboured.

The July 1990 conference in Logan Hall represented a sort of mirroring of the original founding of the Muslim Institute. Thus, the prospect must have looked like a return to the glory days in a certain respect. Consensus and deliberation regained their position as central to the preparations being made. But now Kalim was a much older man, a seasoned veteran of revolution and war. This was no longer young men discussing, dreaming and writing of a world that they could one day live within. This was the historical founding of a new nation set to rival the revolution in Iran, counted alongside other similar revolutionary establishments of other new worlds. These discussions were intellectual in the highest regard but aimed at practical action and physical creations, not mere philosophy.

Over the months that followed an organ materialised, an organ by which the Muslim people of Britain would take the power owed to them. But what to call it? Learning from the failures brought to the British Muslim people by parliamentary democracy, it had to be better, yet it needed legitimacy. Kalim was a master of getting headlines and he knew one headline that would stir a presumption that would strike fear in the heart of the British establishment. The age-old tool of the decade long fear-mongering Conservative rule was now being used against itself. A foe worthy of equality. A threat. A rival. Why simply lift up the authority of the British Muslim people when a simultaneous chipping away at the infallibility of the UK government can also be accomplished? Proof that a false god also bleeds would be just the fear that would cause a nation to doubt its parliament. After all, the opposite of faith is doubt and the only thing that made it the Mother of all Parliaments was confidence. Therefore, the organ of power would be dubbed The Muslim Parliament of Great Britain. The Mother of all Parliaments had a sibling, so it would appear.

But, as is the case in many of Kalim's endeavours, one side of his motivation was to strike against the opposition, while the other side was to create something tangible and usable for those who come after him. Creating a Muslim parliament was radical new thinking, described by Kalim as a non-territorial Islamic state; a concept that allowed Muslim minorities to establish a political system, generating their own power in a space where they could not legally or politically govern. Muslim majorities needed to create Islamic states. Muslim minorities could now, through his blue print, create Muslim parliaments.

Often the pursuit of power by a minority is observed as a 'take-over', a gross term for a dated age. The misunderstanding of certain right-wing minded individuals is that power is a zero-sum game. Power sharing, to them, appears a loss, or even more worrying, a victory for the other. Yet it is a fundamental element of democracy, and all the more the case of the supposedly civilised and sophisticated democracies of the West, that all voices be heard and have the power to ensure their freedom and pursuit of a good life. The well-established institutions of the West sealed a snapshot of power sharing from an antiquated age. To Kalim, this meant that these structures could not be changed, but for the sake of the philosophy that brought them about, new structures would need to be established to uphold their moral tenets in the modern age. Thus, where Muslims are the majority, the Western structures they use to govern do not work and a new Islamic state is needed. Likewise, where Muslims are minorities, they need structures to ensure their rights, and this is where Muslim parliaments need to be established.

The Muslim Parliament of Great Britain was not so much a parliament at all, really—more so the anti-Parliament or a bizarro-Parliament. On the outside it had the look of such similar bodies, yet within it, ran on something distinctly Muslim. As it would come to be, that something was very distinctly British Muslim. Perhaps Kalim saw it as his mockery of the establishment, his re-enactment of Imam Khomeini's mockery of Plato. From the outside, the idea was for it to look just like the British parliament from having both an upper and lower house, all the way down to special committees, resolutions and even published white papers. It was also a representative body where different constituencies from all over Britain would meet in London.

Yet no sight of democracy could be found—at least, the Western style of democracy. All representatives would be chosen by appointment and all motions made in unanimity. The constituencies of the representatives, or Members of Muslim Parliament (MMPs) began through the establishment of groups that were set up in various cities and communities up and down the country. Through these groups, the local Muslim community were invited together to participate in a 'Big Conversation' on the objectives of Kalim Siddiqui's new creation delivered through a manifesto. The enthusiastic and dedicated members of each 'constituency' were selected to preside over their 'seat' as MMPs. This was just the right flavour of democracy for these fledgling communities to rise above their minority status in a structure by which they were not perceived as minorities, but given an equal voice with their other MMPs and the greater British Muslim community.

And stranger still, Parliamentary Procedure would govern the proceedings of the parliament. The creation of the Muslim Parliament of Great Britain was the forging of a symbol, one Kalim Siddiqui would waste no effort in exploiting to its fullest extent to conclude the final act of his stage play: the revolution against the oppressive and cruel dominance of the Western world.

Kalim Siddiqui displayed his finest skills as choreographer on the fourth of January 1992. The inauguration of the Muslim Parliament of Great Britain would be a show for the ages. Starting with the venue, Kensington Town Hall, a brutalist house of bricks that exudes oppression, also home to the borough council and thus a house of power. The whole event was lined with flashing cameras and eager journalists from every source Kalim could think to invite. Chum in the water, for he would have his headlines come morning. And then within the massive hall. Walls of brick darken the room while the yellowish lights add a cinematic tinge of drama.

In trudged the MMPs, Members of the Muslim Parliament. They are the right honourable men and women hand-picked to represent their constituencies from across the whole of Great Britain. A few of the crowd members are international spectators, hoping to check their chance at observing history in the making, looking on in expectation for another successful revolution as so many hopeful eyes did in so many congress halls and parliament houses in times past. A mild variety is found in formal wear amongst the assembled parties, but a general theme prevails. Aged, checkered blazers of a size bigger than necessary, from a fashion era on the way out, dyed all the pastel colours of the rainbow, some coordinated with a taste irreconcilable with contemporary fashionistas. Thick, dark ties with overly elaborate yet not terribly distracting patterns fasten mostly white, pocketed collared shirts. Bug-eyed and thick, yellowish lenses occupy eyebrow-to-cheekbone covering glasses that form a bridge between the upper limits of beards, ranging from jet black to snowy white.

What hair remains on the heads of the male MMPs is cleverly manipulated across bare scalps, attempting to hide the years. The females are clad in ornate yet formal head coverings. The women sit together, front and centre, a parliament in and to themselves. The room is rife with commotion, the typical final words amongst the audience being exchanged and the last ruffles of seat shuffling working against the unforgiving clock. Most of the noisy fray is drowned out by the constant click of photographers' flashes signalling a beginning of sorts. The flutter of cameras is at a rate by which the negatives ought to produce a motion picture. All of this is coming from outside the main hall, but the flashes grow closer and closer.

Into the main chamber walked a man holding proudly and elegantly, the Holy Qur'an. Slowly and deliberately, as in a religious procession, the Word made its way along the brick wall, a side aisle from the door towards a wooden framed panel with two levels. The set-up recalled the stage of the United States House of Representatives. In the centre of the top row of the panel was a large man with white hair, a hefty beard, and a formal head dressing: our Speaker. Beside him was a woman in *hijab* taking furious notes. On his other side, another man in a suit, and on the lower level, a couple of other representatives. Before the panel was a podium, where the man carrying the Qur'an stopped, lifting the holy revelation up before the crowd, before carefully placing it down. In the front row, all women, heads covered, no accident. Kalim had planned all of it for maximum effect. In his new world, the women would have the prime seats, the old men could sit at the back. The Speaker clomps his gavel calling for the recitation.

A tall, thin man in ornate Arab formal wear stepped forth and gave a recitation in lyrical Arabic. After his reading, the words were translated into English. Upon finishing, the Qur'an was given a respectful resting place upon the panel, an attendant in this historic gathering. At a table towards the front, beside the front row of diligent and attentive women, sat Kalim himself, watching proudly as his set up played on. To his side, ever taking notes, sat Ghayas, no longer the young activist in waiting but now the number two man, his focus, it would seem, holding the whole thing together. The Speaker then called upon the Leader of the Muslim Parliament of Great Britain to deliver the inaugural address, legitimised upon the tapping of his gavel.

Kalim strode to the podium, wearing a wool sports coat of an unremarkable pattern, his white collared shirt not accompanied by a tie but more casually left open. Something different, something new. The robust man stood tall, a Muslim Orson Welles, with a thick white beard that gave him the stature of a wise, aged lion. He paused at first, his hand tucked awkwardly in his coat pockets as he surveyed the assembly. A smile of pride did not flash upon his face. Stoicism was called for at this cue. Let them take the pictures, for soon pens will furiously scribble the words he was about to let loose upon the British public.

From his coat he drew his half-moon glasses and perched them upon his nose as he pulled out a leaf of paper. For what, it remains to be determined, if it weren't in fact simply a blank piece of paper, as he would never look to it for reference. Move over Winston Churchill, for a new orator stands before his people in an even darker hour. His first words prick at the spine in the way Rod Sterling's introductions both opened and closed old *Twilight Zone* episodes. His address was equal parts university lecture, doomsday warning, and uplifting victory speech. His voice was loud, clear, and with the resonance that must have reverberated through every seat in the room. Would the brutalist walls they found themselves within have been able to withstand such vibrations? His tongue danced as elegantly upon the Queen's English as it did Urdu and Arabic, languages he seamlessly jump-cut between over the course of his speech. Accompanying the aural presentation was the visual of his hands jumping up and reaching out, grasping for and conquering the attention of all who looked upon him. That was when his hands were not busy peeling his glasses off and replacing them after having twirled them about in a seemingly rehearsed manner.

After having given his extensive blessings to the assembled group and their mission, he began, "History, it is said, repeats itself. Perhaps it does. But the inauguration of the Muslim Parliament of Great Britain today is truly without parallel. We are responsible for the most original and innovative piece of social engineering in modern Britain. After today, British society will not be the same again." He spoke to the growing complexity of the world and the transformation of consciousness on various levels. Islam was the prism by which the light of the past was to be brought in and imparted upon future generations yet to come, the born-in-Britain offspring of those present. The community must draw consult from the Qur'an and *sunnah*. He elaborated on the example laid down by the Prophet Muhammad.

Kalim spoke to the great uncertainty ahead, but assured that no corners had been cut and no shortcuts taken. He expounded upon the forces that stood in opposition to that community; a hostile media, recalling the still fresh Rushdie Affair. He explained the double standard in which they had declared Scorsese's film *The Last Temptation of Christ* blasphemy, yet allowed Rushdie to write hate against the Muslim people. This new structure was to be a political system that allows Muslims to take their place among the British Establishment and deprive the liberals of their favourite weapon: the defining power of law. He asked the parliament, what power did they have? None, he answered, concerning military or police authority, yet upon the courtroom of moral standing, they held all the power. Despite this, they had no way to influence and persuade the general public to be good. This parliament was to be the voice that the community greatly needed. He voiced concern for the scattering of the community into nationalistic and ethnic ghettos and the limitations of the mosques to create unity. He called on all listeners to reflect on their responsibility for the failure of the Muslim community. The parliament would seek to end that historical narrative. The moral and spiritual high ground the Muslim people had access to would finally bring them to the decision-making table and grant them dominance in Great Britain and beyond.

He highlighted the importance of education and producing scholarships to develop top graduates that would put Muslims within the highest levels of British society. Meanwhile, on the ground, Islam would guide the Muslim people as it always had, to care for the underprivileged through the sophisticated cultural heritage all Muslims held in the concept of family and *zakat*. The caring nature of the Muslim people would not stop at their own community, for Britain was as much a great bond to their neighbours as to any historical sense of identity shared with their brothers and sisters abroad. Thus, it was to be the Muslims who lifted up all of the disenfranchised in the UK. Kalim called upon the Muslim community to work within the structures of British society, but not to grant those structures any ability to oppress. Muslims were to take control of their future and not allow it to be dictated by the mainstream. That body would provide for the exchange of ideas and debate that enriched all society. He dreamed of a day when the Muslim Parliament would no longer be necessary, but for the time being it would stand up and, if need required, take the Queen's government on in the international courts for their crimes and violation of inalienable human rights. To that veiled threat, the assembly gave a resounding cheer. That may require the committing of symbolic disobedience, Kalim cautioned. These were the parts of Kalim's speech meant to sting the ears of listeners, to take those headlines.

Next came Kalim's appeal to revolutionary language in the style of Malcolm X. With an eye on the next morning's headlines, Kalim called for civil disobedience when he said, "Let us make it quite clear that Muslims in Britain will oppose, and if necessary, defy, any public policy or legislation that we regard as inimical to our interests. The dictatorship of the majority, dressed up as democracy, is unacceptable." Coverage in the evening's news and in the newspapers was all but assured. The Muslim Parliament was born in a blaze of global media coverage and not a penny spent on publicity. Kalim was a spin doctor before the term had even been invented.

He gave breath to the dictatorship of the majority within normal notions of democracy and the struggles before them as they swam against the tide. He reassured the room that Western civilisation was, in fact, the modern world's sick man. Islam was the antidote to that moral illness. He spoke to an atmosphere of moral anarchy, specifically calling for Muslims to stand up against the abundance of gambling, prostitution and homosexuality. The Parliament would be the harbinger of institutions to protect and uplift the Muslim people. And then his tone moved to hope and the future. The Muslim Parliament would establish a proper agenda. First on that list was the establishment of a truly Islamic university in Britain, for it is in the re-establishment of a bank of knowledge that the Muslim community has the power to undo the Western, disciplined definition of the world. From there he laid out the plan for the work of the Parliament to establish institutions that promoted education and social wellbeing, a remarkably progressive idea for the time.

He then addressed the MMPs on a more personal level, pleading with them. They were asked to abandon petty politics, to not let sectarian ideals inhibit the progress of that body. The assembled were reminded that personal pursuit of power would only cripple the greater community, for the community had to work together to grasp its power from the elites of British society. The Parliament was to stand or fall upon the work of the individuals within their communities. United, the efforts of each member were to be aimed at the community, the one within each constituency, and the greater community of Britain as well. Kalim's slow crescendo suddenly shifted into an uplifting gear of concluding anticipation. The Parliament, Kalim stated, "must solve these problems of the Muslim community that the mainstream political systems and the Government cannot attend to. It is not in any sense a 'separatist' body, however. The large majority of Muslims in this country are British-born. We are here to stay and we must live as fully integrated citizens of this country. This Parliament, therefore, must iron out the problems of common citizenship, it must encourage and help Muslims in this country to play a full part in British society, and, in doing so, it must raise the moral outlook of the entire society. This Parliament must, in short, become an integral and essential part of contemporary Britain."

With that, the community leader turned proper politician might have wielded a power with his words greater than any Prime Minister in the Isle's long history. And in proper fashion, the Leader yielded his time to the Speaker as the room filled with applause and mild cheer. Kalim sat, as he shook the excited hand of Ghayas. In most instances, we might immediately transition to a young, scruffy British urchin with an oversized hat and well-worn shoes, hawking newspapers only half his size with the familiar "Extree! Extree! Read all 'bout eet!"

But no; Kalim took his seat, leaning forward, attentive, for the show had not yet concluded. The restlessness of the assembly cooled to a warm hum as Imelda Ryan, a British convert to Islam, wearing her hijab proudly, took to the podium. A strong yet pacifying voice rode the moment of Kalim's call to action. She spoke to the duty they all had to serve the community at all its levels. She underlined that the future is British-born, and that Islam was here to stay. The progress and advances made by the Muslim community were to be spread to the rest of the country. She compared Great Britain to a large family, emphasising the role of the family and the Muslim's responsibility to provide for the family, lifting all of society up towards a better future. She warned against getting caught up in rhetoric of change, reminding all of the work ahead.

Kalim leaned back in his chair and a smile, the one of a proud father, overtook the lion's mane. He watched as the excitement reached throughout the townhall. At that moment he might as well have been given the entire British Empire. He had conquered the world. Ghayas would joyfully jab at Kalim's side, joining in the applause, as his staple chin following grin contorted his well-groomed beard into the shape of happiness. But the crown weighed heavy upon Kalim Siddiqui. Heavier still the crown placed upon his head by that community, now unified. Indeed, much work lay ahead for all of those assembled in that room.

The inaugural meeting of the Muslim Parliament of Great Britain closed with an emphasis on the high stakes, those being the power over the future. And Kalim brilliantly ended with a shot to the heartstrings as his young niece, complete with head covering, took to the podium. She was the image of Islam's Future. Kalim had given her the stage to become the poster child fit for a Shepard Fairey opus, only missing the British flag waving behind her to make a brilliant piece of propaganda. Standing before the podium she only would have needed to raise a fist of power to have caused the entire Parliament to erupt with passion and revolutionary fervour set to ripple out to the rest of the world. Emboldened, she gave a sharp, innocent glance to her uncle, and then looked forward to the world waiting in attention. Her words were those of a wise intellectual, yet her pitch and voice would have melted the coldest of hearts. Her adorable lisp won the history of human revolutions. You were left to wonder if Kalim even told her to fumble her words at the one fourth mark along her speaking time, for that added imperfection of authenticity. She could have literally said anything for her image and presence was all Kalim needed to seal the deal and get his point across. Yet words like revolution and *kufr* jumped from her lips, words with such consequences one would never hope for them to come from children innocent of the sins of the past. He might as well have sent the poor girl to take her place at 10 Downing Street upon her speech's conclusion.

The maestro took his bows in his head. The Muslim Parliament was now real. Kalim's revolution was upon the world, but revolutions do not end. At least they do not end in the declaration of peace. There was much work to be done and now the focus had pivoted towards the homefront: the community.

Chapter Seven

WE'LL HAVE THE SALAD

SPECTACLE. SHOCK AND AWE. Hear us roar. This may well have been the intended reception of the Hollywood premiere-like event in which Kalim Siddiqui presents "The Muslim Parliament of Great Britain, An Inauguration!" And, although the short history of the physical organisation carried forward into the contemporary world is a fading memory, the little Parliament that could, in a strange way, did find some of the power it so desired. It was in the initiatives ignited by the engine that was the Muslim Parliament which allowed that power to continue long beyond its passing from the earth. The Muslim Parliament did not so much as fall or die as it evolved, just as it needed to with the changing times.

The Muslim Parliament, powerless to rule through law, reigned through thought provocation and a stirring of the entrepreneurial spirit suppressed within the British Muslim community. When an empire dies, its satellites live on. As the Muslim Parliament no longer stands assembled in this era, its committees, works, inquiries and fostered community camaraderie continue the struggle for recognition and representation in British society.

One of Ghayas's proudest achievements from this period, indeed ranking high amongst his lifetime achievements, did not really begin with him. Ghayas was just a man after all. He could not be everywhere, nor have his ear infinitely pressed against the ground. Rather, the story of Ghayas the activist begins with a complaint finding him, upon which he then rides in with his organisational talent and restless spirit to do whatever he can to recalibrate the levers of justice. Ghayas's proudest moment began not with Ghayas, but rather with his wife, Talat. While Ghayas had been waving the flag of revolution abroad, it was Talat who remained to turn Britain into a home for their family and, in so doing, created quite the reputation for herself.

Talat Siddiqui had adapted quickly to Chesham. The move from Corby proved to be a far less drastic culture shock than that between Karachi and London. Chesham was a small village, much as it remains to this day, but it had everything necessary for the day to day. As the 1980s became the 1990s, the high street in Chesham had all the shops one could hope for and all the traffic that accompanied such accommodations, at least during peak hours. Chesham was special in that it is the end of the line for London transport, having both a tube station as well as a bus terminus. Therefore, it acts as a gateway for commuters from out of town. Convenience stores flourished because of this and the little town also has the metropolitan luxuries of a healthy stock of cafés and even a Waterstones bookshop. Footpaths run like secret passages between houses taking pedestrians through town, safe from the traffic of the high street, allowing for a relatively uninterrupted brisk dash against time to the less than frequently docked tube. The town centre has a lovely pedestrian only road allowing for a robust bi-weekly market as well as a few nice restaurants. The schools are ranked high and the size of the town provides for everything to be close at hand for regular errand running, but central London is only about forty minutes by tube so business commutes and day trips can be easily had. It also houses the befitting requisite number of churches and pubs, Chesham of course being an English town.

It was in this quiet English town that Talat would become a community teacher and counsellor. In her work she was rapidly sought out as quite the community leader herself. While Ghayas was the name known for taking care of business in universities, revolutionary meeting halls, and government offices around the globe, in Chesham, the Siddiqui who could assist in the resolution of problems was Talat. In fact, in Chesham, Ghayasuddin Siddiqui was only associated with his highest honorary title. At various gatherings, Ghayas would only be recognised as Mrs. Siddiqui's husband.

Chesham was doubly ideal for the Siddiquis because it had the two essential landmarks for any Muslim community: a mosque and a *halal* butcher. The mosque provided a civic centre and the halal butcher kept his patrons in obedience to the dietary restrictions set down by the Qur'an. Halal literally translates as that which is permissible within Islam. At face value, halal is a broad term that can, if one so desires, be applied to just about anything. Thus, everything to a Muslim could be reduced to a scale extending on one extreme from halal, the allowed, to *haram*, best expressed in the German translation of *verboten*, strictly forbidden. Halal is most often used, especially in the case of our butcher, to refer to food. Halal food simply asks that all food consumed by Muslims must be in their purest form. Major examples of non-halal or haram food include pork, the drinking of blood, or intoxicating consumption such as alcohol. Beyond that, the specifics of whether something is halal or not can be a bit subjective.

Naturally, this can make grocery shopping incredibly difficult, especially in the world of preservatives and processed foods where often non-halal materials are injected into traditionally halal items. This is where the butcher becomes a major and essential element within the community. The knowledge of the butcher and the community's ability to trust in their judgement was essential for day to day flourishing. When diasporic Muslims first came to Britain and other non-Muslim countries in the 1960s and 1970s, the halal-ness of their butchers back at home had been taken for granted, and because halal meat shops were so few and far between in those days, intermittent vegetarian lifestyles were often adopted. The opportunity to make a trip to the nearest halal butcher was indeed a cause to celebrate. Fortunately, advances in refrigerators and machines later allowed for bulk buying of meat and the possibility of more carnivorous meals for the family. Of course, the limitations of space made it only a matter of time before the inevitable fall back into the vegetarian lifestyle. But by the 1990s, halal butchers had become fairly ubiquitous, especially in London and other Muslim population centres throughout Great Britain. Yet, there existed no unified system to measure halal-ness. Thus, consumption of meat in Britain was a risky proposition as different butchers had different standards, and the demands of maintaining a business in a competitive capitalistic society had turned many a virtuous soul.[39]

Halal scandals were not new for Muslims in Britain. The history of Muslim interaction with the outside world has been riddled with tactical abuse of halality and the weaponisation of haram. The Chinese have a history of making life difficult for Muslim minorities by coating door knobs and everyday utensils in pig blood. In 1857, the British Empire in India nearly collapsed a few decades early for using pig fat as lubricant for the weapons they issued Muslim troops. And pork being a cornerstone of the Spanish diet has one particularly malicious origin arising from its use during the Inquisition. These examples all had the commonality of being the Other imposing what they knew was forbidden on Muslims. The idea that a member of the Muslim community would knowingly distribute haram food and betray the community's trust was unconscionable. Few sins are more despicable than such treachery. Nevertheless, a vile rumour was spreading throughout Britain.

Included among the stops of Talat's errands this particular day was a trip to the local halal butcher. When Talat entered the shop, she began by asking the butcher, quite simply, where his meat came from. You see, Talat had heard that some butchers were falsely selling non-halal meat as halal, and at the premium price suited to that label. In some cases, cheaper non-halal animal meat would be added or flat out substituted for what they

134

claimed to be selling. In fact, she had even heard a worse rumour that some butchers would wait at the famous Smithfield Meat Market until later in the day, after all the prime cuts had been sold off, to then collect the non-halal, often non-human consumable leftovers at a great reduction of price, grind it up and sell it as quality halal meat.[40] When the butcher did not give a response, Talat made an about face and politely departed. One item on her shopping list would remain unchecked. In fact, it would be some time before the Siddiquis would enjoy meat again.

Since the inauguration of the Muslim Parliament, Ghayas had been racking his brain, attempting to find ways to redirect their past efforts of being global diplomats and activists so as to carry a more local influence. Talat's return with rumours confirmed fit the bill as just the sort of initiative the Muslim Parliament was created to deal with. The halal meat crisis was a truly British Muslim crisis, requiring the creation of a regulatory body like none seen before in the British Isles. Kalim was overcome with excitement, pledging full support as they now had a truly British dilemma on their hands and an opportunity to give the Muslim Parliament a proper test drive. While Kalim could certainly go out into the community and rouse passion through his speeches and tread the globe offering philosophical wisdom to lead the Muslim world into the future, the halal meat scandal required a different set of skills and an individual whose face would not overshadow the issue at hand. Here was where Ghayas shined.

Whereas the inaugural meeting of the Muslim Parliament was Kalim Siddiqui's Ninth Symphony, the actualisation of the dream of the Halal Food Authority, established in 1994, was the synthesis of Dr. Ghayasuddin Siddiqui's life work up to that point. The mysterious man behind the curtain of Kalim's public celebrity stepped out from the shadows to reveal what an activist could accomplish. The vision was delicate. What was needed was an organisation that had the authority of a government institution but was an independent body working alongside British society for the Muslim community, and one which would not compromise on its Islamic values or fall victim to corruption or bureaucratic arrest. While it may appear a small initiative, the scope would grow to what can be seen today by a visit to the supermarket, including the big chain stores, and looking at the packaged meats to see how the Halal Food Authority seal of approval reigns dominant across numerous brands throughout Britain.

The initial question often killed a movement upon launch. Where to begin? Ghayas saw that another minority community had risen to prominence in British society. The Jewish community. They must certainly have known a thing or two about working with the British government and organising their community towards action? They too had religious dietary restrictions? It would have been foolish to go about establishing a model for halal regulation without at least looking at the kosher model. Ghayas went further and extended a hand of brotherhood to the Jewish community. It would appear that all his days at Kalim's side had not allowed him to lose sight of the fact that every neighbour had a value in the affairs of the greater community. The Muslim community did not exist in a vacuum of isolation. Affairs of this matter required a cooperation with all of their British neighbours.

In Martin Shaw, Ghayas found a friend who would reveal the overwhelming amount of similarities between the Jewish and Muslim communities in Britain. The inter-mosque rivalry and vast diversity within the community often expressed in diametrically opposing opinions in the Muslim community, served as a mirror reflection, if not a funhouse mirror exaggeration, of the division within the Jewish community in Britain. In fact, amongst their talks it became apparent that it was a far less cumbersome task to get Jews and Muslims to agree on something than the Jews or the Muslims to agree amongst themselves! Prior to their meeting, while both gentlemen had dealt extensively within their own community, neither of them had spent much time crossing the lines between faiths. And this interfaith jump could not have been bridged by two more respectful and pure-hearted chaps. Both men saw their meetings as an 'absolute pleasure'. While the global narrative tells a different tale, the interactions of the Muslim and Jewish communities in Britain would prove itself capable of moving mountains. These bridging bonds are the idyllic elements of utopia that manage to trickle into reality and are the soul of a plural, multicultural society desperately reaching towards progress.

While Shaw's background was as a lawyer largely working in fundraising management and consultancy, his work and experience with the British government gave him a preternatural talent for navigating applications and government protocol. His work in dispute resolution between synagogues and his thrust in collaborating with the British Muslims would make him a great mediator amongst and within both the Muslim and Jewish communities. He would also work as a consultant to the British government on minority and race issues which became of greater importance in the new millennium. A key ally, Shaw provided the legal and political touch to the Halal Food Authority. Seeing Ghayas's dedication to the cause inspired Shaw to help out in an endeavour that had little bearing on his everyday affairs. Ghayas not only benefitted from an ally, but in making a friend within the wider British society. Now with a model in mind, it was time for Ghayas to turn to the Muslim community and do what he did best.

While Ghayas had a talent for organising and rising to the top as a leader, he never allowed himself to be the solitary worker. From his student activist days in Pakistan, he had learned early on that no great accomplishment can be achieved alone. This work of the Halal Food Authority (HFA) became not only the preoccupation of Ghayas, but also of a dedicated team who between them worked tirelessly to uncover the extent to which the halal meat scandal was affecting the community and worked on the blueprint of what would become the HFA. It was a community and thus, fundamentally, a family affair; something that perhaps the revolutionaries of old never thought to consider. The revelation, largely by way of various parties' refusal to comply, was that this crisis was far more prevalent than they had first imagined. Over the period of time it took to create the HFA, Ghayas still had to keep up appearances as Assistant Director of the Muslim Institute and a prominent MMP in the Muslim Parliament. Both Ghayas and Talat found themselves at several eating engagements among various other members of the community, but deep down they knew that halal did not necessarily mean halal. For a good two years or so, Ghayas, Talat, and their children had become vegetarians. Whenever they went out to dinner at friends' houses, Pakistani or Indian restaurants or attended weddings where the menu was overwhelmingly built upon their signature carnivorous dishes, the waiter would walk around the table, collecting each person's order. Pen in hand, the waiter would turn to Ghayas who would chime in with what became a classic line: "We'll just have the salad, thank you."

The next hurdle was the term itself. Halal. While the big no-no's were clearly defined—pork, blood, and alcohol—the minutiae proved a bit more difficult to pin down, especially with the nineties being a revolutionary age for food processing and preservation. The scholarly debates in Islam at the time were not equipped to keep up with the radical changes arriving in the grocery industry throughout Europe. How would the *mullahs* feel about genetically modified organisms (GMOs), or the administering of growth hormones, or the artificial sterility that oozed from mass farming? While the scriptures spoke of the necessity of purity in food, the very nature of purity was changing. Science, a field unfortunately left in the dark in the Muslim world following the golden age, was now an ill-equipped antagonist. Many Muslims were now lacking the thorough understanding needed to engage in the more sophisticated debate of distinguishing halal from haram in light of these new technologies. The empire and colonialism were seemingly dead, removed from popular parlance, and globalisation was the newest wave upon the horizon. Foods not before seen in Great Britain were arriving in local groceries, and in large quantities. How would the ancient and enduring notion of halal, contemporarily confined to the realm of subjectivity, manage the strange world of the 1990s?

A wealth of scholars and religious leaders were brought together and a discussion ensued on a scale often reserved for fatwa and Western sentiment. The debate extended beyond the food itself and into the butcher's duty. What was the official method for animal slaughter that would be imposed by this regulatory body? The prayer, the direction of the slaughter and the welfare of the animal were all key considerations. How do you regulate the butchers? In the fires of dialogue, a clear code of definition and propriety was established which would become the backbone of the HFA. It was clear from the beginning that not all matters could be solved in one go. This would have to be a constantly reiterative process that kept the debate alive as new technologies and behaviours presented themselves.

One of the most notable issues was whether or not stunned meat could be considered halal. Stunning was the process by which an animal is rendered unconscious prior to slaughter and was popularly considered a more humane method of slaughter. The HFA partnered alongside senior animal welfare and meat scientists at the University of Bristol and other institutions to develop appropriate stunning parameters, such as electric frequency and amperage allowed. The endgame was to determine the point at which an animal is not killed but rendered insensitive to pain. Careful monitoring protocol was also established to create a safeguard for the specificities of the process. Any animals with a questionable halal status were to be removed from the line. While scientific experimentation would assist with some of the technicalities, a good deal of ecclesiastical debate would be required in establishing the HFA guidelines. Whilst scripture advises using the 'sharpest knife' for slaughter, which was commonly understood to ensure minimal pain to an animal in the context of the sixth century, today that same principle translates for application in the debate on whether or not animals that are stunned (and even to what degree and what method of stunning is allowed) before their slaughter still fit the definition of halal. At the launch of the HFA, a final verdict on the stunning question was not attained and debate on the subject continues to rage to this day. Ironically, scientific evidence shows that the more literal adherence to the scriptures results in the most painful slaughter for the animal; a total misunderstanding in the spirit of the Islamic concept of halal.[41]

Thanks to the help of Shaw, the framework for applications, licensing and oversight would be set down in accordance with British law. Shaw and Ghayas both knew that if this worked, it would catch on and have the potential of becoming a sizeable institution. So, Shaw assisted Ghayas in taking the proper steps to develop an infrastructure that would sustain the growth the HFA would experience over the next three decades. It was clear that the body would even need to be run independently and thus be sustainable beyond the support of the Muslim Parliament.

The HFA was ready, the rubric set, but now an entire culture needed to be changed. Ghayas, always the activist at heart, knew that the true test stood at this juncture. He needed to mobilise the people. With Talat and the rest of the family standing behind him, he embarked on a campaign both to spread the word of the HFA and to rid the network of corrupt halal butchers. Quite naturally, the halal butchers, both good and bad, resisted the HFA. It was an assault on their integrity, another attempt by the authorities to diminish the good name of the local community leaders. Suffice it to say, things got a little ugly. It would be incumbent upon Ghayas to not only hold the line, but explain to the local butchers that this was from the community and for the betterment of the community. The enemy was not him, it was the few bad butchers who stood to ruin the reputation of not only a niche industry, but an entire minority population that needed no help in finding turbulence in the modern world. It would be the people who stood behind Ghayas that made his message strongest. Those who continued to refuse, driven by pride, would note fewer and fewer customers at the first sign that a change was afoot, whether they were ready or not. The greedy ones who abused the title of halal butcher had themselves become the hunted. Eventually, the butcher community would come to see that this was not so much an imposition from the top, but a method for normalising the halal butcher for the benefit of the community and greater society. Once the first tags and seals could be seen on the meat going on sale to the Muslim community, Ghayas's victory had been attained. But while Ghayas may have mobilised the people, his satisfaction was not shared by the people. There was still more work to be done. The HFA became something greater than the revival of trust amongst halal butchers. It was both a rallying point for the power and influence of the Muslim community and was prepared to take Great Britain by storm.

By definition, what is halal contains within it the prerequisites of being kosher. Thus, a push for greater sales of halal products extended beyond the Muslim community and quickly became an increasingly British desire. For the larger companies, they found that to have two separate operations, one for halal and one for non-halal products, was a prohibitively expensive endeavour. Since halal products required their own system so as not to be sullied by the non-halal products, many large and small operations simply switched the production system to producing only halal, since, in the mind of the capitalist, halal is just cleaner meat and thus everyone would be happier if everything was halal.

Of course, the 1980s had ended but nationalist sentiment and racist worldviews would not so easily be left in the past. An anti-halal movement quickly struck back, spewing venomous rhetoric about how halal food was somehow imbued with magical chemicals that would spell the ultimate doom of white, Christian Britannia. These fear mongers seriously underestimated the fight an already mobilised Muslim community was ready to put up. A public relations campaign quickly diminished all arguments, instead explaining that halal merely demanded a higher quality of meat that is beneficial for all of British society. They also quickly explained that they had no intentions of ridding grocery stores of their pork items or alcohol. The New Year's ham was safe and the Muslim community had no desire to upset the integrity of the full English breakfast. Though one ought to, at least once, perhaps try it with halal turkey bacon! The HFA stamp began to be seen not just in the local butchers and groceries, but was turning up in major chain supermarkets. In fact, the threat of boycott quickly had the major corporations falling in line.[42] Even KFC, one of the kings of the American Fast Food Empire, bent the knee, kowtowing to the pressure and desires of nearly a third of the world's population.[43] Its halal compliance policy is brilliantly illuminated on their website.

The HFA was the first regulatory body of its kind in Europe. It now stands as an independent, non-profit organisation dedicated to the oversight, certification and inspection of halal products all across the United Kingdom. The organisation plays a major role in trade between the European Union and other countries assuring that its standards are upheld abroad as well as at home. The HFA has become a model used by similar organisations throughout the continent and the rest of the world. The HFA seal is prominently shown on food, beverages, and now cosmetic products from local shops to the mega-corporate superstores. The foundational principles set by Ghayas, the Muslim Parliament and the army that saw this movement actualised, still maintain the integrity and trust that was almost lost between one of the fundamental cornerstones of the faith and the British Muslim community. All packaged with a lovely seal, for consumer convenience.

Ghayas could sit now in his chair, looking out as the sun set into the moors on the edge of Chesham, a smile stretching along his jawline. Revolution need not be a bloody affair, he had proven. In fact, blood is rather haram. At last the Siddiqui family could return to normal and Talat could stir up delicious dishes from the complete compendium of options she brought with her from Pakistan, carnivorous mains included. Though, perhaps for dinner tonight, we'll just have salad for old times' sake.

Early childhood: As a 9-year-old boy (left) with younger brother Zafar, in Sukkur, Pakistan, in 1949.

Student activist: after BSc graduation in Chemistry, in Jamshoro, Sindh University, Pakistan, 2nd October 1960.

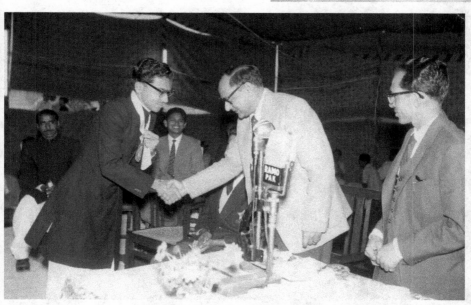

Recognition: receiving an award at Sindh University in 1961 as secretary of the union.

Motherly migration: Batool Fatima, in Sukkur, in 1962 where the family settled after partition. She expected their stay in Pakistan to be temporary, returning to India once things settled down. She would never return.

Father and Sons: With father Muhammed Saeeduddin and older brother (right) Ahmed Fariduddin, Karachi, 1977.

A lighter moment: enjoying a joke with friends at a meeting of the Sheffield University Islamic Society in the mid-1960s.

Muslim Teddy Boys: after a FOSIS meeting in Leeds University in the mid-1960s.

Group photo: Sheffield University Islamic Society in mid-1960s, seated centre front row.

Living legend: Malcolm X exchanging words with Ghayas who had arranged for him to speak at Sheffield University on 4 December 1964. Also in view Ahmed El-Kally (far left) and Sheffield University Student Union Secretary, Neil Rackham. Malcolm would be assassinated two months later in New York.

A new beginning: Ghayas marries Talat Anis on 27 June 1970 in Karachi. This photo is taken a few weeks later before Ghayas returns to his studies in Sheffield and Talat returns to complete hers in Rawalpindi. Talat would graduate a year later and join him in the UK.

West bound: Getting ready to travel to the UK to take a place at Sheffield University. Picture taken in Karachi, 1964.

First job in the UK: Ghayas at his desk in 1971 at *Impact International*, the news magazine he helped found. The office was on Seven Sisters Road in Finsbury Park, London.

Making history: with Kalim Siddiqui at the 7th
Islamic Thought Conference in Tehran held on
29–31 January 1989 where Kalim was a guest
speaker. It was on this trip to Iran where Ayatollah Khomeini would issue his fatwa on Salman
Rushdie.

Solidarity with Bosnia: with Dr Mustafa Ceric,
Grand Mufti of Bosnia, attending a session of
the Muslim Parliament in May 1994 during the
height of the Bosnian war. © Muhsin Kilby

Bosnian delegation: attending the World Conference on Bosnia and the Global Islamic Movement,
13–14 November 1993, Džemaludin Latić (left of
Ghayas), spokesman of Bosnian President Alija
Izetbegovic at Kalim's office in Slough.

Muslim Parliament of Great Britai

Show of unity: Closing ceremony at the
Muslim Parliament's World Conference on
Bosnia and the Global Islamic Movement,
Logan Hall, Institute of Education, 13–14
November 1993. Includes Yaqub Zaki,
Kalim Siddiqui, Haroon Kalla and Inayat-
ullah Zaigham. © Muhsin Kilby

Preparing for conference: with Kalim
Siddiqui at one of the many sessions of the
Muslim Parliament, May 1994.
© Muhsin Kilby

Making a point: addressing a session of the
Muslim Parliament, May 1994.
© Muhsin Kilby

Innovators: Halal butchers signing up to the newly launched Halal Food Authority's regulatory scheme in Birmingham, 25 May 1994. The HFA team includes Haroon Kalla (far left) and Mansour Ansari (far right). Ghayas was its founding chairman (1994–2015). © Muhsin Kilby

Meat me in paradise: one of the many public meetings held by the Muslim Parliament to call for a clean up of the UK halal meat industry, held at Streatham Islamic Centre, London, 7 June 1994. © Muhsin Kilby

Right hand man: with Kalim Siddiqui at his
office in Slough in 1990. Ghayas would first
meet Kalim in 1972 and strike up a friendship
that would last a lifetime.

Contemplating the road ahead: at the Kalim Siddiqui Memorial Conference, Logan Hall, Institute
of Education, London, 2–3 November 1996.
© Muhsin Kilby

First Anniversary: Kalim Siddiqui Memorial
Conference held in Pretoria, South Africa on
28–30 March 1997 with Zafar Bangash (far left)
and Iqbal Siddiqui (far right).

Campaigning for Chechnya: with Jaffar Clarke,
Dr. Marie Benningsen and a wounded Chech-
en soldier, London, 2000.

Championing Chechnya: at the City
Circle on 3 December 1999 held at
Toynbee Hall, East London.
Speakers include Yaqub Zaki, Rehan
Khan (chair), Yusuf Islam and Dr.
Marie Benningsen.

Public meeting: A Stop the War meeting
in Clerkenwell, London, in 2002. Speakers
include veteran campaigner Asad Rehman,
Shahed Saleem and Shahedah Vawdah.
© Salim Bhorat

Hands off Iraq: at the huge anti-war demonstration at Trafalgar Square organised by the
Stop the War Coalition on 2nd March 2002
with George Galloway (far left, back to camera), Tariq Ali and Jeremy Corbyn.
© Salim Bhorat

Bush and Blair's War: with Jeremy Corbyn at
the climax of the anti-war demonstration.
© Salim Bhorat

Speaking out: at Trafalgar Square, 2nd March
2002.

With old friends: with Mufti Abdul Qadir Barkatulla and Ziauddin Sardar at the Muslim Institute Third Annual Ibn Rushd Lecture at the Art Workers' Guild Hall in London, 10 June 2015. © Rehan Jamil/Muslim Institute

Another milestone: at the Muslim Institute Tenth Annual Winter Gathering at Sarum College, Salisbury, with Fadlullah Wilmot, Nasser Butt and Ziauddin Sardar, 17th November 2018. © Rehan Jamil/Muslim Institute

Fifth Annual Winter Gathering, 2nd December 2013, Sarum College, Salisbury.
© Rehan Jamil/Muslim Institute

Life's story: one of the many interviews with author Scott Jordan and Talat Siddiqui at the family home in Chesham, July 2019.

Where it all began: returning to 6 Endsleigh Street, Bloomsbury, 27 April 2019.

Chapter Eight

VETERANS

JUST BEFORE MIDNIGHT on the third of June in 1989, the sun's absence allowed for a brief pause in the temperature's month-long rise towards the hottest day of the year. Ten years after his return home and the glorious revolution, and only months after condemning Salman Rushdie to death, the Supreme Leader of Iran, Ayatollah Ruhollah Khomeini, had suffered his fifth heart attack within the last ten days. The Imam would pass from this world before the clock struck zero, ushering in what might just have been the most sorrow filled day in the short history of the Islamic Republic. Imam Khomeini was eighty-six.

To say a nation was plunged into mourning is a grotesque understatement. While his enemies might well have drunk secret toasts to the death of the revolution in the far corners of the world, at home in Iran and especially in Tehran, everyone had lost a father. The nation was inconsolable. Portraits and floral arrangements of the late Ayatollah popped up at every street corner, public weeping commonplace and normal. Almost spontaneously people all over Iran flocked to the cities and flooded the streets in vast public expression of grief. In quick step, Ali Khamenei was made successor as the Second Supreme Leader of the Islamic Republic, but it was of little effect. The cities of Iran were at a standstill before the animated and dramatic displays of bereavement. In the hot summer sun, fire trucks had to be called in to cool the people down and prevent them from succumbing to exposure. The wicked heat was not the only danger to the desperate people. At least ten mourning Iranians were trampled to death along with thousands of others sustaining injuries in the chaotic festival of sorrow overtaking the streets that summer.[44]

Caught in the fray of utter pandemonium stood two casually dressed British Muslims, invited as guests of honour: Drs. Kalim Siddiqui and Ghayasuddin Siddiqui. And never would the two men experience such culture shock in the very capital of the country they had been exporting revolution from over the last decade. Indeed, the Sunni and Shia Muslims had lived together through many empires and maintained a good track record of peace and harmony prior to more contemporary times. Yet, it was in response to death that the Sunni and Shia divide became night and day. Ghayas had always known Shia traditions to be more overtly emotional, perhaps a bit too emotional in their religious spirit for his preference. The use of emotional here is subtle, similar to how Romance languages predisposition their speakers to greater expression and conveyance of emotion than speakers of the Germanic tongues.

But what Ghayas was witnessing in Tehran bordered on incomprehensible. Was it a competition? To see who could show the most distress over the Supreme Leader's death? Could this have been an act? After all, dissenting opinions in Iran were not of high regard at the time. No, truly this was authentic feeling and it had both Ghayas and Kalim at a loss for words. Both men had been aware of the Shia practice of mourning, *maatam*. While they thought it a bit excessive, they respected the self-hitting practice for it was the Shia people suffering alongside Imam Hussain, the grandson of the Prophet Muhammad, or to die alongside their brothers at the Battle of Karbala. In fact, upon further reflection, physical expressions of grievance were quite natural; the Shia people had just devised a channel for the aggression. The compassioned mutual suffering alongside the passing of Khomeini was a truly emotional and violent affair.

The Imam's body, as per tradition, was cleaned and dressed all in a white shroud and his simple wooden coffin put into an

146

air-conditioned glass box, propped up for display in the Musalla, a place in northern Tehran. On the fifth of June, hundreds of thousands of mourners came to pay their respects to their beloved leader. Overnight, the crowd swelled to well over a million people. On the sixth of June, the glass case and coffin were opened before the Grand Ayatollah Mohammad-Reza Golpaygani, who delivered a final prayer, the *salat al-janazah*, which lasted over twenty minutes. Ghayas and Kalim watched on, in prayer for the man they had come to know well since 1979. Peaceful in their respects, they must have looked an odd sight amongst the devastated crowd around them. The idea was to then transport the coffin through a procession that led to the cemetery where Khomeini's body would be laid to rest. The sheer size and unruliness of the assembled masses proved this no easy task, but the Islamic Revolutionary Guard Corps (IRGC) had a back-up plan. An Islamic Republic of Iran's Army Bell Huey helicopter was brought in. The Imam's coffin was secured by tether line to the helicopter and elevated off the ground to proceed overhead to the Behesht-e Zahra Cemetery in the south of Tehran.

Ghayas tilted his head back and twisted it as the Imam's coffin flew over him. Before it could get very far the desperate people, refusing to let their leader go, jumped upon the flying coffin, tearing at the shroud covering it. Every shred became a prized possession worth more than life itself—forget what amounts of gold could be gathered from around the world. The architect of the Imam's simple coffin did not bear in mind the weight of additional human beings violently swinging from it in his construction. The IRGC members who tied his coffin to the helicopter similarly did not anticipate this additional carrying capacity. For it must have been a great deal of shock to various parties when the Imam's shrouded body flopped out of the simple coffin to the hungry mourners below. Like piranhas, they took to his shroud and tore away at it, refusing to accept his death and making their own momentums of his glorious life. Again, Ghayas would look up as the now mostly naked body of the Imam crowdsurfed overhead. Despite the macabre, this was the highest honour the community he gave his life in service to could offer his memory. Ghayas was left shocked before the presence of such raw emotion, such raw humanity.

The IRGC were powerless before the tear-drowned mob. They would have had better luck parting the Strait of Hormuz than this crowd. People had thrown themselves in the hole prepared for the Imam's grave. Unable to make head or tail of the sea of human anguish, the Imam's body was quickly whisked away to be cleaned and again enshrouded. After a couple hours' delay, there was to be a second attempt. This time the IRGC held firm that the Ayatollah must be put to rest. This was the last order from their Supreme Leader and failure was not an option. The helicopter moved quickly this time for the grave. In a scene hearkening back to countless rugby matches, the IRGC met the mourners, tooth and nail, two mighty forces opposing each other, waiting for the one moment when it would all go tumbling down and the line would break. This time the IRGC held their ground as the body arrived at the grave. One man quickly tore the coffin lid off and the Imam's body was hastily laid to rest within the grave plot. The earthly tomb was then rapidly covered in concrete slabs and a large freight container. The Imam was at peace. The mission had been accomplished and now the IRGC could join their mourning brothers and sisters in a grand lacrimation that could well have lasted for many more days.[45] It wouldn't be until 1992 that the construction of the Mausoleum of Ruhollah Khomeini would be completed at this very site.

Incredibly exhausted and emotionally spent, Kalim and Ghayas returned to London. The passing of Khomeini brought a looming cloud of doubt to the revolution's survival without him. The revolution would undoubtedly undergo a change and based on the atmosphere in Iran, there would be instability which would demand a purge of sorts, and there was no telling what the Islamic Republic would look like at the other end of that storm. The politics back at home had become particularly vicious as well. The subtlety of Saudi and Iranian influence on the Muslim community through its organisations had become so pathetic that it was blatantly obvious to anyone who cared to pay it any regard. Kalim was also feeling it. The adrenaline jab of globe-trotting was fading and the damage done to the body was beginning to show just as the weight of the banner of Islamic revolution grew heaviest under dead arms. Ghayas recalled the Imam's Farsi à la Urdu comprehension. The sentiment of having all actions done in service to the community rang out. Where had the community been left these last couple of decades? Ghayas found himself fighting along with Kalim to defend the community as the entirety of the ummah. As if two men could stand up for nearly a third of the world population, let alone take on that which is the Western world.

Perhaps it was time to go home, Ghayas would advise with a reassuring pat on the shoulder. But they were going home, and Kalim knew better than what his old friend, his brother, was suggesting. They could keep going, fighting the war that will never end, perhaps even become martyrs for the cause, but what would be accomplished in that? The hope that resided within the subtext of the Iranian revolution was fading. Revolutionary politics on the domestic side and muscle flexing as a display of regional power kept foreign affairs regional and with each new conflict, the image of Iran giving global Muslims a seat at the table of global affairs grew more and more distant. The project of Islamism was failing before the ever-corrupting character of power. To fight for the Islamist cause was to find oneself a bedfellow to militant tyrants, Western appeasers and puppets. This was the sombre tone that Kalim and Ghayas's conversations took as the 1990s burned towards their midpoint.

As Kalim and Ghayas gallantly rode off to battle abroad, the situation of Muslims in Britain grew desperate. How could they be doing any good if they were leaving the homefront to ruin? After all, the United Kingdom was their home now. And now that the transitioning age was ending and a generation of Commonwealth subjects had given birth to true-born Brits, the affairs of the house had to be addressed. The Muslim Parliament for Great Britain still had the power to do this, but its foundation and historical continuance of the narrative was too great a ship to chart a new course. At least, Kalim knew it could not be done in his lifetime. His efforts would not slump for a moment, but he was not so delusional to overlook the fact that his time was quickly approaching. In fact, he lived the last two decades of his life knowing he was standing on borrowed time. Yet Ghayas, his trusted brother and heir apparent, 'the man who comes after me' as Kalim never shied from noting, could square the circle and spearhead this pivot. They were community leaders and it was time to go and lead the community. The titanic battles of geopolitics were having little effect on the brothers and sisters at home. Ghayas was back doing what he did best with the HFA, the activist fighting on the ground floor once again. Work was seemingly endless due to the barrage of issues facing Muslims in the UK. This acceleration was aided by the Muslim Parliament developing a charitable wing, Bait al-Mal al-Islami, an organisation which made issues pertaining to children and women top priority.

The Bait al-Mal al-Islami was established as a registered charity in 1993, a year after the launch of the Muslim Parliament. A body looking to break ground for advancing the British Muslim community required an equally game-changing leader. Suraiya Mullick, an initial trustee of Bait al-Mal al-Islami and a lifelong veteran of charitable causes and champion of the less well-off, effectively ran the day to day operation of the organisation. Her sheer dedication alone made her the best choice to become the Chairperson. Her vast list of contacts in the business and various local community networks allowed her to raise funds from a considerable pool of Brits for the cause. Her own level of personal engagement made her stand out even amongst the most compassionate within the British charity community. Far from a distant managing entity, Mullick had even hand written thank you notes to many donors over the years. Mullick served as a leader and a metaphor for the beautiful work this charity has accomplished since the mid-nineties. It was the first British Muslim organisation to suggest that zakat should primarily be spent locally on UK Muslims, as opposed to being sent back to ancestral homelands, and highlighted the dire socio-economic position of British Muslims. This idea is now more commonplace amongst British Muslim charities, yet was a radical departure from the thinking of the time.

From the get-go the Bait al-Mal al-Islami launched a student loan scheme that would provide hundreds of British Muslim students from poorer backgrounds interest-free loans to go to university, pre-dating any British government student loan programme or any such formal scheme with the British Muslim community at the time. A decade later in 2003, the Bait al-Mal al-Islami would launch its Media Scholarship Programme to fund talented young people looking to launch their careers in the media. The focus on education was a primary means of empowering the Muslim community; the Muslim Parliament and Bait al-Mal al-Islami would hardly ever turn away a student in financial need. Ghayas would read letters from students, from home and abroad, who were struggling to complete their masters or PhDs due to financial issues, and his mantra always remained: 'stick to your studies, we will find you the money'. Ghayas's own personal experience of struggling to attain a proper education and struggling even more to fund said education fuelled his understanding of how difficult it is to be away from your natural support system in your home country. Ghayas held education as one of the most important endeavours of one's life. This made every student's plea for help not only a personal call of duty, but something on the level of a human right owed to those who wished to expand their knowledge, and through which, improve the station of the whole community—the ummah.

The Muslim Parliament would draw attention to the issue of investing in the UK and in the British Muslim community. This was one of its biggest contributions toward changing the community's mindset, that of seeing the UK as home and the responsibilities that come with that realisation. This community would not just be a loose gathering of South Asians, Arabs and Africans, but would unite under a single community. Proudly British Muslims. The use of the word 'parliament', which drew a huge amount of limelight on the organisation, was being used to shine light on these ideas and causes. A clever play on words was the crux of Kalim's redirection of the energy generated through hate-filled anger from the Rushdie Affair into a profoundly creative force for the Muslim community and the greater community of the entire United Kingdom.

So, upon returning to London, Kalim and Ghayas's conversations constructed a framework to build up the Muslim Parliament and use it as a vehicle to advance the community that had been there all along, but rarely given a name: the British Muslims. Yet, no matter the diligence and focus Ghayas put into the projects dearest to his heart, he could not ignore the cries of injustice.

And just as the momentum had tipped towards the British Muslim community, the world fell apart. One small, seemingly insignificant chunk of land suddenly put everything on the line. The question of religion, of humanity, of Muslims, of Europe, of genocide, of war, of revolution, of everyone's future. In 1914, one gunshot in Sarajevo nearly ended the world, pitting all of humanity on the brink of annihilation. Just shy of eighty years later, shots again were being fired in Sarajevo. It was widely accepted that the Cold War ended the day the Berlin Wall fell. As the story goes, it only took two weeks for the East German army and volunteer construction workers to put up the 'Wall of

Shame'. Starting in the summer of 1990, the wall took nearly two years to fully tear down. In the common consciousness, it was believed that once the rubbish was cleaned up, a new world order would magically appear out of necessity. A clever writer's deus ex machina. This was not the case. The Cold War, for so many, would not end for many decades to come as former Soviet blocs dissolved and the institutions and individuals lifted and oppressed during the regime recalibrated under supposedly democratic terms. For some yet, the Cold War hasn't and perhaps never will end. Revolutions, by definition, never really do. The ideas and hatreds fostered during that dichotomous era in European history would prove themselves to have a much longer half-life than anyone would care to admit. The rise of the radical right and fascist sympathy in Europe did not arise out of thin air. It was in the kicked-up dust of the Soviet Union's fall that the first major European conflict since World War II sprang up.

Yugoslavia was one of the longest holdouts of the old communist republics and had always been different amongst the company of the other communist states that clung closer to the USSR. This goes back to the historic difference between Joseph Stalin and Josiph Broz Tito, but also because of the cornucopia of ethnic groups that found themselves within the borders of Yugoslavia at the conclusion of World War II. In fact, a resurgence of nationalism in Yugoslavia is what led to the falling apart of the socialist republic while the other states were more so driven by economic depravity. The division of Yugoslavia had numerous historical borders that could easily be sliced up in 1990, forming such states as Croatia, Serbia, Macedonia, Slovenia, Montenegro, and Bosnia and Herzegovina. The problem of Kosovo highlighted the issue of the wrong ethnic group finding themselves on the wrong side of one of these new borders. The problem with these new, independent states arose with the introduction of electoral representation and equity insurances amongst the ethnic groups. For Serbia and Croatia, the Serbs and Croats quickly took majorities in their respective governments. Bosnia and Herzegovina was presented with a problem. As a former outpost of the Ottoman Empire it had established a cohesive multi-ethnic society, yet this crowning achievement was quickly revealed to be fragile on the scale of appearing as though it hadn't actually ever happened. At least this would be its appearance after decades of Soviet style governance led by Croat and Serbian dominated rule.

During the 1990 elections, Serb and Croat parties took major blocs of power, leaving little for the Muslim population of Bosnia, the Bosniaks. Whenever new borders are drawn, disputed lands naturally arise. Serbia's claims over Kosovo revealed that the former leader of the united Yugoslavia, Slobodan Milošević, now leader of Serbia, might not be so willing to surrender the power he once held. What was to stop him from using the Serb population of Bosnia to rule the territory remotely, or to stop him from simply crossing the border and invading the country? After all, Bosnia's military population was split three ways between independent Croatian and Serbian forces bordering their respective states, leaving the Bosniak army flanked in the middle. As the politicians attempted to draw up agreements to resolve the potential for conflict in Bosnia, nationalist tensions did the heavy lifting for them, dissolving any semblance of multi-ethnic harmony the Turks had brought to the territory only a little over a century prior.[46]

Just as the retired revolutionaries, Kalim and Ghayas, had prepared to comfortably hang up their hats and leave the wars of the greater world to go as they may, the Muslim world was in grave danger once again. Not just that, but it was being broadcast through the media the world over. The first genocide in Europe following the Second World War would not only be committed against Muslims but delivered right to the comfort of one's living room for your viewing entertainment. For Kalim, it was not a question. Back again into the breach, for it was a matter of duty. The efforts of the Muslim Parliament quickly set their eye on the situation in the Balkans. The Muslim Parliament organised and ran the World Conference on Bosnia and the Global Islamic Movement in November 1993. The over 3,000 strong assembled attendants of the conference were encouraged to either take up arms in the latest global jihad or donate to protect the Muslims of Bosnia. This was an emergency rescue mission and the Muslim response from the UK had to be swift and loud.

The arms embargo placed on Bosnia prevented weapons from entering the country, where much of the atrocities of the 'Balkans War' was occurring. Yet, arms were largely concentrated and allowed to freely flow into Serbia and Croatia, a place many of the aggressors called home or received their aid from. Bosnia, the largely Muslim populated region of the former Yugoslavia was denied the right to self-defence while the world appeared to turn a blind eye to those committing what amounted to a flat out, carte blanche massacre, a genocide. The Muslim Parliament even hosted the Grand Mufti of Bosnia, Mustafa Ceric, in London for the May 1994 session of the body. For Kalim, it was essential that the British Muslims were the first to shine light on the genocide being committed against Muslims, and rally the banners as it were.

Where Kalim may have seen opportunity, it was in the next generation that ideological revolutions were reaching critical mass and a generation was coming of age before a television that sang the song of global indifference. These were the first British-born Muslims. Whereas Kalim and Ghayas' generation came to age at the twilight of empire, this new generation was entering adulthood with an extracurricular lesson in apathy and passive racism. The seeds gestated in the Rushdie Affair found fertile soil to take up roots in the Bosnian crisis's ontological emphasis on the new identity of British Muslims in the 1990s. Muslims of a new, and once perceived modern and enlightened era, realised not only that racism existed but that it was so institutionalised that the voices that remained silent did almost as much damage as the shadowy bigots and xenophobes.

While many of this generation took a more reasoned yet informed approach to their identity, radicalisation, both of a justified response to current affairs and of a toxic nature, began to spread throughout Britain, and to a certain extent, throughout Europe's Muslim communities. The genocide in Bosnia lit a flame that burned bright through demonstrations before Lord Nelson's triumph calling for jihad against the West for ignoring the cries of their brothers and sisters. Drudging up the memories of Britain's hand in destroying the supposed Caliphate in 1924, extreme cries called for assassinations and chaos from Trafalgar Square to No. 10. Various communities organised throughout Great Britain to collect funds to arm the Bosniaks. While the scales of moral justice may be quick to judge these acts, the steps taken by those who raised funds, even those specifically for arming the government of Bosnia, was legal under the context of the UK in the early 1990s. The violent and harsh rhetoric mixed with the cracking down on Irish terrorism quickly painted the Bosnian jihad fund a dangerous train of thought, especially when the Bosnian-blinded powers that be in the British establishment caught wind of such charitable endeavours. It was clear that Bosnia needed weapons, not food, for food would only make the lamb fat for slaughter. These lambs intended to fight back.

Europe's insistence on non-intervention only fed rumours of a European conspiracy to eliminate Islam from the continent. Radicalisation was fuelled further by the images coming from the Balkans. These were white, blonde-haired and blue-eyed Muslims being executed by death squads. The fatal bullets did not discriminate between the all-too-European casual faithful or the devout. If this is what Europe was allowing to happen to the 'assimilated', what terrible fate would befall those who looked and acted the part in line with Europe's stereotypical imagination? How ever this new generation of British Muslims was to fall, there is no doubt that the genocide in Bosnia not only opened their eyes to a disgustingly true state of the world, but might just stand as the definitive moment for the first British-born Muslim community, just as they were all coming of age. What Rushdie stirred up would remain adolescent angst in comparison to the childhood ending finitude of what happened in Bosnia between 1992 and 1995.[47]

Ghayas saw an opportunity for a new way that would usher in the activist of the new millennium. Ghayas and Kalim were getting old and the world was changing. There were new tools to be utilised, which were having a tremendous effect on public opinion. Broadcast news was making its ascent towards the 24-hour news cycles that delivered instant gratification as would continue until today. This was the future of activism. If Ghayas could find himself or other members of the community before a camera, this was perhaps more effective than marching on Parliament Square.

Ghayas also saw that they had allies—once perceived enemies, now powerful friends—who could bring about actual change. While the government of the time was in favour of an arms embargo on the region, they resisted military action and worse, threw the blame for the conflict equally on the Serbs and Bosniaks. What was interesting was the rest of the world disagreed! America's Bill Clinton pushed for strikes against Serbia, adding strain to their 'special relationship'. Meanwhile, Clinton was also looking to solve the Irish situation. The government of Great Britain was licking its wounds and the time was optimal for the Muslim Parliament to flex their influence. Even continental Europe saw the importance of the Bosnian War's outcome. The European Union had a massive stake in the outcome of the post-Cold War states. The Holocaust of Nazi Germany was still fresh in everyone's mind as well, and after 1945, the phrase 'never again' carried a lot of weight. It appeared that other world leaders and the once ignorant and selfish West, might just, at least for this moment, hold the value and dignity of human life above politics and power. Ghayas saw an opportunity to partner the old revolutionary us-against-them vision, with a new community centred mission. For Kalim, it was off into the fray yet again, while for Ghayas, it was the transition the community needed, the transition that not only correctly oriented the organisations he helped grow with Kalim, but elevate the community beyond the local and, though it sounds rather corny, actually try to save the world.

Ghayas decided to clear off the war room desk and put away his suitcase, for it was time to again don his activist hat. Talat was ever ready for the next project, having her own activist credentials through her work in Chesham and her contributions to the Muslim Women's Institute, the women's committee of the Muslim Parliament. She was the quintessential great (perhaps even greater) woman the phrase referred to whom stood behind great men. Their four children, Faiza, Asim, Uzma and Salman, were coming of an age where they too could play a hand in helping with their Abu's activities, and they would in their own individual ways. From bake sales, sponsored walks to demonstrations, the Siddiquis helped in pushing Chesham to join alongside other communities throughout Britain to aid their Bosnian brothers and sisters confronted with the horrors of genocide. They represented one of the many constituencies throughout Great Britain, led by their MMPs to give their all to the Bosniak cause.

From the outside, the community projects of these groups had the seemingly innocent community camaraderie of any other bake sales and fundraising efforts. The discovery that the selling of chapattis was being used to fund the arming of foreign fighters did not sit so well, especially with the ever-pressured Charities Commission of England and Wales. Although nothing would compare to the scrutiny they would face in the noughties, the early 1990s was no cakewalk. Since the mid-1970s, in response to increased threat of attack from the Irish Republican

Army (IRA) and other nationalist organisations deemed 'terrorists', Parliament had rushed through a series of legislative acts. These anti-terrorism acts would come to a head in 1990, giving British police greater power to arrest and detain. Border security was clamped down, organisations would be blacklisted and those found to be funding 'terrorist' efforts could face limitless fines and potential jail time. The speed with which these measures were conceived and rushed to the vote demonstrated an unabashed stance on the Irish question.

Equally unabashedly carried out was the extrapolation of these laws to those who were just calling for jihad against the UK. Jihad is a broad Islamic term which in its essence stands firstly for the constant spiritual struggle each individual faces against one's own self in the pursuit of perfecting one's character. Secondary, this struggle part extends outside of one's self to extrapolate the fruits of these concepts into the wider society in the form of equity and justice. This would clearly encapsulate community welfare work and activism. Only one aspect of the term jihad pertains to actual warfare, with vast religious legal rulings on the circumstances in which a call to active combat could be made. The main overriding factor, as was made clear through the Rushdie Affair, for Muslims in the UK being that one cannot breach the laws of the land. The Muslim community saw active protesting, lobbying and fundraising for a legitimate government of a sovereign state as all part of the legal form of jihad permissible by both the laws of the land and encouraged, if not enjoined upon them, by their faith.

The full extent to which Islamophobic motives were brewing at the time would not be realised until these anti-terrorism acts were reaffirmed in the chaos of the noughties. The powers that be in Whitehall saw the threat these 'jihadis' posed to British society and perhaps even anticipated them becoming more of a problem than the IRA itself. A word so complex as jihad was easily simplified under the label of 'foreign' and thus, in the tradition of both empire and the way the English language works, in accordance with the dictates of fear, the powers that be sought to define this word for the English speaking world, lest it be allowed a chance to exercise power over its own fate. Jihad was equated to terrorism, and the call for global jihad which has had various blooms throughout the history of Islam, was veiled in its potential danger before a lesson could be taught. The potential lesson jihad could teach was what happens when blatant injustice is allowed to run rampant, what happens when one group of human beings is denied their basic right to exist. Just when the West had a chance to really investigate the Other, it chose the comfort of orientalist sentiment. While those called to the duty of global jihad ranged from social justice warriors, to Islamist and militant zealots, they were all seen as equal in the eyes of Otherness. Naturally, the powers that be in the United Kingdom followed the trail of demonstrations to find a locus for jihadi activity and in the early 1990s, Bosnia was the x that marked that spot. So it would appear that those pushing the Bosnian issue were to be feared, and just like that, the beautiful complexity of the jihad going on in the hearts and minds of each British Muslim at the time was reduced to xenophobic passion.[48]

In accordance with the international arms embargo, the Charity Commission had Bosnia put on a watchlist where only monies for peaceful purposes could be collected on their behalf. But the Bosnians needed arms to defend themselves, not sticking plasters or tea scones. They were being brutally slaughtered. Men and women. Even pregnant women. Children. All equal before the blade and bullet of their aggressors. Something less than human and needing to be rid of from this earth. And the worst thing about it was that despite the ubiquity of the Fourth Estate's visual framing, the West ignored this horror. It could have easily acted, yet it did not. Was such violence in Europe after World War II so incomprehensible? Are the conspiracy theorists correct in saying Europe detests Muslims?

Despite how ridiculous the conclusions that were drawn may appear, they carried a scary logic before the causal reality of European action in the early 1990s. Seeing the establishment's move, the British Muslim community countered. It would not remain silent; it would find a way to help. As crazy as the world looked in this particular instant, it was not hard to see that this assault was targeted and that only Bosnian lives stood to be lost in this conflict. Muslim lives. Such carelessly allowed violence should frighten any sane individual, despite their descriptors! The British Muslims, alongside others, chose to act. And the fundraising efforts were instead funnelled into the new Muslim Parliament Bosnian Jihad Fund. A challenge was set to the government. Would they ban jihad? In a clever bit of bureaucratic juggling, the money raised was given to the elected government of Bosnia under Alija Izetbegović, not a charity bound by the Charities Commission, to spend on their priorities to prevent genocide of their people. The community had taken a stance, abiding moral right and the laws of the land, that justice was something worth fighting for and they would help in whatever way they could to prevent the destruction of human life and stop mindless, flagrant ethnic cleansing. If a charitable event was shut down by the local police, no resistance was to be had and the event was to be moved to the neutral venue of a mosque. Here the police had no jurisdiction. If the community wanted to give, no technicality was going to stop this.

A tectonic shift was occurring that few would have been able to pick up on except in retrospect. The first generation of British Muslims—and here I refer to those Muslims born in Great Britain to the parents of the global diaspora—was coming of age. No longer were they giggling and playing in the other room while their parents planned and organised. They were now educated and finishing their studies, preparing to enter the professional world, ready to make their mark from the new platform their parents had attempted to set up. The causes their parents fought for were now to become the causes of the sons and daughters. Likewise, their failures and frustrations would echo through the generations. The Rushdie Affair made them intellectuals. The Bosnian War made them warriors. Yet, as each maturing British Muslim waged their own jihad within themselves, the question remained: what would a warrior look like in this modern age?

Sadly, some would run full speed down the dark path of fundamentalism and radical thought, seeking all that could be sought to give their lives meaning. Still more took the warrior spirit and channelled that into both bettering themselves and their community. Now an accountant or a doctor could be as committed to the cause as an imam or even a scholar. The mantle's passing was at hand. Never is it the intention of the parent to create a burden for their children in the weaving of legacy, yet it is a naturally occurring phenomenon. The daughters and sons, and especially those first British Muslim children, were to find their moulding in how they were to fill their parent's shoes.[49] One option was to live a parallel life where a son makes a name for himself in a fashion separate from his father's legacy. Another option came in taking on the apparent birth right, standing and delivering before the jury of history.

Yet another option was to be so crippled by acts of the father that the son could never imagine living up to such expectation; so afraid of flying, that they were unable to land once they found themselves airborne. The Siddiqui children would go on to live their own successful lives, but in the early 1990s, the groundwork for the patrilineal succession seemed apparent. Inspired by their father, his four children would go on to found and run their own community groups. Asim helped set up *The Challenge*, a Muslim youth news magazine in 1992, and, along with Faiza, the City Circle, a network of young Muslim professionals in 1999. Asim would blog at *The Guardian* and *New Statesman* and regularly be invited to TV studios as a sensible voice, particularly after the events of 7 July 2005. *Time* magazine would put Asim on its cover in February 2008 as part of a feature on 'Europe's Muslim Success Story' and be referenced in books written at the time on the development of British Muslim communities.[50] Faiza would drive the work of the Muslim Women's Institute through its Muslims in the Media Scholarship programme. Uzma would volunteer as a Maths teacher at a Saturday school, a counsellor at the Muslim Youth Helpline, a mentor with the Prince's Trust Mosaic Network, and be an adviser to the Muslim Women's Advisory Network. Salman was a driving force behind the Muslim anti-war group Just Peace, and co-founded the Oxbridge Muslim Alumni and MUJU, a Muslim and Jewish theatre company.

All the children would take a keen interest in their father's work and support his activities. However, Ghayas had no interest in carrying on a family dynasty of community leaders. He only wanted his children's hearts to be in their selective career paths and stand to better themselves and those around them. In Kalim's son, Iqbal, Ghayas saw the other side of this tricky coin. The revolution was killing Kalim and, whether or not he would agree, he would admit it was a worthy thing to give one's life in service of. And whether or not he realised it, he had also pressured Iqbal, especially in the last few years. A hard father whose rhetoric shook the foundations of Western civilisation would indeed be one no one would wish to refuse.

Kalim was a leader and the type of leader who bore a talent for charisma and manipulation. Ghayas knew he himself had certainly been pressured to fall in line with Kalim, but he, unlike Iqbal, always had his one condition and could walk away at any point. Ghayas's heart was in the cause and the community and therefore, any pressure he felt from Kalim was justified. However, towards the boy, it just didn't feel right. Kalim expected the world from Iqbal, as any father expects from their son. What differed is that Iqbal's heart did not seem to lie in his father's endeavours, but Ghayas got the impression that he was helpless to deny him. Kalim's health only made this more manifest. Iqbal's own life on hold, he became his father's personal assistant, driving him from point a to point b and back, carrying the bags, becoming his secretary. One day Ghayas approached Iqbal and with the respectful tenderness of a wise teacher, told him that he was not bound by some destiny that demanded he do as his father commanded. If Iqbal's heart lay in other dreams he ought to seek them out, for in his happiness he would find success and another avenue by which to attain his father's pride—if a father's pride even required concrete evidence (which I assure you it does not). Iqbal simply shook his head as the many young people before him had, and Iqbal and Ghayas continued on with the day's business.

The Bosnian War represented something deeper for the first generation of British-born Muslims. It was a call to arms, a chance for the up and coming generation to partake in the post-colonial struggle which their parents had fought in. Above all, it was a chance to fight for the community. The Rushdie Affair was a chance to let out youth's angst. Yell and shout, perhaps pound the wall a few times. Set something on fire. This, though, was the chance to walk the talk. This was to be where they found their definition in the annals of history. This was all their war. And the stakes were apparent. After all, if genocide could once again occur in Europe even after suffering one of the worst examples of such terror, what would stop it from happening anywhere? It thus had to be resisted by everyone, no matter where they found themselves at the point of initiation. It was not uncommon for foreign mercenaries to become involved in such conflicts. In fact, there was quite a purse to be made through the independent contracts floating around. Wishing in no way to prohibit the next generation from joining in the glorious revolution, the Muslim Parliament compiled a registry of individuals willing and able to join in the Bosniak military. This registry never came to be more than a symbolic call to arms, however.

In 1993, Ghayas travelled to Bosnia. There he saw the destruction first hand and heard the gruesome stories of how snipers were posted in hotel rooms using pedestrians as target practice, or how the military would capture one man and force him to call for the rest of their family, saying all was safe, so that they would come out from hiding to be shot on sight.[51] Yet again, Ghayas found himself the eyes to witness the depravity of human acts. But while he could only play spectator and commentator for Bangladesh and Iran, now he bore power once only thought to reside within a state: military assistance. While in Bosnia, Ghayas wanted to reassure the Bosniak people that the Muslim Parliament of Great Britain was working on their behalf to both reveal and rally the globe against the atrocities occurring throughout their country. He also offered the registry and thus the military support of the British Muslim people. A general in the Bosniak army thanked Ghayas for the support, but explained that overseas volunteer fighters with no experience of war or knowledge of the landscape would be more of a burden than a help. They would need to be trained and disciplined and there was no time for such preparations as the war was all around them—in fact, they were sending such boys who had turned up back to the UK since they were so ill prepared and lacked any military training. Besides their sincere offer of support, they were just another group of vulnerable civilians that the already overstretched Bosniak forces had to protect. Ghayas also delivered an invitation to the first President of Bosnia Herzegovina, Alija Izetbegović, to attend the 1993 conference on Bosnia hosted by the Muslim Parliament. Izetbegović had to respectfully decline for he was needed by his people and if he was to leave, there was little guarantee that he would be allowed to return.

Upon his return to London, Ghayas and the Muslim Parliament would continue their work, speaking out against the plight of the Muslim Bosniaks, raising funds and educating the public on the matter. The hope was to change the collective narrative towards the Muslim community, by tying the Bosnian situation to the larger historical struggle of Muslims in the world while reconceptualising what it meant to be a member of the British community and the larger European community. The lessons in neighbourly love and the Muslim revolution against Western oppression were not easily received. A multitude of other organisations throughout Britain, including those within the British Muslim community, were very critical of the Muslim Parliament's approach and efforts towards the Bosniaks. The opinion of being on the side of peace often spoke out against the Muslim Parliament's support of arming the Bosniak people or calling for the states of Europe to join the US in striking against Bosnian Serb positions. The wider rhetoric that the genocide was as much the fault of the Bosniak people as the Serbs only made matters murkier.

It would only later be learned that the UK government was engaged in operations to support the Bosniak military against the Serbians. Of course, the UK government could not both be supporting a militant resistance and be sending troops as a part of the United Nations Peacekeeping operations—what an irreconcilable contradiction that would be. Though perhaps not, for it was the revelation of US President Clinton's when remarking upon his time in office that many US allies in Europe said they opposed lifting the arms embargo on humanitarian rationale, stating that more guns going in only spells more bloodshed for all. What they wouldn't care to admit was their true intention: to keep Bosnia locked right where it was to befall whatever fate may result. After all, it would be unnatural for Bosnia to stand as the only Muslim country in Europe. And yet we scratch our heads as to why Turkey didn't gain membership in the EU when it was at its most secular-liberal period in history. Let us not forget that even as the UK contributed to peacekeeping operations, a joint mission with the Dutch resulted in a horrific massacre in the Bosnian city of Srebrenica. The peacekeeping troops had failed to neutralise a

Serbian-backed military unit of Bosnian Serbs, the Army of Srps-ka, before declaring the city a 'safe zone'. The military unit took the city after over eight thousand Bosniaks had been gathered there for their protection and then forced the Brits and Dutch to leave. With the UN out of the way, the Army of Srpska proceeded undisturbed in their cold-blooded slaughtering frenzy.[52]

Hits to their reputation were only the beginning of the arrows the community would face as the 1990s rolled on. The support for the Rushdie fatwa had left a sour taste in the mouths of the Peace Pledge Union, the pacifist landlords the Muslim Institute was renting 6 Endsleigh Street from. The perceived militant policy in regards to Bosnia must not have helped in their decision to decline a renewal of the lease. Fortunately, the Muslim Institute had one other property they had purchased and still owned from the early 1980s. 109 Fulham Palace Road was a building largely used for storage and letting up to that point, and by the 1990s found itself in a relatively rundown part of Hammersmith. At the time, the building was described by Zafar Bangash as somewhere he wouldn't even keep a horse. Still, it was within a reasonable distance from the intellectual capital of London and Logan Hall where many Institute events, lectures and conferences were held. So, in 1994 the Muslim Institute, the larger than life Muslim Parliament, and the newly established Halal Food Authority, would move into 109 Fulham Palace Road.

As for Bosnia, well-estimated casualties ranged from 25,000 to over 300,000. Judging by the fact that Sarajevo's most easily seen landmark is the stretches of land decorated with white tombstones, marked with death dates between 1992 and 1996, the numbers are modestly calculated. Although Bosnia Herzegovina filed suits against Serbia and Montenegro for genocide in 1993, it would not be until 2007 that the International Court of Justice would deem it genocide, and even then the decision would state that the genocide was not the direct act of Serbia and Montenegro. Don't worry, though—they did get a firm talking to as the court did recognise their failure to prevent a genocide from occurring. The International Criminal Tribunal for former Yugoslavia was established by the UN in 1993 and by 2008 would find several of the Serbian leaders, both military and political, guilty of war crimes. Slobodan Milošević would die in custody at the Hague in 2006 before his sentence could be reached.[53] So, in conclusion, small crumbs of justice came. Eventually. To some. Perhaps this should be the motto of the international courts.

Like clockwork, just as the universe was throwing every sign it could muster to slow down and turn back to the local community, Kalim would suffer his third heart attack requiring yet another bypass surgery. The first one lasted twelve for the ten years it was cautiously given by doctors. In his last book, *Stages of Islamic Revolution*, Kalim details his last major stay in the hospital, receiving the bypass surgery, suffering six instances of cardiac arrest and a long, solitary, bedbound recovery. The severity of this one is the sort that is emphasised by the replacement of 'if' with 'when' in the doctor's monologues. Kalim knew the end was upon him, but he held to the famous *hadith*, in which the Prophet asserts, "If you are planting a tree and see the end of the world coming, don't stop planting the tree." After all, his last stint lasted well past the use-by date. He was not so naïve to think that he could test death a second time, but his ambition alluded to his intentions to use every minute of this last ten-year lease of life. The global Islamic Revolution still remained to be seen, although he knew that he had words left to write and that he would need to slow down.

During the final years, Kalim and Ghayas would sometimes talk about the future direction of their organisations. Ghayas felt changes in thinking and approach were needed. Kalim was open to change, but the change must come after him. He was too old and weak now to change direction but at the same time did not want to step down or take a backseat. Any change would be for his successor, Ghayas, to enact after him. His admission that his final book would need to be updated after five years or so spoke to his understanding that the world was changing rapidly and thus, thinking and ideas would also need to evolve. Kalim's opus called for a secession of the Muslim interregnum that had continued since medieval times. Allowing one's philosophy to ossify, frozen in time, would not progress the ummah. Both he and Ghayas knew and preached that education was a lifetime's work. New information and questioning need its due accounting. The greatest disservice Ghayas could do to Kalim's work and the greater ummah would be to allow it to ossify within such an intellectual ice age. Evolution needed to occur where necessary. This final reflection was the snowball destined to become an avalanche in Ghayas's political thinking as well as for the future of the Muslim Institute and Muslim Parliament. Reiteration, editing and adaptation. Kalim was after all a perfectionist, even to the bitter end.

Kalim's home away from home was in Pretoria, South Africa, where he was always welcomed as a most honoured guest under the auspices of his friend Ismail Kalla, who he had first met in July 1973 at a conference in Libya. It was highly advised by Ghayas and his doctors that Kalim pass on his invitation to a conference in South Africa taking place in the April of 1996. But how could he refuse one last chance to both see Pretoria and to attend a conference on 'Creating a New Civilisation of Islam'? Do not worry, Ghayas bhai, Kalim said, on his return they would discuss the change to come, the community and the future. That conference might just give him an idea or two. Kalim walked on. But that long conversation would not take place. Kalim would not survive his final trip to South Africa.

On the evening of 18 April 1996, Dr. Kalim Siddiqui had been resting at Ismail's home, where he and his wife Suraiya had been staying for this visit. Kalim got up to make *wudu* (ablution) to get ready for prayers. He and Suraiya were to leave for the airport back to London that night. The conference had been a huge success but had pushed him to his physical limits. Kalim was the star attraction and everyone wanted a piece of him. Shortly after 6pm, the *maghrib adhaan* sounded. Kalim, accompanied by Suraiya, left the annex they were staying in to walk together to the main house for the congregational prayer. As they walked between the buildings, Kalim suddenly felt strange, then collapsed into Suraiya's arms. As Ismail rushed to assist, it was too late. The paramedics would report that his death was instantaneous. Dr. Kalim Siddiqui had left this world with the adhaan ringing in his ears.[54] Ismail immediately ran into the house, picking up the phone. A call ran from Pretoria all the way to Toronto. On the receiving end of this phone call was Zafar Bangash, who had recently returned to Canada from attending the same conference. Ismail broke the news to Zafar who said that Ghayas needed to be contacted immediately to receive word on the next actions.

Just after tea on that Thursday, as Ghayas was finishing up the day's work, the phone rang. Zafar broke the tragic news to Ghayas. An era had ended. Kalim was dead. Knowing the words would one day come did nothing to prepare the heart for the dagger's plunge. Shock still comes for the most thoroughly prepared. Ghayas responded with stoicism. Such was the magnitude of the loss that there was no time to mourn in the sorrow of knowing a friend, or rather, a brother, had died.

It will never be known how much more work Ghayas had intended to do that day or how late he would have otherwise stayed in the office, but all other matters and conversations and gestures fell silent to memory before the backdrop of the news from Pretoria. There was now so much that needed organising: bringing the body back, organising the funeral, notifying the members of the Muslim Parliament and the contacts worldwide, inviting dignitaries to speak at the funeral, preparing the press releases that would need issuing. But first, Kalim's children would need to be told the news. For all he had known, an infinity might have passed between Ghayas dashing back from work and arriving back in Chesham while contemplating the awfulness of breaking such news to the now fatherless children.

Upon entering his home, Talat was not only the first to greet him, but also the first to learn of the day's sorrow. Ghayas's phone rang. It was the BBC. Not an all that unusual call by this time for Ghayas. After all, the BBC, Channel 4 or other media outlets would often ring if they needed Ghayas or Kalim to make a statement on one happening or another; sometimes they would even be invited down to the studio for an interview or panel discussion. Yet that day's ring did not have much in the way of opportunity. They had alerted Ghayas that they understood that Kalim Siddiqui had passed away earlier that day in Pretoria. They wanted to inform him that this newsworthy item would be reported during that day's nine o'clock news.

Upon hearing this, Talat's heart suddenly skipped a beat. We need to go to Slough to convey this news to the children in person before the BBC does, Talat would say firmly to Ghayas. Kalim's two daughters, Shama and Lubna, were staying in the family home with Shama's three children, potentially in the dark concerning the shadow on the day. Few injustices measured to learning of the loss of a parent, a child, even a good friend, through the banal ennui of the evening news. The unimaginably difficult task of informing the children that their father would not be returning from South Africa fell on Talat and Ghayas.

The sun still lingering above the horizon, the Siddiquis made the oh-so-familiar car ride from Chesham to Slough. Ghayas had taken this trail countless times since his first trip two decades past. Though this time the trip was alien, for the destination would no longer be that warm home of Kalim's favourite cup of 'subpar tea' be that the 'smelly' or 'disgusting' varieties he would joke of as he sipped away, his face once warmed by the steam. That home would no longer be the same one, once filled with the olfactory tantalisation of South Asian cooking, or intellectual illumination. Parking up outside the house, Talat, driven by a preternatural instinct, knew just what to do and just what to say. Greeted by Shama and Lubna, it appeared to them a wonderful but unusual surprise visit from Talat Auntie and Ghayas Uncle. Talat took Lubna into the kitchen with Shama as her children played. It was late; they had better finish cooking dinner. Normalcy had a ticking clock placed upon it. The preparation of dinner would continue alongside the usual chatter. The meal went off as so many lovely dinners had in the past. Despite the weight of grimace's tug upon Ghayas and Talat's hearts, all seemed business as usual. Following the meal, Talat told the daughters of their father and the news from South Africa. A conversation no one would want to have. Talat stayed with the daughters while Ghayas began working the phones, and together they all watched the announcement of Kalim Siddiqui's passing on the nine o'clock news.

Ghayas and Talat returned late to Chesham. BBC *Newsnight* began around 10:30pm that night. At around quarter past eleven, it was announced that Kalim, the revered face within the British Muslim community, the man famous for fiery support of Iran's revolution and swift support for the fatwa against Salman Rushdie, the man who may not have worked well in organisations but would have his opinions heard, had died in South Africa at age sixty-three.

Kalim had two celebrations of his life. Upwards of two thousand people attended the next day's *janazah* prayer after Friday prayers in Pretoria. The following day Kalim Siddiqui's body was flown back to London. A massive gathering assembled on Sunday the 21st of April for janazah prayer at the Stoke Poges Country Club in Slough. Solemn words were read on behalf of Ayatollah Ali Khamenei, the leader of the Islamic Republic of Iran, Dr. Hassan Turabi, an influential Sudanese politician, and the Hizbullah of Lebanon. In attendance were many of Britain's top Muslims—friends, allies and rivals—along with a colourful variety of characters of controversy and intrigue. Yusuf Islam, famously once known as Cat Stevens, was also in attendance. The two-hour service spoke of Kalim's achievements and milestones as well as the fights left to be fought. He was hailed as 'the leading Muslim of his generation' and 'Britain's most prominent Muslim community leader'. After the prayer and words, Kalim was laid to rest in Slough Cemetery.[55] As his body was committed to the earth, the looming emptiness of the void he left behind began to sink in.

At this moment it would have felt like the entire Muslim world had turned their eyes upon Dr. Ghayasuddin Siddiqui. Less in invocation of condolences and more like an opponent upon release of a chess piece, signalling the end of their turn.

Chapter Nine

A VERY BRITISH MUSLIM COUP

BEING THE MAN that Kalim Siddiqui had introduced as 'the man who comes after me' made it clear that Ghayas was the heir apparent. Regime changes can be horridly messy affairs, but after the passing of Kalim the community needed another authority figure to stand behind. The law of the conservation of energy in physics explains how energy can neither be created nor destroyed, only transferred. Political power abides by similar principles. This truism has left many an establishment on the brink of oblivion when first leaders pass without a solid system of succession. For all of Kalim's efforts to plan for the post-revolutionary future of the ummah, he failed in preparing both the Muslim Parliament and the Muslim Institute for the post-Kalim world. Such failures have doomed empires, casting their fragmented territories into long periods of interregnum, confounded by war and chaos, unable to easily move on.

Yet Kalim had explicitly stated that all of his efforts reached for something greater than himself and all who helped him. He had clearly warned against the evils of personal pursuits of power and petty factioning in his inaugural address before the Muslim Parliament. Such were the ways of the corrupt Western systems, something the Muslims were above. Also, those Kalim left behind knew that the Muslim community would not often come across such a charismatic and strong leader. Despite his flaws, the man took charge, so much so that his demands would continue to be abided after his passing. And in 1996, the transition followed rather peacefully, without a hitch. Perhaps this segment of society had figured it out; the revolution could continue passing from one administration to the next, resistant to the usual pitfalls of the affairs of power.

In fact, the mourning had barely just begun when the trustees of the Muslim Institute journeyed one final time to Slough to discuss the future of the organisation, where Kalim himself was made its first Director. Kalim had passed on Thursday and the board of trustees met on Sunday the 21st of April, just before his funeral. They met in Kalim's office, a mighty seat of power, which neighboured his house in Slough. The meeting of the board had one noticeable absence, Dr. Mohammed Moin of Nuneaton, who could not make the long journey on such short notice. At the Slough meeting, Ghayas was made the new Director of the Muslim Institute and Zafar Bangash was made the new Assistant Director. Notably, two new trustees were elected to the board, Kalim's son Iqbal Siddiqui and Haroon Kalla, brother of Ismail in South Africa. A week later, the members of the Muslim Parliament would meet to elect Ghayas as their new leader. The future was now secured and consensus attained regarding Kalim's successor.

Such was the high profile of the Muslim Parliament that when Ghayas was elected its leader it made global news. The news was also splashed across the front page of *Crescent International*: "If the enemies of Islam thought that the death of Dr. Kalim Siddiqui would mean the end of the institutions he helped bring into existence, they must be greatly disappointed. Muslims in Britain moved quickly to fill the void created by the departure, last month, of Dr. Kalim Siddiqui. At an emergency meeting of the Muslim Parliament of Great Britain on May 5, Dr. Muhammad Ghayasuddin was appointed its new Leader."

Ghayas had hitherto not used his surname to avoid any suggestion that he and Kalim were related and to not distract or confuse people from Kalim Siddiqui, the main show in town. Ghayas's book, *The Impact of Nationalism on the Muslim World*, published in 1986 by the Open Press (the Muslim Institute's publishing wing) names him on the cover as M. Ghayasuddin only.

Ghayas accepted his new position without hesitation. Though he may have been made out as the timid man lurking in Kalim's shadow, he quickly revealed to everyone that he had no aversion to the spotlight. It was fair, theoretically, for Kalim cast a large shadow and those closest to him would be almost hidden in that mystique. But Ghayas was most certainly not timid. Often the rash mistake quiet for ignorance and cowardice. Ghayas was just, as it so happened, listening—a novel concept. And listen very carefully he did. Kalim taught this man how to debate, how to politic, and how to take the reins and lead this community to the future and, it must be said, while the student Ghayas may have been easily distracted by the cries of the people, when studying, he is otherwise very focused and quick on the uptake. After all, during his years of distraction he had become a master of pausing and picking up right where he left off when the time came to return to work left unfinished.

And let it not be forgotten that one of the key pillars of Kalim and Ghayas's efforts had been to foster a robust foundation in education as the key to overcoming the great oppressors around the globe. While Kalim and Ghayas were the meeting of heart and mind, Ghayas, his body weight composed mostly in kilos of heart, had all along kept his mind's plasticity topmost as to capture any new lesson that came before him. Kalim had created the Ghayas who took the podium days after his body was laid to rest. And Ghayas owed the fulfilment of their final conversations to both Kalim's memory and the greater community, that which the Imam told him was what mattered above all else. Change needed to happen.

The direction shifted as the two men had agreed and this time the community had to not simply be shown the future, but be guided there. Kalim was not blessed with the time needed to properly make the pivot; more thought and further global development was needed to transition his thinking properly. A new administration allowed for a sharp new direction. Kalim never allowed his education to be completed and knew the greater education of the ummah had a lot to learn after his time. Ghayas was aware that he could not do this alone and in truth that the effort was not so much his as it was something which belonged to the community. Therefore, the community may leave him behind if that was what must be.

He knew that the next generation needed to be empowered and saw his entire tenure as, in a manner of speaking, a transitional period. He just had to slowly reveal the transition so that he could sit back or walk away or be taken by God himself, but the community would continue on, seeing that they had to continue the walk of progress. In the very definition of progress, no one ought to ever see it completed. Like revolution, progress is in perpetuity, but it is a perpetual bettering, whereas revolution is simply change, violent in nature and restricted by dichotomous vocabulary doomed to never be sated. Ghayas knew the revolution had to die. The notion of them against us, the perpetual fight against the Other was not the way. The British Muslim community needed to itself, be empowered to take on the future. Britain was no longer a refuge to provide these men to think freely. It was now home.

For too long, Ghayas had fit his political ideals to whatever ragtag group would accept his assistance. His one condition was his shield and one of many structures that kept him honest through all those years before. In truth, he had never needed political patronage as Ghayas the activist was a force unto himself. And now he could truly play the part. He would prefer the more uncompromising approach to other's opinions and most especially, governments. Governments, global movements and grassroots efforts remain incompatible with each other when forgetting that they are built upon the fundamental principles of humanity's desire to help. The narratives are becoming confusing, so perhaps they will one day be thrown out so that everyone can once again, just simply be human.

Ghayas had been a first-string player suddenly given the conductor's baton by the maestro himself, expected to keep the dynamic and complex symphony going. He needed to play the game very carefully. The first moves would be most essential in setting up what would come next. A period of mourning would be required and thus he called for a Kalim Siddiqui memorial conference to be held. Hopefully the others would take Kalim's thoughts and extrapolate them in their own ambitions and efforts. The conference was a resounding success, coming together at lightning pace and bringing all those Kalim had inspired together at good old Logan Hall in November of 1996. Ghayas also knew that as the second leader he needed to make a strong statement that the Institute and Parliament would continue beyond its first leader. Kalim would have had it no other way. Ghayas took to the podium, reassuring the assembly that all would remain business as usual. The MMPs' individual efforts in their constituencies would be most essential at this time.

Upon becoming leader, Ghayas also reupped the fatwa. Much as Ali Khamenei assured the people of Iran that Rushdie would not be rewarded the forgiveness time sometimes allots, Ghayas reaffirmed the support for the Ayatollah's death sentence to Rushdie. Secondly, on his first visit to Tehran after becoming leader, he was invited to meet with the Iranian President, Hashemi Rafsanjani. The meeting, held on 9 August 1996, made headlines in the Iran News and Kayhan International, Iran's leading dailies, and the evening news. Ghayas told the president that the Muslim Parliament stood for the unity of all Muslims and was on the side of the oppressed against the oppressors.

Thirdly, he made mention of a passing comment Kalim had made during his inaugural address to the Muslim Parliament. Kalim, ever so clever as to flirt with making a radical statement without implying condonation, inferred the possibility of civil disobedience if the UK government continued to ignore the Muslim voices within Britain. Ghayas rather directly stated that not only would civil disobedience become commonplace if the UK government did not recognise the British Muslim voice, but that the community would be willing to go to jail for their respect and access to political power. Ghayas too, it would appear, now knew how to get headlines. While Ghayas did not have the charisma or oratory talent of Kalim (few do), his calm, friendly presence and willingness to engage the popular media assured the fight for the community was still alive and well. The legacy of Kalim Siddiqui appeared to be in good and ample hands.

The time for change had to come. 109 Fulham Palace Road was overdue a spring clean. Under Ghayas, the revolution needed to die, and thus the Institute's direct role in the affairs of foreign states needed untethering. Ghayas was not so brash as to announce the revolution fulfilled or to denounce the Islamic Republic as a failure, but to instead slowly turn the levers. The focus was Britain and her Muslims, and therefore the corrupting influence of foreign players looking out for their own self-interest needed to be rooted out of the garden. Rumours of members holding questionable allegiances and suspicious money flowing in and out of the building needed to be addressed. Several members were revealed to have been under the bankroll of the Iranian government and were rapidly relieved of their positions.

The Institute would serve the British Muslim community from that point forward. Iran, Saudi Arabia, and whatever other state wishing to claim any of the attention rightly owed to that community, was asked to depart. A rather bloodless affair by way of purges, but the new office sentiment was not shared by all in the Institute. The pivot that Ghayas initiated in both the Parliament and the Institute put him on the offensive. It was now the duty of these organisations, in their service to the community, to expose and investigate the problems within Britain's Muslim community. For Ghayas rightly saw that corruption was not merely a game played by those from abroad, but was also incubated within the various Muslim institutions of Britain. Ghayas was criticising the mosques and the imams and peeling away at the veneers of the community's self-righteousness. Whereas Kalim's fight was with a united ummah against the oppressors, Ghayas knew that the first step to saving the world begins with a look in the mirror. The saving of the community at home made efforts beyond that stronger, by having a stronger foundation to stand upon.

Ghayas's actions naturally rubbed both the community leaders and, more importantly, a few of the trustees the wrong way, especially when he put the whole of the Muslim Institute before the mirror's gaze. The intellectual spirit that first brought Ghayas and those young students to Kalim's house in Slough all those years ago had been replaced with politics and some romanticised notion of glory that reeked of something close to nepotism. Ghayas and Dr. Zafarul Islam Khan had begun talking with Kent University in the spring of 1997 about possible areas of cooperation. By April, he announced that the Muslim Institute was to be relaunched as a centre of academic excellence, beholden to its original university-like origins. Of course, this was not seen by all as a return to basic principles. The non-academics within the Institute's board saw this as a giving away of Kalim's progress and a threat to their sphere of influence within the organisation. Zafar Bangash, Ghayas's Assistant Director, and Iqbal Siddiqui were key members of the concerned party. To them, Ghayas appeared to be pulling the whole place down, brick by brick. What, then, would he do to the Muslim Parliament?

Unfortunately, the Muslim Parliament functioned at its highest levels when unified in an all-encompassing effort. Global efforts have a power here; the Rushdie Affair and the war in Bosnia, if either served any good, at least brought the Muslim world together. It is a sad, natural reality that tragedy brings people together. The United States witnessed this in the response to the September 11 attacks in 2001. With the Cold War apparently over, the world had little evil to unite against. The 1990s was sorrowfully met with the fact that the world could not handle peace time. The rest of the twentieth century was so built upon military and nationalist might that it didn't know what to do when peace was attained. Peace seemed far too utopian and because of that, no one could trust it. Anxious and suspicious, the 1990s provided the ideal backdrop for the violent beginnings of the twenty-first century.

Ghayas found that the need for introspection did not taste as sweet as unification in jihad against the West. Could the jihad continue into infinity and beyond? Ghayas saw that the Muslim Parliament was running into a common tendency amongst Muslim groups. As the organisation would age, the old leaders would maintain control through the perseverance of the ritual of respecting one's elders. Without new life blood, the mission and direction of the organisation would slowly atrophy and ossify into dogma as a result of inaction.

The attempt to make the Muslim Parliament function as a multilateral body did much of what Kalim feared democratic processes would do. The Muslim Parliament did not reach its full form during Kalim's own lifetime as an upper house was never established and attendance at Parliament sessions had begun to dwindle. Ghayas pivoted the Parliament away from ideology and towards pragmatic efforts. Ghayas worked against isolationist initiatives and the promotion of political Islam. The Parliament as such needed to act more as a lobby group to campaign for the justice of all, and not just the Muslim community. This was the original mission of the Muslim Parliament: to act as a body to demand justice for those left behind by the majority establishment. Ghayas held to the fundamental tenet of Islam whereby a Muslim is duty-bound to help all of the disadvantaged, despite their differences, especially those who are his immediate neighbours. The focus now was on bridge building, human rights and social justice. Great initiatives were to emerge around media scholarships,

women's rights, anti-war, anti-fundamentalism and numerous re-
forms proposed to tackle the rising problem concerning Muslim
marriages and problems in British *madrassas*.

The Muslim Parliament held a European conference on Islamophobia in October 1997 at their regular venue of Logan
Hall in central London, which was to become the first conference to highlight specific anti-Muslim hatred and to introduce the
term 'Islamophobia' to a mainstream audience. Ghayas worked
towards a greater joint effort between the Muslim Institute and
the Muslim Parliament to see that things were done. The new
direction for the Parliament attracted more grounded activists
and campaigners less concerned with the greater ummah and
more with the state of greater humanity. It was by the mid-2000s
that Ghayas formed the view that the name 'Parliament' was
now more of a hindrance than a help (the original limelight bequeathed by the name was no longer adding value) in attracting
people to the cause as the new potential recruits were now more
mainstream progressive activists who would not want to become
'members of a Muslim Parliament'. Therefore, he took a decision
to slowly transfer these projects to the Muslim Institute quietly
and without any fanfare.

Well into the new millennium, the Muslim Parliament would
continue its efforts in a more activist fashion through campaigns
concerning Muslim marriages, child abuse in madrassas, and other growing injustices throughout Britain. The Muslim Parliament
as it was at its inauguration and as it was dreamed to become in
Kalim's original inception might well have died with him, but the
community needed it to continue on, for the fight for the Muslim
community was only in the prologue phase leading up to the new
millennium. The Muslim Parliament was now more of a lobbying
body, campaigning from the local grassroots for British Muslim
issues. Ghayas, for the sake of the community, needed the Parliament to live beyond itself into the noughties. What Ghayas
did with that name alone had a lot to say about the workings

of power in the United Kingdom. Though, with the change of the Muslim Parliament's tone, a growing discontent riled within some of the Institute's trustees.

The disturbance rippled into concern during Ghayas's first major divergence from Kalim that was voiced, rather ironically, at the Kalim Siddiqui Memorial Conference back in 1996. There Ghayas spoke of a need to reflect on the community's strengths and weaknesses. He called for a toning down of the revolutionary rhetoric and averred that the process of change must be more gradual and calculated. Where Kalim wished to take on the world full stop, it was now time to move from ideological battles towards more pragmatic efforts. Ghayas needed to lead this community, without compromise, into the future if he was to ensure that the community would not only survive in Britain, but thrive.

Following the purges on Fulham Palace Road, to some, every small thing Ghayas was doing appeared to fly in the face of Kalim Siddiqui's intentions. The words that came from Ghayas were not words the Kalim everyone knew would say. Kalim, now frozen in time and memory, lost his sophistication and intellectual fortitude for change. Change, that harbinger of uncertainty, had just as much chance of destroying all of their progress as advancing it. To many of the trustees, Ghayas was tearing down everything Kalim had built in his life. Had he given up on the great historical project? Was the revolution condemned to fall before the might of the oppressors? Was his intention to have the community assimilate and slowly lose their identities before the tyranny of the majority? Was Ghayas leading them quietly into the dark? And then there was talk of turning the Muslim Institute into a centre of academic excellence, dedicated to research and teaching. This future had no home for the non-academic, and thus threatened, they had to act. Ghayas's honeymoon period was brought to a sharp end when the trustees called a meeting, the night before Ghayas was to meet with Kent University to begin the Muslim

Institute's transition. It appeared dark clouds were gathering over Ghayas's home in Chesham.

Home. It is a concept that traverses all human history and culture. It is a fundamental survival mechanism derived from shelter, but made something transcendent as humans separate themselves from other animals. It is the fundamental building block of society, the place from which all notions of thinking, social and political, emanate out of. Whilst its particular definition has taken on a creative diversity of meaning from culture to culture and generation to generation, its essence remains fully intact. A house is one physical manifestation of home. In truth, all buildings throughout the history of architecture are houses, adapted for other uses. From the tallest buildings of the world, reaching towards the heavens, to the smallest most primitive huts, they all bear one common feature. A heart.

The heart of a home, a building, is where the soul resides. Commonly we refer to the hearts of houses as family rooms or the living room. In the past, the living room was often centrally located, for it was common. It is where the sun's warm light is allowed in to illuminate the satellite rooms. It is where the fire can be made at night. It is where all are welcome. It is where the life of a home is lived out. Often it is where the day begins and where the day ends. In a living room, a family celebrates its highest moments and endures its toughest hardships. It is a room designed for socialising. It is where guests are welcomed. It is the site of tea, coffee and snacks. Where the greatest conversations are had. Where quiet contemplation can be nurtured. It is where the children walk their first steps and say their first words. It is where phone calls are received, bringing tidings of victory and delivering news of misfortune and loss. Like a family, the living room also ages, bearing the memory of all joys, arguments, fears, excitements and camaraderie. And love. When a family moves, the living room waits, still occupied by the memories left behind, but always ready to take on more from the next family to take on its walls.

Few societies have perfected the living room as have the British Muslims. The high standing the community gives to the concept of family demands nothing less than suitable accommodation. The British Muslim living room in particular is a manifestation of the clash of civilisations blended into a harmonious cornucopia. There is a sense of hallowed ground present in this room, a sanctity that politely asks one to remove their shoes before entering. Upon the floor an ornate yet proper rug beckons back to an ancient furnishing necessity. A couch will be found, often well broken in, revealing its age (if its vogue of a lost age of fashion hadn't made the fact abundantly clear). Though one couch is not enough, for a British Muslim living room must be prepared to accommodate vast numbers of guests, as all are welcomed here and become a member of the family under their ancient guest-right custom. Objects of art and living plants decorate, often themed around a masterful work of calligraphy to express an appreciation of beauty and the living earth. Tables are a must for it can be safe to assume food of one variety or another will only be awaiting presentation if not already perched in place. Also, one needs a place to let their tea or coffee rest as speaking is done as much with hands as it is with the mouth. A liberal variety of books will accompany relics, awards and photos of family, both present and distant in both space and time. A window lets natural light flow in, bringing natural life to what could otherwise be construed as terribly artificial. Most remarkable of the British Muslim living room is that it seems to simultaneously feel a new place each time it is entered whilst also being a frozen snapshot of everything that it ever housed within its walls.

The living room in Chesham, home to the Siddiquis, is a bona fide example of the British Muslim living room. Its south-westerly facing windows provide a stunning view from atop the hill, allowing spectacular sunsets to be experienced, particularly with the nakedness of the trees in winter. Sharing the classic elements of a British Muslim living room, it is most defined by the memories that have been made within it. It was in this room that Ghayas and Talat worked for the world they desired. It was in this room that their children grew up. In this room, they learned of marriages and the passing of family and friends. And in this room, with Kalim Siddiqui at rest, Ghayas would chart out a new direction of travel, one neither would have ever expected taking. From across the Atlantic Ocean to just the other side of London, the trustees travelled to Chesham, just as in more ancient times the nobles rode across England or the tribal elders traversed deserts to hold council. An issue demanded resolution and it was to be had in this living room, atop a hill in Chesham.

It was February 1997, less than a year after this very group had selected Ghayas as their new leader. The image was the distorted reflection of the old meetings in Slough. Talat had taken the role of Suraiya, conjuring magic through the power of the culinary arts, mixing the daily recommended amount of diplomacy and shared history into her *biryani* and *bindi ghosht*. Whereas the children once played in another room, Asim listened eagerly from his room a floor up, careful not to reveal his eavesdropping. Where once these gentlemen sat around Kalim who helmed the conversation through the proposition of questions and the cross examination of the student's thoughts, now Ghayas sat, the quiet listener, before the tidal wave of accusations hurled at him by his surrounding brothers. Taking all of it in, Ghayas retained the seemingly timid stereotype he had shed before the Muslim Parliament in the recent past. The inquisition in the living room would have made the Prime Minister's Questions appear a calm and dreadfully dull affair.

The room split between the silent old friends of Ghayas and the newly constituted vehement opposition. He was destroying Kalim bhai's legacy, dismantling everything he stood for. Shameful, dishonourable, despicable. Ghayas listened, his heart breaking, as men he considered closer than brothers took turns to either plunge their daggers in to taste his blood or merely watch as others indulged. There was nothing Ghayas could do. He knew this. The plot was well thought out in advance and the script was set. Unlike Kalim, he was thrown from the conductor's post, now a member of the audience, only capable of watching as the performance went on.

Ghayas's first defence was that this meeting was inquorate. Illegal! For once again, Dr. Moin was absent and not given the legally required time to appear and have his opinion heard. The first retort came from Zafar Bangash who said that if this meeting was illegal, then so too was their meeting in April of 1996 just before Kalim's funeral. Therefore, the very installing of Ghayas as the new Director was done through illegal means and needed to be immediately rendered null. This technicality was of little matter, though. The opposition trustees had a quorum and the votes. No confidence. A letter of resignation had practically been written for him. Zafar Bangash, Ghayas's Assistant Director and mentee turned leader of the opposition led the inquisition with Iqbal Siddiqui at his side, the man once a timid boy before his father, standing up before 'the man who came after'. Out of nowhere the prince had found a narrative to latch onto, his mind conquered by the simple idea that the Institute and the Parliament were his birthright. The Ghayasuddin Siddiqui Administration was to end. He had served his community well, but now it was time to retire. Zafar would become the third Director of the Muslim Institute and Iqbal would be his deputy. They did allow him to retain his trusteeship for he would always be remembered for his efforts to the revolution, but the revolution had come for him.

Yet before the bell was to toll for him, Ghayas had one wildcard up his sleeve, one more chance to put it all on the line. His condition aside, this was for the future of the community. That was all that mattered. So, he gave one last defence. A true bombshell. He listened to their accusations and verbal assault and contemplated whether or not to throw the card down. His face contorted, for he loved these men, but they were going to force him to play it. When the tsunami winds calmed, Ghayas spoke. Yes, the trustees were free to think and do what they had laid out, but Ghayas would not go quietly. If the meeting which named him Director was not legal, then the induction of the two new trustees, Iqbal Siddiqui and Haroon Kalla, was also not legal and therefore the two voices calling for Zafar as Director were not legally valid. Null. Ghayas would not abide such treachery for he had seen it tear many an organisation and movement to pieces. The community deserved better and it was for them that he would fight. Every word spoken was like a bone being broken. Here they were, the men he called brothers, casting him to the dirt without so much as a thank you very much. All notions of power and control in that living room had ceased to exist. The only valid trustee voices were those who existed at the time of Kalim's passing. Dr. Moin, a grown up, would have none of this childish nonsense, overriding Zafar Bangash who now stood alone.

The bombshell dropped, Kalim had, posthumously, given Ghayas just enough power to thwart the would-be coup. No further words could be mustered and this was far from the end of the conflict. For the time being, all that needed to be said had been said. Ghayas waited in silence as the would-be revolutionaries filed out back to their respective homes, out there in the world. As the dust settled, the tasty notes of herbs and spices lingered in the air. Ghayas's family, shocked at the assault that had just transpired in their home, would join him in the living room. He had survived his first assassination attempt.

Martin Shaw had always delighted at any opportunity to meet his friend Ghayas, though he knew this meeting would not be the typical, lovely cup of tea. Ghayas was in need of help. Of course, Shaw would help his friend in any way possible. Had he known what he was getting himself into, he might not have been so gung-ho. Shaw had quickly forgotten that the men who started these organisations did so without a proper understanding of the legal intricacies of starting non-profit organisations. Shaw unravelled a messy history of paper work and documentation, like a terribly tangled string. He carefully parsed it out, resolved the knots, and brought order to the jumbled mess. Due to the distrust of the government, the operation and management of the community lacked the elements of legitimacy and legal precedent needed for a quick resolution to the problems at hand. The earliest governing documents were appalling and wrought with error. Their original solicitor gave them poor advice and established no fall back in the event that what had happened would happen. They had underestimated the complexity of the charity system in Britain. Despite their good intentions, their cultural dynamics clashed with the governing system of Great Britain. In fact, the best way forward was to put a full stop to the mess and start from scratch, doing a proper job of it.

Beyond the research, the arbitration amongst this group was a new kind of beast that Shaw had not come into contact with very often. The worst sorts of dispute resolution are those pursued amongst old friends and family. That and the cultural norms of this community made it not only hard to organise everyone in one room, but difficult also to get down to brass tacks. The *salaams* and other customary exchanges of respect and processes of dialogue were foreign and frustrating to Shaw. Objectivity and concise action need not apply. Neither side would state their case out of fear of disrespecting the other's reputation. Aside from that, Ghayas would not see these men, his brothers, come to any consequence for he loved them. Potentially, assets could have been forcefully taken and the losers put out on the street. Ghayas's dedication was to justice and the wellbeing of the whole community, even those he found himself in stark disagreement with. The legal battle for the Muslim Institute would last nearly a decade.

London rang in the new millennium with a Muslim Parliament expunged of the old guard, with the Muslim Institute's troublesome young Turks removed and newly liberated offices at 109 Fulham Palace Road. The scalp of Ghayasuddin Siddiqui would prove a hard one to secure indeed; as the Director of the Muslim Institute and Leader of the Muslim Parliament he would weather several further assassination attempts upon his character. He had indeed become one of the Talking Heads and his celebrity and notoriety great. Despite the decks of cards that were stacked against him, Ghayas resisted and his community standing and high profile demonstrated a force to be reckoned with. His beliefs would not waver and it was for the community's victory that he fought. Rebirth, much like birth itself, was a process rife with pain, but the opportunities after the fact and the beauty to behold in metamorphosis made the whole endeavour worth it. One evening Haroon Kalla would ring Ghayas from South Africa, where he had returned to from the UK a few years after Kalim's death. Ghayas answered with the salaam he gave each caller. Okay, Doc, you win, uttered Haroon. What do you want? To which Ghayas responded, "I just want you all to act reasonably."

The new millennium was the ultimate opportunity for all to walk into 'the future' and make a better world for themselves and others. For Ghayas it was another decade, one in which Muslim communities might get it right. This first decade was set to be a decade of change. A wonderful potentiality lay before everyone, something stood to be learned and progress to be made. City by city from East to West embraced, drank, cheered and watched as the fireworks rocketed across the sky. The computers turned their calendars over to the year 2000 without the slightest hitch. Civilisation did not plunge into chaos and apocalypse. Ghayas sat back in his chair, watching the sun set into the distant moors.

The world continued to spin and there were trees that still needed planting.

Chapter Ten

CANDLE IN THE WIND

31 AUGUST 1997 started as a typical Sunday morning in the Siddiqui household. Ghayas rose with little urgency, as usual on the weekend. He slowly collected himself and made for the lower level to enjoy his morning tea. As he sat reading the morning's issue of *The Observer*, he exchanged sentences for bites of his breakfast. Meanwhile, Talat prepared breakfast as the kids, now college age, slowly trickled down on their way to go about their weekend business. Talat's two sisters, Iffat and Seema, were staying in Chesham with their children for the summer. Seema, Talat's youngest sister, and her family had moved to Ireland from Pakistan a few years earlier and would visit Chesham regularly. Iffat and her family had travelled all the way from Chicago to spend their summer with the Siddiquis. In the background the news continued, neither aware nor concerned with the Siddiquis' morning routine. Suddenly, a breaking headline shot across the screen.

Diana, Princess of Wales, had been confirmed dead as a result of injuries sustained from a car accident in Paris, in an attempt to evade the paparazzi gone horribly wrong. The Siddiquis paused along with the rest of the United Kingdom. Diana was a symbol of many things to many different people. She was a strong mother of two boys who were the future of the British monarchy. She was an institution of charity and goodwill across the globe in herself. She was a sweetheart. She was an icon. She was a role model. She was not without her controversies. But, most of all, and often left underscored, she was a human being. Later dubbed the 'People's Princess' by then Prime Minister Tony Blair, her loss was the loss of a glimmer of hope in a world otherwise devoid of such sentiments.[56]

To Ghayas this was a tragedy. That poor woman. As he had done many times in the past and would continue to do throughout his years, Ghayas cast everything aside. A good woman had died and that was all that mattered. Something must be said. Respect must be given. The Royal family, the British establishment, the nightmare history of colonialism, the current mess that was geopolitics, Islamophobia—none of it mattered at that particular moment. Two boys had lost a mother and an entire nation, including the British Muslims, had lost a strong spirit. What did matter was that Ghayas had some letterhead at home that read Dr. Ghayasuddin Siddiqui, Leader of the Muslim Parliament.

Asim quickly fired up the computer and set upon dictation of his father's words. Ghayas now had an office within the comfort of his own home, that could run 24/7 complete with two phones, two secretaries (Asim and Faiza), and plenty of letterhead. As Leader of the Muslim Parliament, not even the legal battle mattered at this time. As Leader of the Muslim Parliament, Ghayas expressed his sorrow at the loss of a gem of the charity sector and a champion of human rights and international diplomacy. The Siddiqui family operation at that moment was the voice of the British Muslim community and Ghayas's letters was one of the first letters of condolence made public concerning the death of Princess Diana. While Tony Blair shined in the spotlight over the hesitation of the Queen's words, Ghayas honoured a life without question, without desire for personal gain. It was the right thing to do and he was a community leader, in spite of his titles being a matter of dispute. Interestingly enough, the title of Leader of the Muslim Parliament would follow him for many years after the Muslim Parliament had ceased to be a 'parliament'.

1997 was an interesting year for Great Britain. In a landslide victory, the Labour Party took control of Parliament for the first time since Iran's revolution. As part of that victory, Tony Blair became the youngest Prime Minister in British history and the first Muslim MP, Mohammad Sarwar, was elected. Also, a record breaking 119 women were in Parliament following the election. The birth of Dolly, the first cloned sheep, was announced. Scientists confirmed the link that triggered the Mad Cow Disease scare. The BBC launched a full-time online news service updating its first websites from the 1995 budget. The news was no longer restricted to its key time slots; now it was always ready, a mere click away. The United Kingdom transferred sovereignty of Hong Kong to the People's Republic of China, ending the 99-year lease and effectively, the British Empire. Both Scotland and Wales also held referendums allowing for the creation of their own national assemblies and tipping sovereignty away from home rule. Ghayas had officially outlived the British Empire. And perhaps the Muslim community could work with this new government. At least there would be a new host of potential allies. No doubt, times were rapidly changing and a new kind of community leader would be needed to handle this crazy futuristic world of the new millennium.[57]

The new millennium left opportunity for a new style of Islamic intellectual discourse in London. Asim Siddiqui dreamed of a free network of British Muslims that could come together to discuss the issues of their day. This was not the grand narrative endeavour of his father and their generation; a group united against a common enemy, aimed at a common cause, with a manifesto, a strategic plan, enough ideologies and philosophies to fill several tomes. No, Asim's idea was something more freeform. A meeting of people from so wide a variety of backgrounds and characters you would wonder what in fact drew them together in the first place. They might have appeared as old university mates catching up over a meal or a football match. For this group, there was no manifesto or plan, let alone much of a structure at all. It was simply a free space for thought on Muslim issues amongst inquisitive professionals. One cold January night, City Circle was formed, and young Muslim professionals had a free and independent network to discuss contemporary topics. The events were open to the public and since 1999, topics spanning the spectrum of thought have been discussed, from women as leaders in British Muslim society to the very question of if one can equally be both British and Muslim. City Circle rapidly became the finger on the pulse of Muslim intellectual thought in London. This network respected religion and tradition, yet was down-to-earth and accessible. Through City Circle, Asim and his friends changed the game of discourse within the British Muslim community. Yet the greater game of British society itself was also adapting to the new century.

The new game called for leaders to go out and become a face, or as popularly dubbed, a talking head. Where once Kalim could orchestrate his own publicity and produce his own news, Ghayas's approach was to become one of these talking heads. Force them to hear what you have to say and they will grow to respect your voice, for you are playing on their terms. Whilst Ghayas was not the most energetic personality the cameras loved, his calm, well thought out and reasoned responses won him the calls of all the major news organisations. He was not a screaming fanatic shouting to crowds or burning things; he smiled and let his words be sharper than his image. The British Muslim community was a growing segment of the population and their opinion and voice needed to be present at every occasion. Following Ghayas was the title, Leader of the Muslim Parliament, long after the Parliament's last meeting. In British society, title is everything, even if it has no actual meaning. One could not go on the news with the title: Ghayasuddin Siddiqui, some guy, or Ghayasuddin Siddiqui, concerned Muslim. After all, Ghayas had not used his PhD credentials for work in over thirty years, but he would always be Dr. Siddiqui. Despite being in a begrudging legal battle with his former colleagues, the activist spirit could not be silenced. And

Ghayas did nothing short of flourish as he became a member of the rotating cast of talking heads, reasoning with the public to bring a voice to the under-represented and snuff out ignorance at one of its major origins: the media circus. All the while, his family, supporters and co-workers stood at his side. The Siddiqui family was an organisation unto themselves, helping out whatever causes they came across and making sure the public record included the voices of British Muslims. As Ghayas came into his own before the television camera, it would appear the world was, unfortunately, beginning to take ever more interest and curiosity in what was going on with the often-misunderstood Muslim people.

Sometimes, the more things change, the more some things seem to stay the same. By 1999, the Middle East was as volatile as ever. At the twilight of a new millennium, Ghayas took on a new role. Muslims were no longer just another among the Other discarded to the generic label of blackness. Muslims were rapidly becoming the other of special interest both to the state and public in the United Kingdom. By the end of the 1990s, the Western world had no monolithic 'evil doer' or 'bad guy' to claim as its enemy. So that which the West least understood were prime candidates to fill the void of the 'them' for 'us' to take on and win the day! Ghayas knew that the new brand of leader the British Muslim community would need had to do whatever they could to keep public opinion in favour of their Muslim neighbours. Different leaders chose different methods to achieve this objective. Many leaders chose to cooperate and collaborate with the UK government. This proposition was particularly appetising to them with the new Labour government in power, although even with a popular and charismatic Labour government, issues of racism, xenophobia and ignorance would not be resolved overnight.

Ghayas billed himself as one of the predominant talking heads of the British Muslim community. His job would be to come on the news, radio, or speak to the papers about issues within the Muslim community and keep the general British public aware that the British Muslim population was not only fiercely loyal to the UK—their home—but that they too possessed the same rights as all Britons. Ghayas's work was cut out for him as he had to become the calm voice of reason amongst some of his contemporaries who continued their cries for jihad and promoted isolationary and antagonistic rhetoric fundamentalist tendencies. He spoke out against discourse that alluded to Islamophobia, or any brand of xenophobia for that matter, and dismissed any assumption that the sum of the world was a battle between a supposed 'us' and 'them'. As it had always been, and as he thought is should be in Britain as well, Ghayas was only concerned with justice and justice for all. As chaos reigned in the Middle East following the Gulf War, whenever a Muslim would go home or take a holiday to the land of their ancestry, there was always potential for fear and foul play as perceived by the Foreign Office and other governments.

Terrorism was a word of accelerating usage in the English language. Terrorists were no longer just the Irish. Just as anti-terrorist policy had migrated from concern of Irish aggression to the jihadists, so too had the skin tone of the stereotypical, imagined terrorist.[58] Regardless of which party controlled Parliament, the anti-terrorism legislation evolved from vague statements, easily used to entrap undesirables and hooligans, to target anyone who threatened the powers that be in Great Britain. The earliest instance of the evolution of anti-terrorism policy was displayed in the UK's extradition policy. Many states in the Middle East and North Africa had more sophisticated anti-terrorism laws in 1999 than the UK. So, when British citizens of Muslim background unwittingly and erroneously found themselves in trouble abroad, the UK was less than keen to intervene. The British government claimed this was the diplomatic gymnastics needed to maintain order in the region, but for many, including Ghayas, these British

Muslims had rights and it was the duty of the government to protect the Kingdom's subjects abroad. The reports of abuse and unlawful trials made the gravity of the injustice all the more apparent and fired up the spirit of Ghayas all the more. Regrettably, there were individuals moving between borders and rousing trouble, making everything more complicated and harder to sort out. Yet, the bad actions of a few should not condemn the others and this was Ghayas's message from station to station. Ghayas would soon find out he was not alone in his quest for justice.

After all, Ghayas wasn't the only British Muslim standing up as the 20th gave way to the 21st century. Where Dickens' tales fill the snowy streets of London with unfortunate, yet good-willed carollers, Ghayas's tale finds the wintery London streets of 1998 being roamed by a band of activists. The leader of this band, the young and energetic lawyer Rashad Yaqoob, was determined to rally the Muslim Britons to action. Having travelled from his hometown of Birmingham he knew that one door in particular, when knocked upon, would fulfil the hope that drove him out into the cold. That door was at 109 Fulham Palace Road. Not only did Ghayas warmly welcome Rashad and his merry band of young activists in from the cold, he ordered pizza. Together they ate on the floor of the office, comforted in the knowledge that their newest bandmate, sitting there beside them, was the very community heavyweight, Dr. Ghayasuddin Siddiqui. Such a name, a face, and a voice would help Rashad give legitimacy to his group within the community, to the press, and with the authorities. Rashad would push Ghayas back into international affairs.

In 1999, three college-aged British Muslim boys were detained by Yemeni security forces. They were grouped with five other Britons arrested earlier in the winter holiday season. Together they were dubbed the Aden Eight, named for the town of their arrest, and put on trial alongside one Algerian accused of plotting a bomb attack. They were university students studying abroad in Egypt and went to Yemen for their winter holiday. Only one of them spoke Arabic and they were put before a trial that was mostly for show. The need for an example to show a hardline anti-terrorism stance by the Yemeni officials was desperately needed. Around the same time as the Aden Eight's arrest, sixteen Western tourists were taken hostage by a radical group that resulted in the deaths of three Britons and an Australian during a botched rescue attempt by the Yemeni forces. The boys were subjected to interrogation and torture, seen in their wounds and general dishevelment. They also alleged sexual misconduct.[59] Little beyond the rhetoric claiming that 'people are working on it' was seen by way of effort out of the UK's Foreign Office. Ghayas was dismayed at the lack of action from the government to protect its own British citizens. Ghayas had to see for himself, so, along with an Amnesty International delegation, he travelled to Yemen—the only community leader to do so—for three weeks in January 1999 to witness the boys' trial and evaluate their conditions. It did not take him long to realise these boys would get no justice in Yemen.

Upon his return to the UK, Ghayas became a reasoned and firm voice to bring the boys home to Britain to have a proper and fair trial. One of the students was the son of the infamous British cleric Abu Hamza al-Masri. His own alliances and activities abroad piqued the interest of many foreign leaders and organisations adding to the controversy of the Aden Eight. Were they working for him? This was quickly put down as a rumour. Ghayas had had one conversation with Abu Hamza upon his return from Yemen and found the man completely incapable of holding a civil conversation and thus cared to lose no further time attempting to reason with his boisterousness. Yet, despite Ghayas's opinion of the father, no son ought to suffer because of a father's acts. It was a logical fallacy to posit that a son's destiny was set by the life lived by the father. For Ghayas, it was not whether or not the students were guilty or innocent that drove him. It was the fact that their trial was a farce and guilty or not, all humans, especially British citizens, have a right to a fair trial. Ghayas believed that these boys would only receive justice through the United Kingdom's judicial system and that was where he made his argument. Later, the boys would join the ranks of Brits caught in hard times in foreign countries and used as bargaining chips to progress the chess game that is international relations. This was conduct unbecoming of a government that represents the interest of all the British people, including the British Muslims. Yet this was only the beginning of the nightmare the noughties would become.

All was not right in central Asia. It was the summer of 1999 and the mountainous Caucasus region of Chechnya had just been invaded by Russia. The small Russian republic of Chechnya had had a rough and less than peaceful eight years since their declaration of independence from Russia upon the fall of the Soviet Union. The Russian Federation wasted little time in reclaiming that piece of strategic real estate. The price tag on the property was the death of tens of thousands of Chechens and a gruesome display at Grozny during a failed invasion in 1994. Chechen command of guerrilla warfare tactics proved a more than capable defence against an impossibly oversized military advantage. Bad press, humiliation, and widespread international opposition to Russia's plans forced the then Russian President, Boris Yeltsin, to declare a ceasefire with the Chechens in 1996. Aslan Maskhadov was a commander in the Chechen army that led the successful guerrilla campaign. In 1997, Maskhadov was elected President of Chechnya in what was regarded as a free democratic vote. He subsequently signed a peace deal with President Yeltsin which was seen as a victory, with Russia partly renouncing its claims on Chechnya. A quick glance at the nearest world map will reveal that this was not the fairytale ending all had hoped it would be.

As the signatory ink dried on the 1996 peace treaty, jihadi warlords emerged in the land of Chechnya. The leaders of this jihadi group, Shamil Basayev and the Saudi-born Ibn al-Khattab, were both veterans of the Afghan jihad from 1979 to 1989 in which British and US forces, alongside Saudi Arabia, aided the Mujahideen in opposing the Soviet Union's invasion of Afghanistan. No stranger to Russian strategy and unafraid of their superior war machine, they sought to unite Chechnya with neighbouring republics in an Islamist central Asian dream state. Their first target was the neighbouring Republic of Dagestan. In 1999, Basayev and al-Khattab led a series of raids that became known as the invasion of Dagestan. National hero Maskhadov condemned the actions taken by the jihadis, but the then Russian Prime Minister, Vladimir Putin, had already pinned the blame for the invasion on Maskhadov and declared his government illegitimate. Putin promised the Russian people that a quick and decisive victory would restore justice to Russia. Maskhadov quickly sought amends by offering a peace plan and a strategy for cracking down on the jihadi warlords. It was swiftly rejected. Russia was again going into Chechnya.[60] This time, Putin's political climb was to be set off and accelerated as he made good on his promises. His narrative as national hero began to materialise, eventually winning him the presidency of Russia. Meanwhile, Chechnya wept.

The British Empire had discovered, cultivated and recklessly used the simple yet deadly tool of Islamist radicalism for centuries, and played a key role in bringing the Saudis and their wahabi ideology into power. In the 20th century, the US would take the lead in using the 'Islamic card' to promote their own interests, be that from controlling global oil supplies to its most explicit display in a war against the Soviet Union. In 1979, Afghanistan found itself as one of the many venues of the world tour of proxy wars between the US and Soviet Union. The Soviet Union was the enemy of enemies, bringing together the CIA, the Saudis and the Pakistani military like old chums in support of the Mujahideen. Or, as former US President Ronald Regan called them, 'the Holy Warriors'. Arms were as effective weapons and tools to these soldiers as the Saudi wahabi ideology of jihad. Once the Soviets gave up and went home, the Mujahideen turned on themselves, setting the stage for the rise of the Taliban, who in turn provided a home for Al-Qaeda—trained, of course, by the CIA during the Afghan jihad against the Soviet Union. The West had thought it could tame a wild animal, and after losing interest disregarded it as it grew too great for the cage it was kept in. Other international players were happy to try their hand at utilising the beast for their own ends. In acting upon their nature, Shamil Basayev and Ibn al-Khattab voluntarily handed over the pretext Russia need to re-invade Chechnya.[61] A new manipulation was afoot.

For Ghayas, the global political machinations were one thing, the humanitarian cause was another. When two forces fight, it is the little people who lose no matter who wins. The mighty historical narrative of Russia. The proud, pious and righteous slayer of infidels the jihadis had painted themselves as. Yet, in the middle, it was the Chechen people being murdered as a result of senseless violence or having their homes and lives destroyed by the hammer of war. In Grozny, the graffiti on the walls read 'Welcome to Hell: Part II'. Amnesty International estimated that between 20,000 and 30,000 civilians have been killed in the First Chechen War (1994–1996), mostly by indiscriminate attacks by Russian forces on densely populated are as. It also estimated a further 25,000 civilians were killed in the Second Chechen War (1999–2009). Fifty-two mass graves are among the reported in Chechnya. Combined with the military forces, historians estimate that up to a tenth of the entire Chechen population died in the conflicts; that is, 100,000 people out of a million. Some scholars estimate that the brutality of the Russian attacks on such a small ethnic group amounted to a crime of genocide. Without doubt, the committing of war crimes was a given.[62]

A little further east perhaps, but to Ghayas it had appeared that it was happening again. The ghosts of Bosnia continued to haunt the land. This time it was a major global player playing the role of aggressor. If a state as insignificant to the global game as

Serbia could get away with it, how much easier could the powerful state of Russia play the same hand? Even worse, they could use the tried and true sound-bite of the matter being a 'strictly domestic affair', so perfected by America and the UK for past atrocities done to their various 'Others' at home without their territorial boundaries. For Ghayas, this was where a clever line needed to be walked between the interpretations of law and government opinion. New legislation prevented the funding of rebel or terrorist causes. If Ghayas was going to act in the face of the cries of suffering people, he was going to need to be his most creative.

Around this time, Ghayas crossed paths with fellow campaigner, Dr. Marie Bennigsen. She was the leading expert on central Asia with a focus on Muslim communities. Her connections allowed Ghayas to meet with Maskhadov's personal representative to the UK, Colonel Omar. Since Bosnia, the allure of the jihadist option had become ever more attractive to young British Muslims and Ghayas needed to lead them away from such destructive temptations. Time was ticking, people were dying, and the anti-terror laws loomed ever present with each action Ghayas might take. Ghayas began by launching a nationwide campaign to raise funds for the democratically elected and internationally recognised government of President Aslan Maskhadov. It was the one advantage the Chechens had over the Bosnian situation. These funds would be used by the government of Chechnya for the well-being of their people. As with Bosnia half a decade earlier, here was a way to combat war crimes in a way that could not be labelled as terrorism by the authorities.

Whilst the Muslim Council of Britain was lobbying the government to take action, Ghayas was taking action himself. He also had a colonel up his sleeve. During the second half of 1999 Ghayas would travel up and down the UK in his red Ford Mondeo, along with Colonel Omar and a translator, speaking at mosques and community centres to explain what was happening in Chechnya, raise funds and channel collective anger into something constructive. Parallel to this, UK jihadist sympathisers began raising funds for Shamil Basayev and Ibn al-Khattab as the only true Muslim leaders of Chechnya. If left unchallenged, this would have had the effect of delegitimising the Chechen cause in the UK. Up and down the country Ghayas would drive, one man against the jihadis for the sake of the Muslim community and above all, to protect the innocent of Chechnya. One man. A colonel. A translator. And a red Ford Mondeo. Over £100,000 was eventually raised over the course of this campaign.

The Ghayas-Colonel Omar road trip did not go unnoticed. Leaflets began appearing all throughout the country with a Ghayasuddin Siddiqui mugshot. Beneath his photo read the caption: "Do you trust this man?" The leaflets were being circulated in the tens of thousands. A classic propaganda technique put Ghayas's ability to be trusted with other's funds on trial. Accusations flew around of him mismanaging the organisations he had been involved in. The culprits behind the paper smear campaign remains unclear up to the present day. Interestingly, the appearance of the leaflets coincided with several of the old guard of the Muslim Parliament being relieved of their duties. The more one looks into the matter, the clearer it becomes that this was a plot against Ghayas the man, regardless of what destruction it might cause. To Ghayas the insult was that the lives of brothers and sisters in Chechnya would be risked over a matter of petty politics. It seemed a hefty effort to go to such trouble to snuff out one man's voice, who was less an enemy than a fresh, differing opinion in relation to the jihadists. At the end of the day, while Ghayas was opposed to the tenets and methods of the jihadists, they both had the mutual enemy of Russia and Russia's influence abroad, as well as perhaps other plots fuelled by Islamophobia and other degrees of xenophobia.

With Ghayas's ascension to prominence in British affairs, his list of political opponents also experienced a growth spurt.

Ghayas would be the first to say he had no true enemies, but he was not in control of what others would make of him. Now head of the Muslim Parliament, he had a historical rivalry with the MCB that dated back to the Rushdie Affair. His ability to act so effectively did leave the MCB organisation seemingly weak and largely ineffective in its abilities. Yet to Ghayas, many of the MCB leaders were still the students he remembered from his school days in Karachi all those years before. And they had to have known that financially he was of the cleanest and most transparent on such organisational matters. Had they underestimated his worth as an opponent? Silence ruled the debate that remained open but for the whispers of gossip and hearsay. So, Ghayas again found all his old friends either on the other side of the table or not present at all. No matter though, for it was not Ghayas who needed their backing, but the people of Chechnya. Ghayas's next move was therefore no choice. The fundraising could not be cut short or allowed to fall victim to such child's play. Back to the Ford Mondeo it was, although this time he had a new but familiar passenger.

Ghayas revived the campaign for Chechnya with a quick visit to Dr. Bennigsen. With her assistance, Ghayas was able to invite the Foreign Secretary of Maskhadov's government, Ilyas Akhmadov, to London. The Muslim Parliament would host a collection event. Come one, come all—that is, all who support the cause for Chechnya. Publicly proclaim your loyalties. Bold. Why make them kiss your ring to win a temporary loyalty, when you can ask them to put their money where their mouths might have resided? Question their morality, their piety, and what might remain of their humanity, for in such times, these qualities appeared to be increasingly few and far between. This was the moment of truth. For the Muslim Parliament, MCB, or anyone else who said they supported or believed in the Chechens' plight, this was the one and only chance anyone could properly support the cause. To boycott would be absurd. All Muslims raising funds to help the Chechens had to attend, lest they be labelled treacherous or abandoners of fellow believers. That jaw-stretching smile must have run across Ghayas's face as he watched the leaders of Muslim Britain present their funds to Ilyas Akhmadov. The character assassination campaign of Ghayasuddin Siddiqui had swiftly met its end, but the campaign to fund Chechnya was allowed to live on and deliver tangible help.

Not only did that move flex the abilities Ghayas possessed for the causes he took on, but it served to position the Muslim Parliament as the main champion of the UK's Chechen cause. The MCB having the institutional connection regularly met with the Labour government of Tony Blair and felt obliged to invite Ghayas along on the subject of Chechnya. This meeting occurred on 8 December 1999. Keith Vaz, the Minister of Europe, was the MP who would meet with Ghayas and the MCB delegation. Vaz, his family also hailing from India, had crossed paths with Ghayas in the past. He had clashed with Kalim Siddiqui when he was attempting to rally Asian Muslims to join mainstream political parties to have their voices properly heard. Of course, this was when the dream that would become the Muslim Parliament was swirling around in Kalim's head. Why dance before the establishment for their entertainment, when the Muslim community could well enough stand on its own and establish their own institutions and channels to act through?

For Vaz, the playing field had been entirely renovated. Now Vaz was a minister of the Crown and enjoying the position of power, especially when the mighty Kalim Siddiqui was no longer around to say otherwise on the matter. As the delegation of community leaders strolled into the meeting room, he perhaps thought Ghayas the quiet, ineffectual shadow that Kalim left behind. Ghayas had been seated next to the MCB head, Iqbal Sacranie, perhaps so that the MCB could appear Ghayas's equal, yet also so that the MCB could keep Ghayas closer than friends or enemies, as the saying goes. Sacranie spoke, diplomatically and in platitudes. Could the British government not do more? Then came Vaz's turn, and he played his role better than one could have forecasted. Patronising to the bone, in a manner that would have monarchs and former government heads applauding from their graves. Of course, the government was doing all it could to improve the situation. You leaders and your community need not worry, for the state has their interests at heart. And then came the ultimate insult to intelligence and dignity: relations with Putin's Russia are also of importance to Queen and Country.

Ghayas listened carefully, but even his patience had a limit. Ghayas explained to Vaz that the British government's actions or lack thereof displayed hypocrisy of the highest order and directly contradicted New Labour's commitment to an 'ethical foreign policy'. The vitriol that drove Ghayas to not only speak but speak up, and nearly reach the level of shouting prompted Sacranie to place his hand on Ghayas's leg, signalling that perhaps his tone had risen a level or two too high. Ghayas ended his speech, leaving no room for rebuttal. Time would be needed to recover from the shock of Ghayas's fury. Sacranie would not invite Ghayas to speak with the government again.

In 2000, Ilyas Akhmadov arrived in London and was hosted by Ghayas at the Brondesbury Park Hotel in north-west London, owned by his old friend Yusuf Islam. Ghayas had held his daughter Faiza's wedding at the hotel a few years earlier where Yusuf was guest of honour. Here, Ghayas invited the great and the good from the British Muslim leadership. Here, he publicly handed over a cheque to the foreign minister comprising the funds he had raised with Colonel Omar, a translator, and a Ford Mondeo. The other Muslim organisations followed suit. On this day at least, justice came in the form of a cheque, the journey of which existed beyond the numbers written upon it.

Throughout the course of his life, Ghayas had abided a lot of insane and extreme ideas in his attempt to reconcile his religion, this life, and his pursuit of justice. Yet few could have anticipated the degree of carnage and fury that would dominate the destructive display of the clash of civilisations on the 11th of September, 2001. The firework residue and empty champagne bottles that ushered in the new century had barely been cleared up before the world fell apart. Ghayas was frozen somewhere between stomach-upending nausea and gut-wrenching sorrow as he looked at the images on the television screen. The planes that struck the Twin Towers in New York. The fire and smoke. Mindless destruction, completely devoid of care for human life. Madness. Yet the terror was in the details. It was the images of those who survived the impact, stranded in the towers, who decided it was better to plunge to their own deaths than suffer burning in the falling Twin Towers that imprinted upon Ghayas's memory. This was the horror show. The penultimate act before the apocalyptic world demanded this new age of extremism.

Ghayas reflected as the atrocity played out on the screen before him. Extreme and confrontational interpretations of Islam would only lead to further clashing of civilisations. Next time, maybe on more violent terms. A near unconscionable thought at the time. His youngest son, Salman, had been working for a bank at the World Trade Center in New York the week prior. Ghayas needed to be the loudest of the talking heads, especially against politicised Islam. A lot of lost ground needed to be made up for. A survey of history up to that point was a testament of failures and what was done next would determine the fate of the world in this strange new era.

US President George W. Bush addressed the United States and as it so happened, the rest of the world. Calm and collected, Bush announced that he was launching a war on terrorism. To Ghayas this was indeed a strange announcement. How could one fight an idea such as terrorism, let alone declare full-on war against it? Did he mean to declare war on Islam? That would be a foolish notion. Perhaps Bush did not see the 9/11 attacks as a retaliation to the West doing essentially the same thing covertly. Did he think doing the same thing unabashedly would garner a different result?

The speech was intended to lay out a new foreign policy and rally patriotic fervour in the US. A different form of terror struck Ghayas. The intention was not to simply turn the US into a police state in the name of freedom, but to spread the support of this war to other countries to initiate a global effort coming from the West, largely against the former colonised world. The warriors of the colonial age had finally aged out of the fight and now Bush wanted to give a new generation a reason to top off their animosity towards the West. Interestingly, the speech ended with Bush talking of how the mission was to make it so those wishing to inflict terror and harm upon others would be unable to sleep easy at night. Quite the conundrum as he was pushing his country over the edge into the deep, grey sea of moral ambiguity. Terrorists are a matter of perspective. The British will see terrorists in the Irish nationalists as easily as the Middle Eastern Islamists, but who are the terrorists in India, or Libya or China? Eventually, this mission of President Bush would end up being a trap, subjugating themselves to friendly fire. A dark relative of Gandhi's eye for an eye quote would leave those waging war on the terrorists becoming the terrorists themselves.[63] Could President Bush handle the confusion ahead?

Ghayas had no time to ponder this; the time for action was now. The fate of the next generation hung in the balance of what would occur next. It is not hard to imagine Ghayas calling for Talat from the other room and the subsequent phone calls to his sons and daughters. While Ghayas had up to this point spent a great deal of his life demonstrating for various communities at home and abroad, this would be the first time he would find himself organising for the global community, for the youth, and the world they would have to live in after him.

Anti-war movements produce strange bedfellows indeed. It must have been quite the shock when Ghayas showed up at a meeting that had communists, veterans of the old Labour Party, lefties, nuclear disarmament die-hards, LGBT activists, flower children, and the establishment based Muslim organisers. The hardened revolutionary was going to talk to this group about peace. Yet this ragtag group recognised the high stakes and it was their unified understanding that this was for the children—so that they did not inherit a bombed-out husk of a planet that broke the ice—and thus made way for handshakes. Ghayas would not have to restate his conditions for this group, for whilst they all had a great deal to disagree about outside of this movement, Great Britain joining in this 'War on Terror' was the worst possible outcome at this moment in time for all of them. Thus, the Stop the War Coalition was formed in September 2001 with Ghayas a founding member of its steering committee. Two Labour MP old-timers helped bring publicity to the group alongside Ghayas. Ghayas got along well with the two Labour members, Tony Benn and Jeremy Corbyn, as well as their Scottish mate George Galloway. They were dedicated men who knew a war was the worst thing for British society at all levels. They also appeared to have nothing to lose, their party having left them behind with New Labour. It was not like any of them would be rising to prominence in the future. So it was one last hurrah!

The Stop the War Coalition swung into action and an anti-war demonstration was organised. The established Muslim organisers at the time also mobilised their members to demonstrate. It was a pivotal moment in British Muslim history—up until September 2001, there had been little collaboration between Muslim organisations and 'mainstream' organisations. The 'us vs the West' rhetoric was still the norm. But here we were, fighting for the same cause as our non-Muslim brethren, to stop the war in Afghanistan. Great Britain joining this War on Terror was the worst possible outcome at this moment in time for everyone. Surely it was time to come together? Meetings took place to discuss the key theological concern: could Muslims have close collaboration and genuine partnership with non-Muslims for a common goal? Eventually the Muslim Association of Britain (an affiliate of the MCB) would join the coalition. But for Ghayas, any theological obstacles were long departed. There was important work to do, a war that had to be stopped, and here were good people who wanted the same. That was enough. Ghayas no longer felt the need to confine himself to Muslim-only groups and encouraged young, confident British Muslims to join mainstream civic organisations and human rights groups whose aim was to make Britain a better place for all.[64] A regular speaker at anti-war demonstrations, Trafalgar Square and Hyde Park would become Ghayas's new pulpits to promote peace.

Tony Blair was a beacon of hope for Ghayas when he first strutted into 10 Downing Street after defeating the monarchy over the Diana affair. The party he led appeared to care for minority communities and dialogue across religious, cultural and social boundaries. This was especially the case for the British Muslims who also shared a great affection for the man and his party in the 1997 general elections. The trouble with Blair began when he seemed to be propping up the American President. Any fear of damaging the 'special relationship' during Clinton's disagreement with the last Conservative government was quickly corrected between Blair and Clinton, but even that relationship seemed a bit stale in comparison to the credit Blair was giving to Bush after 9/11. To the rest of the world, Bush was a moron with his hand twitching over the button to launch a third world war. However, the British Prime Minister was taking his dangerous ideas and giving them a charismatic and seemingly reasoned and sophisticated voice: his own. [65]

Not long after the War on Terror speech, Bush would introduce America to the real threat out there—the Axis of Evil—in his 2002 State of the Union Address. Now the War on Terror had moved beyond a stateless war of shadows. Now it had sponsors, physical locations you could see on the map and direct your hate towards. Then the unconscionable occurred. Ghayas's opinion of Tony Blair withered as more and more British Muslims detained abroad were left to rot without trial, across the far reaches of the globe. One of the worst examples of this was seen in the case of Moazzam Begg, whom Ghayas campaigned for the release of. Begg was seized from his home in Pakistan by Pakistani Intelligence and handed over to US Forces in Afghanistan in 2002. He was held in Bagram in Afghanistan before being transferred to the infamous Guantanamo Bay detainment camp where he was held under charges of aiding and recruiting for al-Qaeda. He was held by the US until 2005, without trial. He was one of the notable British citizens held by the US without trial for being a supposed 'enemy combatant' or a 'terrorist', the definition of that moniker ever expanding.[66]

Ghayas also campaigned for the release of Babar Ahmad who was detained by the United Kingdom without trial for eight years to prevent him from being extradited to the United States. Once again, he was labelled a supporter of terrorism for posting in support of the Taliban on his website from the UK. Since the site he posted on held one server in US territory, the US claimed jurisdiction over the case. Again, for Ghayas, the guilt or innocence of these men was superfluous. It was a matter of justice. Injustice was holding citizens of Britain without a fair trial, and Ghayas simply demanded they be given this.

But a deeper problem was looming as the United States garnered more and more influence in Europe and the Middle East. Terrorism was the enemy and although on 12 September 2001 that was still a vague concept, a shadow, in the following months and subsequent invasion of Afghanistan, the shadow took form: a stereotypical form of an adult male with a beard and a brown skin tone. As stereotypes tend to, the nationality and other personal details fall subservient to the raw empirical look of an individual. Even the specificity of being Afghani or Muslim faded into the ignorant ease with which Otherness absorbs all in generalisations. The Other was forced into the imagination of the West and this Other was the enemy.

The United States announced it was forming an international coalition to wage war against Saddam Hussein's Iraq. Ghayas had to make sure it wasn't 1990 all over again. It sounded like utter madness. Yes, the United States struck back at the Taliban following the 9/11 attacks. Horrible, violent, and questionably effective, but at least the move had some logic as the US had decided that the Taliban were responsible for the Twin Tower attacks. But why in the world would the United States wish to go to war with Iraq? Did George W. Bush want to finish what his father had started? If that was the case, then at least we would be working in the realm of logic again. Worse still, the Americans, consumed by fear and the need to decimate whatever bogeyman was being presented as a threat to them by their government, overwhelmingly supported the invasion of Iraq. Did they realise what happens when one treads so carelessly into a cycle of violence and war? Ghayas didn't know what to do at this point. Was the United States going to actually follow through on this threat? It was absurdity. And then suddenly, Colin Powell, Bush's Secretary of State, goes before the United Nations and claims Saddam Hussein's government is hiding the production of weapons of mass destruction and for this, everyone should join America's war against Iraq. And then a nightmare flashed before Ghayas's eyes. What if America convinced the international community to not only let them go into Iraq, but actually follow them as allies in the aggression? This could not stand!

A thick tension hung in the air at the start of 2003. The dogs of war were not only prepped and equipped, they were hungry. The United Nations, long considered a defunct international governing body, was the last best hope in preventing the realisation of the nightmare shared by Ghayas and many other founders of the Stop the War Coalition. On the fifteenth of February, oddly enough the birthday of America's first president, Ghayas again found himself shoulder to shoulder with a most interesting crowd of people. The ideologies did not matter on this day, for they were all Britons and their demonstration stood to challenge a decision that would forever alter the course of global events. Police estimates stated that Ghayas was joined by over 750,000 other Britons. Others said it was over one million. Either way, it still constituted the largest demonstration in the nation's history. Starting at Grover Street and the Embankment, the swarm of protesters ground London to a screeching halt. The intended rally point was Hyde Park, but many were unable to make it that far. Those who did found the journey took several hours. Throughout Britain over the two official days of demonstrating, the fifteenth and sixteenth of February, well over a million people took to the streets. Not only this, but the Stop the War Coalition was part of a global coalition in mirror opposition to the US's anti-Iraq coalition. Sixty other countries joined in the global days of protesting, rallying between six and eleven million people. Rome earned the Guinness World Record for the world's largest political demonstration with nearly three million people standing against the war in Iraq.[67]

The thought of what had been organised was as awe-inspiring as the next steps were bewildering. The world holds its breath as weapons inspectors enter Iraq and the weapon stock inventory is released. UN resolution after resolution is accepted by the Iraqi government. With each discrepancy the US beats its chest and moves its armaments into position. It is quickly revealed that Tony Blair is in full support of Bush's endeavours, be that with or without UN mandate. Gordon Brown declares that he is ready to empty the vaults of the Bank of England to disarm Iraq. Only the Attorney General seems to stand between Blair and British forces marching toe to toe alongside the Americans in their quest for oblivion, even as Parliament opposes him. Robin Cook, the Leader of the House of Commons, resigns and the Attorney General, Lord Peter Goldsmith, gives a legal thumbs up to a British

Invasion of Iraq in accordance with current UN resolutions. As France and Russia stand firm, prepared to veto any ultimatums before the UN Security Council, Bush, Blair and the Spanish Premier José María Aznar meet in Azores, mirroring Roosevelt, Churchill and Stalin in Yalta. The seventeenth of March would be the moment of truth; disarm or die. Disarmament did not occur. Saddam did not leave Iraq. On the twentieth of March 2003, the coalition of the willing began their invasion of Iraq. Baghdad would be captured in April. Bush would declare victory in May. The last British troops withdrew eight years later in May of 2011. US troops officially withdrew in December 2011, yet with rising insurgent violence in 2014, US troop numbers in Iraq have swelled and the future of US involvement in Iraq remains a debate in Congress to this day.[68]

And then came peak morning hours for the London Underground on the morning of the 7th of July, 2005. This month had already broken records for being the coldest July in over twenty-five years. Ten minutes to nine in the morning. Liverpool Street towards Aldgate. Edgeware Road towards Paddington. King's Cross/St. Pancras towards Russell Square. The tube explosions had sectioned off central London. The capital appeared to be under siege. Fifty-two people of eighteen different nationalities. All Britons. All dead. Over seven hundred injured. Later that day, Ghayas would discover that his youngest son, Salman, had, while on his way to work under King's Cross, once again narrowly avoided becoming one of the numbers tied to yet another horror show in these extreme times.

The role of talking head that Ghayas was fulfilling at the time had now expanded from explaining how British Muslims were also rights-bearing British citizens, to explaining to the UK as he had been explaining to the US since 2001, that Muslims are not terrorists, albeit some terrorists may proclaim to be Muslim. Past associations across the board were opening everyone up to investigation. The terrible extent to which extremism reach had been demonstrated and the complexity of organisation, from religious to political, in all the nationalism, in all of the postcolonial sentiment, and in its long and diverse history connected to the United Kingdom was revealed to be irreconcilable. Islamophobia did not have its name, but its elusive presence could be felt from Cornwall to Dunnet Head. Questions abound flew at Ghayas, his mind numbed by recent history. How can we be sure we are safe from extremists? Are we to fear the terror abroad or is it being brewed here at home? Do the British Muslims need protection from the state? How do we carry on in a post-9/11 and post-7/7 world?

Ghayas's responses quickly began to run together, unified under a common theme. He would raise his hand in reassurance and look his questioners and audience in the eye. A wise and reassuring friend. It is not a matter of difference. Anything we do to point out our differences only seeks to widen the gaps in society. No one should get any special treatment or double standards. Everyone spoken of in these situations are Britons. All Britons need to live together and help each other as good neighbours do, regardless of any of their differences. We must go on about our days together. Terror is fuelled by fear and we must return to and reflect upon our notions of community and reinvigorate our sense of duty to that community. Together, we can win the future.

Yet the world was at war. Another global attack was always pending. It could happen anywhere, at any time. Vigilance was required by all. The minutiae of sophisticated intellectual notions of justice and equality left the free people of the West vulnerable to attack from their enemies. Even the calm, reasoned diplomatic face of Ghayas, a Muslim leader a long way from the days of Kalim Siddiqui, could not prevent the unbridled emotions produced by laws and their long-term effects on the cultural atmosphere of a society. The UK was no stranger to terrorism prior to 9/11. In fact, the UK government had an almost expert anthropological knowledge of their terrorists, so much so that in

2000, the Terrorism Act gave a solid definition of terrorism. The definition rang with the familiarity of Irish attacks in the past, but not only defined terrorism as acts intended to inflict bodily or property harm to persons or disrupt society or the government, but labelled terrorists as individual actors or those who associate with terror groups. Stop and search policies were also outlined and the images so famously attributed to America under the Patriot Act were already effective and established law in the United Kingdom. Following 9/11 there seemed to be a new legislative act on a fairly regular basis that further defined detention without trial limits, asset control, and the legitimacy of evidence obtained through torture and other human right threatening measures. Each bill was hotly debated in Parliament and met with stark opposition and demanded negotiation of the details in order for the measures and acts to pass the House of Commons. As the debates raged, the attacks continued through Europe and fear rolled through London, thicker than its world-famous fog. The noughties would be a decade of gradual alienation for many Muslims in Europe, especially in Britain.

In 2006, the Racial and Religious Hatred Act would make racial and religious remarks of a threatening nature illegal, but this legislation came in response to five years of unabashed hate in the name of national security, added on from the fear mongering that started in the 1970s and 1980s against high levels of immigration. Multiple generations, alienated and formed into fodder, for the extremist machine and the temptations of fundamentalists. An argument could be made that Blair's New Labour government had the best of intentions. But such pavement made for a fragile road and the destination was not what was originally anticipated. The Western world always found itself one step behind the terror it had declared war on. Instead of stepping back and asking what fed these new terrorists, they simply pushed on, believing they could actually win, when in fact they were running on a treadmill with settings that were under the control of greater outside forces.

The first two decades of the 21st century witnessed a remarkable effort from the British Muslim community in working to clear the name of Islam and remove the stain of hate from society. Reflection and reiteration to make sense of the past and put the trajectory of the future on the tracks of logic and moral grounding has been the underlying project. New groups have risen in response to a collective need for understanding and cooperation to navigate these troubling times.[69] While in Yemen, Ghayas and Rashad had great discussions concerning the next generation of activism needed for the future. Their discussion would plant seeds in Rashad's head that would give rise to an idea that would become City Circle. Rashad's sister, Salma Yaqoob would later march in stride with Ghayas as founders of the Stop the War Coalition. In 2000, Ghayas was invited onto Radio 4's *Any Questions* with Jonathan Dimbleby where he would share a panel with *The Guardian* columnist and environmentalist, George Monbiot. Ghayas would introduce Monbiot to Rehan Khan, then chairman of City Circle. Together they would host a memorable event at the London School of Economics that brought climate change to a Muslim professional audience. And to complete the circle, Ghayas would introduce Monbiot to the Yaqoobs. In 2004, George and Salma founded the anti-war Respect Party.

Beyond this Ghayas would lend support and become a founding trustee of Yasmin Alibhai-Brown's British Muslims for a Secular Democracy in 2006. As a veteran campaigner, Ghayas was always keen to share his insights, always energised to see the next generation of activists charting their own courses. His move from proponent to opponent of political Islam was an inspiration to many. Ed Husain and Maajid Nawaz would seek Ghayas's advice and support in establishing the Quilliam Foundation in 2008. Ghayas was given a position on the anti-extremist body's panel of

219

senior advisers. The times were changing and Ghayas was happy to see himself on what was appearing to be the winning side.

Prime Minister Tony Blair even attempted to do his part to illuminate British ignorance towards its Muslim community by speaking at several events and conferences aimed at giving the British Muslim community a platform and enlisting their help in the fight against terrorism. He spoke of how extremists had sullied the voice of 'calm' Muslims. He also spoke to the similarities between Christians and Muslims and the importance of interfaith dialogue therein. Try as he might, much of the audience wasn't buying the desperate attempts to win political capital on the twilight of his administration. His mind was made up and there was no flexibility on the military option against terrorism. Ironically, he wanted to help British Muslims combat the fundamentalists and the jihadists when Thatcher's government had trained them only a decade past in Scotland. Although, he was intelligent enough to know that he needed the support of the Muslims at home and that social cohesion was in everyone's best interest. His command of language and eloquence would not be enough to pull the wool over everyone's eyes.

Ghayas found himself invited to one of Blair's events in October of 2001 at the Al-Khoei Foundation in north-west London. War in Afghanistan had just started and Blair wanted well-vetted members of the British Muslim community to stand behind him to give him a sense of mandate and righteousness. His adamance for the military option met with a lot of friction, but he would assure them the strikes would be swift and that British troops would not be stuck there for long. He pleaded that these extremists were as much their enemies as the rest of the Western world's, but Ghayas and several others only saw war as a last resort and a temporary solution for an endemic problem. Blair even gave credence to establishing further Israeli settlements in Palestine to maintain peace in the region! Was he expecting a rubber stamping on a total sell-out of all that the Muslims held dear? Ghayas wondered incredulously as the speech unfolded. By the end of the Prime Minister's speech, a consensus ebbed and flowed around the themes of terrorism being the enemy of all equally and prayers for the bombings to end swiftly with a victory for justice.

Following the brief questioning period, Blair flipped into full campaign mode, for he had to sell a war and needed key photos, shaking key hands with key figures. He slowly made his way around the large space, engaging the attendees in responsive chit chat, who were queuing to get their chance at the honour of speaking with and shaking the hand of the Prime Minister. At one point, Mr. Blair, a smile straining to be anything but upon his face, approached Ghayas with his right hand extended. Ghayas would look the Prime Minister right in the eye and respectfully decline the opportunity to endorse the continuation of the cycle of violence that was on offer. Tony Blair would not receive the honour of shaking Dr. Ghayasuddin Siddiqui's hand that day.

Chapter Eleven

ACTIVIST, FEMINIST, BEARDED

IN THE CONTEMPORARY age of social media, data and information overload as well as such phenomenon as fake news and post-truth, an environment has emerged. In this new atmosphere urgency is key, sensitivities are set high, and judgement is fraught with complexities. First impressions, instant judgements of a thumbnail, have replaced much of human interaction and the rise and perpetuation of often outdated stereotypes and clichés have been re-established. As the nineties made way for the noughties and forward into the time of this book's writing, and in spite of the innumerable examples of the exception, so too rode along the stereotypes and clichés of ages long lost. This is largely because stereotypes do not arise from thin air. Globalisation forces what has often been described as a collision, a crash, an antagonism, or to put it most diplomatically, an encounter not without friction. No matter which side you think you are on or claim to support, lack of reflection, both upon oneself and society at large, stifles the progress we hope to achieve.

One man was not only aware of this, but made it an essential element of all his actions, now positioned as a major leader of a Muslim community at the dawn of the twenty first century, and with the hope of helping society realise this tragedy spawning error. Ghayasuddin Siddiqui, a bearded, quickly surpassing middle age, Muslim man, would upon a glance of his mugshot seem one of the least likely individuals to bear this characteristic. Ghayas spent his life attempting to break beyond this dichotomic state. The first lesson of this chapter, that being that one should never judge a book by its cover, should have been realised long before getting to this page for there are plenty more lessons still to be had!

Another stereotype that Ghayas proves exception to goes something along the lines of that each and every one of us is the sum total of the people we surround ourselves with. Ghayas has surrounded himself with both praiseworthy, saint-like individuals as well as vicious scoundrels, yet we would call Ghayas neither an angel nor a scallywag. Ghayas does not follow this logic, nor allows us to judge him by the friends he kept and the enemies he made. First off, Ghayas did not so much as make enemies as simply disagree with people. He was of a very specific cultural and situational upbringing (one that transverses the multitude of cultures that appear on this planet) that produces that rare individual who believes all humans have the capability to be good, regardless of their past actions or beliefs. While he had likes and dislikes as well as a preference for the company of some to others, he never had a blacklist of enemies, even though he himself appeared on quite a few!

Interestingly, he also had a tendency of finding himself seated next to certain individuals whom others would deem despicable or evil. Yet where others would shun the audience of such disreputables, Ghayas preferred to learn. To him, all people had the capacity to teach, and this was what distinguished Ghayas. He was instead the rare synthesis of all the people he found himself in the company of. Ghayas put a lot of faith in the human ability to overcome oneself and, as a result, be good. This faith has burned Ghayas time and again in his nearly eight decades on earth. But, it should be a comfort that maybe, beneath it all, the arc of humanity always bends towards the original state—that of good.

It is a mighty task, no doubt, to not only correct a stereotype, but to both point a mirror back at an entire people and then ask them to do better. The range and frequency of resistance boggles the mind to even begin to contemplate. But Ghayas did not fear resistance or even the potential of the opposition's tarnishing of his name or reputation. From the beginning, education was key for Ghayas and Kalim, if not the quintessential ingredient necessary for empowering the ummah. While a good deal of reading needs to be done and continues needing to be done ad infinitum, education is not merely gained in the knowledge accumulated from books and 'wise' men. An education is also reflected in action and for Ghayas, how we treat our women and how we treat our children—they being our future and true legacy—that differentiates between the civilised and the truly savage. And there was indeed work to be done. In fact, one of Ghayas's great diversions from Kalim's direction was not necessarily in circling the concern from the international ummah and back to the one at home in Britain, but in bringing it right to the fundamental unit of both society and Islam: the family.

To see the talking head Ghayas on the news responding to one amongst his vast portfolio of televised interviews, he could easily have been passed over as just another bearded Muslim man. Sure, he wore Western business attire and his beard ranked amongst the highest percentile of adult Muslim beards, both in its grooming and generally tamed condition compared to his peers. Yet aside from this, he looked like any other of the perpetuated authoritative patriarchy. Many in his generation saw women as property, their only God-given rights being the right to privacy and donning full body coverings in public. The only feminist organisation you would expect this man to sit on would be Saudi Arabia's Girls' Council, a body composed exclusively of men, many overweight and bearded.

If this theoretical, casual onlooker knew Talat Siddiqui or their daughters Faiza and Uzma, they would know that these women would never allow such foolishness. And when the casual onlooker found themselves at the nearest women's advocacy organisation, they would stand to see a lot of appearances subverted. For in the room where such a meeting took place the most independent and empowered of these young women might just find themselves subtly dressed in hijabs, and it might just have been the free and casually dressed with the greatest insecurity about their identity. And the most outspoken and mobilised person, ready to march alone on Parliament Square to demand equal pay across the gender gap might just have been a quaint, older, bearded man. For one's identity, especially that of a woman, and the strength with which one carries oneself through society are completely independent of how one dresses or how others view such choices. An individual's piety or overall goodness is not derived from appearance but, rather, found within the heart, seen in the actions that an individual carries out. It is the Other who sees these things as weird or unusual, yet this is the society most would want to live in. Individuals impose their own prejudices upon people based on how they look, failing to see, let alone care for, the human being underneath.

It was the strong activist women that Ghayas found himself demonstrating side by side with throughout his long career that provided him with a heart-deep respect for women. Ghayas had understood early on that a community needed educated women contributing to the team effort to build a just community and society—it could never be a male-only exercise. Ghayas would have it no other way. He raised his daughters the same way he raised his sons, full stop. This was the example he put to the community, knowing it was radical and equated to telling a lot of Muslim parents they had raised their children wrong. The Muslim Parliament and the Muslim Institute was to be the medium through which Ghayas placed a mirror before British Muslims and asked them to do better.

In fact, the most active, participatory, and lively committee in the Muslim Parliament was the Muslim Women's Institute (MWI). While the front rows at the inauguration of the Muslim Parliament served as a political statement and public relations magic trick, the body genuinely did believe in the empowerment of women and the advancement of women in and for the community. In fact, it is a common misunderstanding that Islamic culture undermines the role of the female, naturally bent towards a more authoritarian and patriarchal brand of society. The truth is quite the contrary. Again, to the outside onlooker, the meetings looked rather male dominant while the women were to be confined to the kitchen, slaves to a cultural sexism. While much can be said about the inherent nature of culture and tradition, that outlook is utterly naïve.

In Muslim society, society would begin, and if she deemed it necessary, would end upon the say of women. The tradition of imposed gender segregation is more out of benefit to the egos of men than the repressive protection of some imagined fragility of a woman's purity. In fact, if the women were not preparing divine dishes for mealtimes, most Muslim men would quickly succumb to starvation. Women are the managers of the house and therefore the essential rulers of the Muslim world. Forget how it looks or what illusions men draw up to help them sleep at night. Childcare, education, meal preparation, balancing of the budgets, and making sure their husbands and sons and daughters can find their way to work or school are all placed upon Muslim women. Not to mention the sophistication and complexity of their social and gossip institutions which leave the male-dominated halls of power looking rather primitive in comparison. Muslim women require no title to flex their position beyond the highest honour bestowed upon them at birth—that of having been born a female. Let men quarrel over their titles and self-importance; they need some activity to fill their days. This, of course, is the basis of Muslim society and unfortunately is as vulnerable to corruption as any other social or cultural system.

Unfortunately, some Muslim communities and states have abused the basic building blocks of society to oppress women, rendering them objects, stripping them of their rights and dignity. In a most beautiful example of irony, it is this grotesque form of patriarchy that is not only an impediment to Muslim societies, but also as much, if not more so, the case for the West. This irony commits a double-cross when Islamic scholars, both men and women, agree that it is not the default of the religion, which has afforded broad freedoms and rights to women. One might take notice of how Muslim patriarchy is at its strongest during the moments when their cultures are in decline or under the blade of colonial subjugation, or as it is seen more recently through tyrannical puppet regimes. And today, fragile masculinity and princeling practices may sound like a harbinger of darker days ahead. In the ever more mobile, contemporary world, archaic and corrupted forms of community have found their way into Great Britain, and it is in witnessing this that Ghayas and Talat stood together in opposition. The rights of the vulnerable in society are rarely ever protected in times of extreme assault on a society's dignity. The physically and politically weakest always fall the hardest. This is why societies must be ultimately judged on how the weakest fare be they minority groups, women, or children.

In fact, before Ghayas received criticism for his alleged undoing of Kalim's legacy, some of his most radical positions and policies asked the Muslim Parliament to reflect upon themselves and the community itself. Ghayas delivered the uncomfortable truth that the Muslim world, particularly British Muslim society, needed to take a long, introspective look in the mirror. The war was not, or at least could no longer be focused on the 'us vs them' mentality of the postcolonial age. After all, how could Muslims say they were fighting on the right side with internal corruption rife within the community itself? Sexism, rape, child abuse and the depriving of universal rights and justice was happening there at home, in the midst of their very communities. Much work lay ahead for the Parliament as Ghayas saw it. Education was going to be essential, for it was the foundation upon which the next generation of British Muslims would be staked. This sentiment hearkened back to Kalim's words, who wanted Muslims in every field and industry.

The key difference was in the simple possibility that the enemy was not out there, the external oppressor, but may reside within the heart of the community. The new chapter of the Muslim Parliament and the new direction of the Muslim Institute was to initiate projects that set the stage for the first home grown generation of British Muslims to flourish not as outsiders looking for a voice, but as native members of a larger society dedicated to progress and justice for all of their neighbours. This was a rude but necessary wake up call for his peers. Otherwise, they would be doing a disservice to their children and their future. Without this, the core of the community would decay and ultimately ensure the annihilation of anything resembling a British Muslim community. Why would the new generation of British Muslims attach itself to a crumbling and decomposing edifice? The British Muslim community needed to be something greater. Activists for change. And change always begins at the most basic unit of Muslim society: the home. Clean the house and then take on the world. This was the spirit of Ghayas's reign as a leader in the British Muslim community. This was the spirit of the HFA and the pivot that has assisted in helping embed the British Muslims within British society. Ghayas's new way is seen in the initiatives and policies that stand strong even in the present, and are continually revamped, evaluated and adapted for decades to come. This spirit is what will outlive Ghayas, as can be seen in the City Circle and the reconstitution of the Muslim Institute into the organisation it appears as today.

Of course, such a shift is easier articulated than enacted.

While in Chesham, Talat herself had become quite the leader in the community. In fact, her reputation as a community leader could be said to have surpassed that of Ghayas's, for in those days, Chesham knew Ghayas more so as Mrs. Siddiqui's husband than anything else. When he was off waving the flag for the revolution abroad, Talat remained in Britain, holding down the homefront. In her own unique way, Talat rose to become a valuable asset to the community rising from the grassroots. As both a community teacher and an assistant social worker, Talat not only came to learn of the local community in Chesham, but allowed for Chesham to find out about the woman they were blessed to have in their neighbourhood. She mobilised the sleepy, mainly Pakistani Muslim community, to dream bigger and was adamant that women and girls ought to set their sights higher.

With her youngest son in school, Talat had the freedom to fully throw herself into the service of others. She began simply by volunteering at Elmtree Primary School's summer school programme. After showcasing her abilities to both educate and connect, the headteacher asked if she could stay on to assist as a volunteer reading assistant during the regular term. She also managed to volunteer at the school where her two youngest children were attending, Newtown Primary School. While she demonstrated great skill in the classroom, social services also saw an opportunity that could not be passed up. They 'head-hunted' her to be an interpreter so that the schools could liaise with Pakistani parents who struggled with English. Talat was essential as Chesham had become a popular settlement for Pakistanis in the 1960s.

Chesham being a small town just outside of London provided a home close to the port of entry and exit, but without the exorbitant costs of living in the city. Its balloon and aluminium factory provided good work opportunities for low skilled labourers, especially men from Pakistan's Mirpur and Jhelum area. The 1960s was a time of easy migration, especially from the Commonwealth countries, as the post-war economy demanded working class labour from abroad. West Yorkshire, East Midlands, West Midlands, Luton, Peterborough, Derby and East London were prime landing ground and fertile soil for establishing homes and families for the new migrant workers. In fact, as this influx of workers became established over the proceeding decades, their outflow of 'sending money back home' slowly built the small Mirpur village into a decent sized town of large villas and shops that carried British products and even accepted pound sterling! While Chesham was a village by British standards, the villages these new Pakistani residents hailed from followed a very different code. These villages were considered the backwater of Pakistan as minimal education and poverty were the norm and religious patriarchy and village politics ran the show. Such attributes have a way of making their way through customs, duty-free. This background would continue to plague the Chesham Pakistani community as an avalanche of social and domestic problems condemned them to underachievement, along with other settling communities throughout Britain.

The first wave of migrants was largely male, who would work in Britain and send money home. After a few waves of men arriving they would spend the 1970s settling and building up their wealth until women and children could follow suit by the 1980s. The population shock of the arrival of women and children would lead to backlash against Britain's liberal immigration policy and the closing of borders, leading to a storm of racism and xenophobia that infused much of the happenings in 1980s Britain. While the first men to come to Britain had jobs and a more welcoming environment to acclimatise to, the women suddenly found themselves a long way from home, separated from the wide familial support networks, with a language and culture stacked against them. To bring with them and raise young children made the burden all the more challenging.[70]

In Chesham an incident occurred where a Pakistani father was interpreting for his wife at a local school and it slowly became apparent that the father was abusing his wife at home. The safety of the wife and their children being of paramount concern to the school officials, an impartial interpreter was needed urgently. Enter Talat Siddiqui. It was not only her first call in her new position as school liaison officer but also one amongst what would quickly become a long list of domestic issues within Chesham's Pakistani community. The school had indeed found a rare gem, as educated and articulate Pakistani women who were also willing to stand up in public were not easy to come by at the time. Talat's abilities were quickly noticed and as word spread, her services were increasingly demanded. Social services had a rockstar in Talat and she began a long career as an assistant social worker, remaining until she took her retirement. Over her storied career she also served voluntarily to set up a local Asian women's support group, a Sunday morning supplementary school, and would also serve as a school governor.

The Asian women's support group, which met once a week, provided a local safe space for women to raise concerns and better themselves and the community. The group provided opportunities for Asian women to become educated, aware of local support services they could access and enhance their skills. Many of the domestic problems in the Chesham Muslim community were linked to the lack of language skills and knowledge of how things worked in the UK. The isolation of many Chesham Muslim women, both mental and physical, perpetuated the overall lack of academic achievement, the rising mental health issues and limited any chance of breaking the vicious cycle. Many of the women in the support group took lessons in Urdu to formalise their language skills while others took essential English lessons. Some even studied for an English as a Second Language Certification. Talat arranged for regular talks with local community services and the Citizen Advice Bureau. She also set about organising environments that were more appropriate and comfortable for Muslim women, such as women only swimming sessions and other exercise events. Her work did not limit her to the confines of Chesham; she also took the ladies out on the London Underground. For many of the women in the support group, this was their first trip out of Chesham, into the City of London. Such events, in response to a blossoming of popularity, even became a recurring summer outing event where the ladies and their children could visit London's various theme parks. These were the small bits of independence and seeds of empowerment that these women desperately needed.

Talat saw the difference this support group could make to the community and set her sights on uplifting women and girls, with Ghayas at her side. The empowerment of women, their children and their families, would be the first step towards establishing an upward trajectory for this community. Talat's dedication to the community did not stop at the women but, long before the Muslim Parliament's White Paper on Education, she focused on a need for proper supplementary education in Chesham. Fledgling attempts had tried to establish Urdu language classes for young Pakistani boys in Chesham, but now Talat was called to aid. Her agreement to help came with the ever-becoming famous condition which the Siddiquis added to their endorsements.

A similar class had to be established for the girls too. Within weeks of Talat joining the initiative, a girl's class was launched and Talat's focus pivoted to this endeavour. The class started as a basic Urdu language lesson and Qur'an recitation for girls, but in teaching the class, Talat realised these girls also needed support for their school studies in the run up to 11-plus exams. English and Maths were added to the curriculum. The two-hour class quickly grew to a three-hour class, after which her daughters, Faiza and Uzma, would continue as volunteer tutors in later years. The primary school English and Maths lessons eventually extended to include local Pakistani boys. Her son, Salman, also taught for a brief spell. The raving success of the Urdu classes made Talat the port of call for supporting the local secondary school, Chesham Park School, as their students prepared for the GCSE Urdu final examinations. Eventually the school provided an Urdu GCSE teacher in-house as part of the school curriculum provision.

Administering the support group and her volunteer teaching helped Talat to make a difference in the local Chesham Muslim community, but it was her work with social services that exposed her to the very worst of troubles that were festering in the British Muslim community. These issues were all too easily brushed under the carpet by community leaders and nearly completely undetectable in the concerns of the British establishment. Talat often assisted at women's shelters serving victims of abuse or in helping children and spouses get back on their feet if they needed to escape from an abusive or forced situation. In her time assisting the community, she came to make several key observations which she would bring back home to discuss with Ghayas. Ghayas would concur, as he was during this period also receiving letters and calls from a regular stream of distressed women facing similar situations. These issues were wider than Chesham; Ghayas was being contacted from women up and down the country from one domestic tragedy to the next.

One unfortunate reality was that an increasing population of young Muslim men and women were being forced into marriage. The situation was dire and needed critical attention. Arranged marriages had been a custom, yet had a long-standing tradition of being a fair agreement between two willing parties. It was a family activity, but the distortion of this institution threatened the very custom. The distance and culture shock between the old world and Britain gave the unique tragedy a colour, painting the whole practice in an often grim light. There was much more freedom in the United Kingdom, especially after the sexual and philosophical revolutions of the 1960s and 1970s. Parents of Asian origin feared the worst for their children, growing up in such a tempting and distasteful culture. Muslim parents were keen to get their children married young to prevent them from succumbing to the pitfalls of dating and sexual activity outside of marriage that was becoming more and more predominant in British culture. The pressure on the children was compounded by the fact that they were bound to family duty in helping to bring their family members to the UK for a better life. Family holidays back to Asia were often set to a familiar itinerary of moving from extended family household to household, each with a potential spouse-to-be waiting for a first meeting. Marrying a spouse from 'back home' became all the rage, be it forced, highly pressurised, or even the wilful longing for a spouse of a perceived familiar background. This was the tradition, was it not? In Pakistan it was quite ordinary for families to line up potential suitors from extended family or between other families of 'good standing' and then allow the wedded-to-be to make the final choice.

Yet when the British Muslims sought their brides and grooms-to-be, they were hit by a culture shock that resulted in serious whiplash. Although the period of adjustment to any new spouse from a different family or clan can be just as fraught with problems as a match between people of two entirely different countries, many marriages of this sort would persevere and, ultimately, be successful. However, the cases in which force was applied only made the eminent disaster all the more cataclysmic. Straight up deception, emotional blackmail, and brute force all found a place in the arsenal of a parent towards son and daughter alike. The irony is such horror found its origin in the innocent desire to give their children, and more often themselves, a more prosperous life.[71]

While the horrors of forced marriage often manifest themselves in the collective consciousness as women being the ultimate victims, boys too held their fair share of victimhood. There were numerous situations where boys would be forced to marry a girl from back home, then bring her back with them to the UK, where they would promptly divorce them, potentially abuse them, or even simply sideline them so that they could continue or commence another relationship with a different girl. Often in these cases, the boys had secret prior existing relationships with girls outside the Muslim community, which ironically was the very fear that launched parents into such extremes as forcing their children to marry someone they had chosen. This was how they were to make honest men out of them! Yet these poor girls would find themselves prisoners, bound by their language and cultural limits and the fear of justice under a false interpretation of dogma.

On the other hand, the girls who were sometimes kidnapped and taken back home to marry often had more of a fight on their hands if they desired to rid themselves of an unwanted spouse. One option was to try to annul the marriage, but often this was difficult due to intense parental pressure. Some of these girls would just accept their situation and continue, only to see their husbands attain UK citizenship and end the marriage, leaving them in the dust. Other times, there would be no other option but to run away, risking life and limb, to seek the safe haven of a women's refuge until they could, if they were lucky, liberate themselves of their 'husbands' or 'family'. Of course, there was also the option most don't wish to speak of, yet high profile cases and newspaper headlines bring the reality to the forefront of our minds. Death, suicide or homicide, often consistent with 'honour killing'. Interestingly, it would be 'honour' that would connect forced marriages, where the woman must marry a person not of her choosing to protect the family's reputation or for their benefit, and these honour killings, where a woman must be killed for harming the family's reputation. Either way, the honour and interests of the family would often play out on a woman's body, owned by everyone but herself.

What to do in such a hopeless situation? The pain of this reality haunted both Ghayas and Talat as each filled their dinner conversations with increasingly horrific stories of what was going on in their community. It was indeed a complex problem. First and foremost was the issue of labelling this as a cultural problem. How can one person say another culture is wrong or bad? At the end of the day, it would seem that you would have more luck proving one's religious conception of God is correct over the other. This was the cultural relativism that made the British establishment completely and utterly useless in such affairs. Social services, educators, the police—all paralysed for fear of offending anyone's religious sentiment. This was a community issue, beyond the jurisdiction of the state. After all, if the state could interfere in something as sacred as the notion of marriage, what would stop them from going further in defining what is and is not acceptable as a religious or cultural practice? The debate would rage on. Yet for Ghayas and for Talat, the condemnation of an entire generation to the brutal terror of forced marriages could not be allowed. In Islam, marriage is a contract, requiring both parties to enter into it in full consciousness of the decision and with both parties willingly accepting of the agreement and its responsibilities. Forced marriages were against the very tenets of Islam and any sexual intercourse that resulted was rape. Any parents or family members who partake are aiding and abetting in sex crimes.[72] Ghayas knew something had to be done, but what? Well, Ghayas never claimed to be all-knowing.

And that is how a bearded, middle-aged man began showing up at political action committees dedicated to women's issues.

In researching solutions, Ghayas and Talat made several illuminating discoveries. Forced marriages were a larger problem than the progressive modern world would care to admit. While it would often be tied to the abuse of the practice of arranged marriage, it was also largely seen as an escape. Indeed, the long tradition of arranged marriages worked from one side of the coin to be a deliberative and democratic process whereby parents and children agreed to pairings that were beneficial to all sides. On the other side of that coin, the filial obedience of children to their parents could be abused through manipulation to force marriages that served to benefit the husband or, potentially, a status or monetary compensation to the parents. Likewise, a great deal of women were being promised the freedom of leaving their home country if they would marry a possibly less than desirable man. In the worst case scenarios, women would find themselves as one of multiple wives kept between a country of origin and Britain, raising the children and essentially an object of pleasure at the whim of the male.

Some young Muslims were also using Islamic marriage as an unregulated avenue to become sexually active with no strings attached. Whilst at the receiving end other Muslims, often unwitting females, due to an improper understanding of the legal status of civil and Islamic marriages, would become entangled in a whole host of potential traps. Their world would unravel twice over when they discovered that their *nikah* had no legal standing in the eyes of the state. While Brits belonging to the Anglican Church have their marriages recognised before God and Queen at the same time, the system is not so simple for Muslims. Those having had a nikah overseas would have their marriage recognised under British law, while those having a nikah conducted in a British mosque and overseen by the imam would not be automatically recognised, for this was the affair of the mosque. The mosque served as the joiner and if the need presented itself, the place to approve of divorce both under Islamic law, although not recognised under British law.

Similarly, Muslim marriages were not guaranteed or automatically recognised by the United Kingdom. As the Muslim contract for marriage is required to be entered into without duress according to sharia law, and must involve a series of conditions between both husband and wife, it would appear the legitimacy must be recognised by the state in Britain. But the process of obtaining a civil union under British common law is entirely different. If a couple undertake a nikah only, then this marriage will not be recognised under British law and hence, neither party will receive the legal protection afforded to married couples. For example, if a civil union is not obtained under British law this can spell disaster in the case of something happening to a spouse, for there is no protection of inheritance under British law if the civil union is not properly obtained. Again, education was needed to ensure that a nikah ceremony be preceded by a civil registration, to make the marriage legally recognised in the UK. And so British law could be relied upon to provide a wife's right to maintenance in the case of a divorce, the protection of spousal inheritance rights, and to give legitimacy to her children in the eyes of the law. Education was needed to ensure that a nikah ceremony was preceded by a civil registration to make the marriage legally recognised in the UK. Only then could British law be relied upon. Ghayas also pushed at this time for imams to register as providers of a civil marriage certification recognised under UK law as part of the nikah ceremony.[73] Ghayas saw these issues as fundamental flaws in the community requiring immediate attention and so he pushed on toward a resolution.

This was a complicated issue but there were two main strands of a solution. One was to ensure that there was better education of what constituted a Muslim marriage in Islam, as it was certainly not the adulterated model that had arrived in the UK from the backwater villages of Pakistan, Bangladesh and India. Both parents and the parties of marriage needed to know where their rights started and ended. The overemphasis on respecting elders had bizarrely turned marriage into a right of the parents as opposed to a right of the marrying parties. Education was needed to consolidate understanding that consent in an Islamic marriage from both parties is paramount, otherwise the marriage is void and any sexual relations in this situation are tantamount to rape.

As part of this educational effort, Ghayas with old friend Mufti Barkatulla drafted up the Muslim Marriage Contract. Ghayas first met Barkatulla after Kalim and Ziauddin bumped into him on their travels to Saudi Arabia during the 1970s and advised him to come to the UK. The Muslim Institute would fund his education here as part of their drive to create religious scholars grounded in both Islam and modern societies. This investment would indeed bear fruit decades later when Mufti Barkatulla became that rare breed of scholar, traditionally qualified expert in Islamic law and able to combine tradition and modernity to produce something new and relevant but rooted in Islam.

The Muslim Marriage Contract laid out examples of the rights a girl could stipulate in her marriage, allowing girls and boys to put into the contract any issues that they wanted to highlight i.e. the right to continue working, the right of a wife to initiate divorce if necessary etc. It was an opportunity to discuss wider issues before marriage to ensure the foundations of the union would be based on certain agreed terms. These were controversial issues to discuss at the outset of a marriage at the time, and it was also not commonly understood that from an Islamic point of view the marriage contract was just that—a contract between two parties and whatever was agreed could be signed upon. There was now the opportunity for the contracting parties to engage in structured discussions to ensure as smooth a start to their married life as possible. As part of this campaign there was also a rise in pre-marriage counselling sessions and marriage courses for Muslim couples to attend in advance of their marriage.

As Ghayas learned from his experiences in establishing the Halal Food Authority, it was one thing to lay down a policy for reform and regulation, and quite another to enact a cultural change that presupposed and required a segment of society to recognise their own wrongdoing and attempt to correct it. Taking on the small subculture of halal butchers proved a dangerous endeavour in its own right, but to take on the mosques and the imams was a dance not for the faint of heart. Imams were well-equipped to take on the adversarial nature of their multicultural, multi-ethnic and multiple opinionated neighbours, but they would prove especially swift in their retort to criticism from within. Though Ghayas, a man whose only admitted enemy, per se, was injustice, knew that rivalries amongst the mosques of London, let alone greater Britain, provided enough animosity within the community. Ghayas needed new allies and new approaches to unite the community beyond inter-mosque politics.

In learning the intricacies of the marriage problem and women's rights, Ghayas came to befriend numerous leaders in the Muslim women's political action community. A champion of women's rights in Britain, Ghayas learned as much from Cassandra Balchin as he could impart or assist. Shaista Gohir, another women's activist, was shocked by the idea of Ghayas, both as a man and a man from his generation and background, running around fighting for women's rights and their access to power. Seeing these women in action and fighting for the community reinvigorated an old, restless spirit within Ghayas. He had seen that these women had done their research in tearing down the misogynist interpretations that had been ascribed to the Qur'an. They sought to set the record straight and return the gender neutrality inherent to the Divine Word on issues like marriage, restoring the right of women in having their say over the matter. Watching them make stride after stride and winning battle after battle forced his signature smile along his jawline. The future was safe in these women's hands.

Ghayas made many new and high-profile friends including Ann Cryer, MP for Keighley in West Yorkshire. Now women and bearded men alike rallied for the British government to take action. Ghayas even found friends on the left through the Southall Black Sisters. Hannana Siddiqui (no relation), co-ordinator of the organisation, was calling out the British institutions for their ignorance by way of cultural relativism. Meanwhile, Ghayas called out the British Muslim community itself, taking the official and incredibly radical position that deemed any sexual activity performed under a forced marriage as rape and people who forced others into marriage as sex criminals. It was just the bold, no-nonsense sentiment that had always been Ghayas's style and was the blunt force needed to wake the community up.

The Muslim Parliament now aligned with several women's rights activists and the Stop Forced Marriages Campaign was underway. The result of this would be a joint initiative by the Home and Foreign Office of the United Kingdom in curtailing the problems of forced marriages. A community liaison office was created within the Foreign Office to work on behalf of the victims of forced marriage. Part of this initiative included setting up a helpline predominantly used by girls, who suspected or found themselves being forced into a marriage either in the UK or abroad. Several high-profile cases occurred in which the British Embassy in Pakistan got involved in bringing girls in this situation back home to Britain.[74]

The first area of focus and success came in reforming the educational approach to marriage. A lot of the problems encountered and situations the victims found themselves ensnared in could have been avoided with better understanding. Numerous educational brochures and pamphlets were produced explaining the different types, technicalities and processes involved in marriage as well as what rights women have in their entering into that most holy union. Public service informative displays began turning up at airports, reminding people that forced marriages were illegal and thus illegitimate under Islamic law, as well as providing a contact number to be safely delivered from a potentially disastrous situation. An entire campaign to educate young Muslims spawned from these investigations. Frank conversations were had and safe places offered for those who needed them. As the world changed and new generations grew to an appropriate age for marriage and sexual activity, the mission was to make sure that the British Muslim youth were armed with the education they needed to fully empower them to make the best decisions for their future.

Alongside the massive effort to build up an educational infrastructure to tackle the issues of marriage in the community, Ghayas used the authority vested in the known name of the

Muslim Institute and the Muslim Parliament of Great Britain to promote, in alliance with the Muslim Council of Britain, the use of an accessible document: the Muslim Marriage Contract. Critics dubbed the contract a damning document that only sought the expanse of extremism through endorsing sharia law in the West. Opponents also came from within the community, though often arising from conservative and literalist groups, decrying kufr.

These attacks conflated the old revolutionary rhetoric with the general efforts to advance and assist the British Muslim community in the new millennium. At the launch in 2008, Ghayas had pulled together a fragile alliance between the Muslim Parliament, the women activists he stood beside, the MCB and the Islamic Sharia Council. City Circle provided a platform for the frank conversations the community needed to have to ensure progress on the issue. The Muslim Marriage Contract simplified nikah, making it more user friendly, mutually understood, and safer for those who chose to be married under the purview of the mosque as well as the state.

Quite contrary to the view of critics, the Muslim Marriage Contract protected young British Muslims from the abuse of sharia law and Islamic custom. The act of marriage itself was made more open to others, neutral of one's faith and casting out the notion that women needed male guardians or *walis*. This was a main bone of contention with the contract. The role of the wali, historically, was intended to be a tool for the protection of women; however, it was increasingly being used as a means to subjugate women. Fathers and uncles would often refuse consent to a woman's choice of marriage partner and instead pressure them to marry elsewhere. This resulted in a clash of literalists wanting to retain the original text—despite it being abused and allowing men to keep control over women—and those wishing to remain faithful to the spirit of the text and protecting women in marriage. In some cases, this was simply a sexist desire for power and control over women, dressed up as greater faithfulness and observance to the text. The contract also allowed a woman to make demands on the husband to root out spousal rape, prevent husbands from taking multiple wives, to deter the manipulations of parents, and make a path for divorce if the terms were not upheld.[75]

Cassandra Balchin's life was dedicated to connecting women and the community with the knowledge and legal assistance they needed for not just marriage, but divorce if need be. Since other political action groups had very visible ties to political motives, the efforts Balchin and her successors, such as Shaista Gohir, dedication can only be described as pure work for the community and for all subsequent generations around the world. In this mission, there is an often lost foundational casting of humanitarian effort that all ought to reflect and learn from.

Unfortunately, the stubbornness of society to both change and recognise change, mixed with the volatility of politics, often overshadows the heart of certain initiatives. Under pressure from within the British Muslim community, shortly after the launch of the Muslim Marriage Contract, the MCB made an about face, throwing the Muslim Institute under the bus by withdrawing its support for the initiative. When asked why they endorsed it in the first place, they commented that they had been misguided by individuals they had once trusted on such important matters. They would set off to make their own version of the contract, 'properly' constructed by clerics and religious scholars. After all, what input could Muslim women or human rights groups possibly have to contribute to such a community matter?

Although, it should be noted that a deeper lesson resided within this swirling situation. Ghayas the bearded feminist was ahead of his time, not as a result of some genius insight into a more progressive future or to try to dismantle the patriarchy, but because he kept his finger on the pulse of the community. Often the best leaders are found just a step back from the community with a more open visual acuity guiding and navigating the empowered individual through a dark wood, not dragging them by a powerless hand to hit every stick and rock in the way. Ghayas did not dictate to a room of women how they would win some war against the establishment, like he could have if he wanted to. No. It was in this method of leading by following, walking with the community he fought for, that the Muslim Marriage Contract and Stop Forced Marriages initiatives rose to dominance in a way that would help the community, not rebuild it in some utopian vision.

Indeed, leadership by walking beside can result in truly forward-thinking action. Being a male feminist broke ground in the British Muslim community of the new millennium, but in the greater scheme of things, was not the most progressive display one could throw up on the chalkboard. In listening and reflecting, Ghayas came across another pressing danger within the community that remains a controversy; one if not addressed will most certainly be a force that threatens to divide the British Muslim community to an extent it will not easily bounce back from.

The Catholic Church ushered in the new millennium with the granddaddy of all scandals. It crash-landed into the public eye with a force that could have reduced St. Peter's to rubble and sent ripples out from the Vatican to the institution's most distant reaches. In 2002 a local paper, *The Boston Globe*, propelled its readership beyond the national level when it began publishing reports of sexual abuse of younger parishioners by priests and other church officials. Not only had these incidents occurred, but had been occurring for several decades, and were still occurring across the United States and the rest of the world. To complicate matters further, the Church may have been complicit in attempting to cover it all up. Meanwhile, Ghayas watched and read as this scandal consumed the attention of international media outlets. What was most striking was that large portions of the Catholic community seemed less than shocked by this news. The general response of 'that makes sense' by members of a given community reveals a dark dynamic within communities—that certain evils would be accepted for whatever reason, be that for the benefit of a greater good or the belief that gossip had just gotten out of hand. Both possibilities here speak to a community being more fittingly labelled as a mob and the ramifications of such a structure can be truly destructive, physically and literally as well as mentally, and to the greater cultural consciousness.[76]

What terrified Ghayas is that he had enough realist sentiment to know the British Muslim community was not so infallible as to be invulnerable to similar scandal. It is in this instance that one reflects on the gossip they have come across in their day to day lives. From the silly to the seemingly impossible, the notion of 'what if' creates truly grizzly scenarios within the mind. After all, Ghayas had remembered hearing complaints coming out of madrassas. Often teachers would be brought into Britain and given visas and accommodations to teach. Naturally, the way of things in Saudi Arabia or Pakistan had diverged from what was acceptable and what was not in British society. Whereas corporal punishment is acceptable in other countries and cultural framings, in Britain it had been frowned upon and made illegal. Ghayas had heard stories of children returning home with welts and bruises or displaying irate and antisocial behaviour in response to their environment. This was more than enough to reveal that the regulatory oversight of madrassas in Britain was grossly inadequate.

Just as in the case of the halal butcher community, oversight of this area would be seen as an insult to the dignity of educators and as another attempt that would be capitalised on by British society to cede power and influence away from the Muslims. By this point of his life, after giving everything for the British Muslim community, Ghayas did not care about such outdated generalisations and ignorance-drenched fears. Once again, Ghayas would take on the imams. Education had remained for the better part of his life, the key to a thriving community and global peace and prosperity. Therefore, a blemish on this institution was a community sin of the highest order, for it plagued the future and could condemn the community to another lost generation.[77] The lost generation of postcolonial Indians can be directly tied to the continued tensions between India and Pakistan still being seen over seventy years after partition.

In March 2006, the Muslim Parliament issued its report on 'Child Protection in Faith-based Environments'. This followed a seminar held the previous year in which the discussions highlighted that most madrassa teachers were unaware of their legal obligations to the children left in their care. This revelation initiated the need for a policy document to be drafted. Before the seminar, Ghayas approached a number of mosques and community centres to ask them to host the event. Most were reluctant to do so. Their objections varied from 'why raise a non-issue?' to 'this will further marginalise the community' and the most ominous, 'this will be opening up a can of worms'. Ghayas realised he was scratching on the surface of an iceberg. His discussions with some ex-teachers indicated that physical abuse was widespread. In madrassas, up to 40% hit or scold their pupils and cases of sexual abuse, around 15–20 per year, were considered by insiders as being an understatement.

This topic was a taboo of the highest order. In the layers of denial Ghayas was attempting to unveil the community from, he had to go much further than halal meat cover-ups and instances of forced marriage. A darker denial lay even deeper beneath the surface, a place not even the most curious of journalists of the time were willing to go. There was very little discussion taking place in the community on the subject at any level. Surely safeguarding of children from harm should be the focus of every community? And here was Ghayas, looking in horror, as madrassas at the time were wholly unregulated and had no policies in place to meet their legal requirements pursuant to the Children Act 1989. Local authorities would not take this challenge seriously for fear of being accused of Islamophobia in the contemporary context, more content to hide under the veil of cultural sensitivities. However, if madrassas were left on their own it was likely that due to poor understanding of child protection law and practice, a large number of Muslim children would remain exposed to significant risk of harm. It was time for action; madrassas needed to implement transparent and accountable child protection policies in order to create an environment which minimised the risk of abuse. It was clear that if left unchecked, this ticking time bomb could develop into a national scandal and the Muslim community could be hit with the same avalanche of child sex abuse scandals, decades afterwards, in a manner similar to that which scandalised the Catholic Church at the turn of the century. The Nolan Report was the Catholic Church's response to the issue of child abuse in 2001, and it emphasised its commitment to place the protection of children at the forefront of its policy. Ghayas firmly believed that this should also be the commitment of the Muslim community and the step needed to ensure this outcome was put into action. The madrassas had to recognise that this was not a matter of choice that could be ignored.

Under Ghayas's direction, the Muslim Parliament issued a similar report to get the ball rolling in 2006. The report noted that thousands of children were potentially being subjected to unlawful abuse in the 700 Islamic schools that served upwards of 100,000 students across Britain. It recommended that the government create a national registration scheme of madrassas coordinated centrally and monitored by local authorities, and ensure that Local Safeguarding Children's Boards provide necessary advice and support followed by effective training to all staff and volunteers. The publication of the report did much to highlight the issue in the Muslim community and the British community at large and was reported in the national media. *The Independent* published a write up of the report. Ghayas had found a friend in Ann Cryer MP. She commended the Muslim Parliament's bravery for tackling the issue and added that failing to protect the children in madrassas because of 'cultural sensitivities' was nonsense. Were we saying British Asian children were not entitled to the protection of the law?

Following the publication of the Muslim Parliament's report and a report by the Government's Chief Adviser on the Safety of Children calling for a ban on corporal punishment in religious settings, which was accepted by the Labour government, the BBC launched an investigation in 2011 uncovering some 400 instances of accusations of physical abuse in madrassas in the previous three years. Due to families being pressured by their communities to keep these incidents quiet for fear that the state would take away access to proper religious education, prosecutors speculated that the number of instances reported likely represented the tip of an iceberg. Whilst internal efforts have been made to correct past wrongs, given no legislation has been enacted as a result, such dangers still loom formally unchecked in the British Muslim community, leaving the time bomb ticking and its explosion all the more inevitable.

Ghayas's efforts calling for better oversight on madrassa education in Great Britain goes down as perhaps his most important work and equally most controversial. Ghayas knew taking on imams was a dangerous business indeed, but while simultaneously campaigning for Stop Forced Marriages and calling for reform in madrassas, he had noted that "mosques choose their imams based upon their piety, not on their knowledge". Ghayas had become quite the wordsmith in his later years, being able to navigate respect and exposure, treading carefully on the line of insult and offence. Ghayas was truly the successor of Kalim Siddiqui. This was a risk he would reserve only for the issues dearest to his heart and most important for the community. Getting education right and doing things for the benefit of future generations was the highest mission Ghayas could hope to accomplish in his life. This was his revolution, not for the self or the here and now, but for the community of the future. After all, what good is the work for the community if the community ceases to exist in the third or fourth generation? Ghayas's work in educational and family reform within the British Muslim community was his most pivotal and, tragically, the most overlooked or simply ignored. Where Ghayas was truly leaps and bounds ahead of not just his community, but the wider human civilisation, was in his ability to look in the mirror and not fear what he might find, but hope that he could improve upon the flaws revealed.

Ghayas knew he would not live forever, but this story was never Ghayas's, it was the community's, and that future was all that mattered.

Chapter Twelve

FLYING LESSONS

IN 2009, TALAT Siddiqui had a bad feeling. It was that super-natural spine tingle of unease, an anxiety that demanded a quick pace back and forth, a mental inventory. It never hurt to just make sure all was as it ought to have been. She was in Dubai for one more night to see her daughter Faiza and her family before returning back to Britain after a holiday she and Ghayas had taken, first to Pakistan and then Dubai. Ghayas had returned earlier, allowing her more time in Dubai.

As Talat paced from one room to the next, her phone suddenly rang. It was Ghayas. He noted that he had not been feeling well the whole day and as a result had been rather dormant, taking a long nap upon the couch. Something possessed him to call, yet the call had no immediate purpose beyond being able for Ghayas to hear Talat and, perhaps more importantly, Talat to hear Ghayas. She had heard him in a variety of states of emotion and wellbeing throughout their nearly four decades together. But this call seemed strange. Everything he said was intelligible, but, as for coherence, there was something off. The stabbing of the spine grew as unease overtook Talat. She asked if he was well. He assured her that he was fine, just fine. Okay, she responded, but perhaps you should stay awake. Drink some water, or call someone to help if you need to. She nearly pleaded with him to have someone check on him. Again, he was fine, no need to worry. Those words often have the opposite effect on those who receive them and they were just the combination of words to drive Talat's intuition over its threshold.

After conferring with her daughter, Faiza, Talat's concerns over the strangeness behind the call were confirmed. With Ghayas having been a diabetic for decades, perhaps this was just a case of hyperglycaemia? They decided to call back and now his coherence had deteriorated further, their worst thoughts appeared to have been confirmed. While Talat kept Ghayas on the line, Faiza tried to call for an ambulance from Dubai, then realising that it wasn't possible, she tried the only other people she could call: her siblings. It was the end of the day at work and Uzma and Salman were both unreachable, travelling home on the various lines of the London Underground. Asim was out of the country on a work trip. Improvising and getting increasingly desperate, Talat suggested Faiza call their neighbour, Akleema, who lived at the bottom of the hill, a woman with teenage children. She did not want to provoke a state of emergency or heaven forbid, a crisis, but she explained to her neighbour how her last phone call with Ghayas had went. By the grace of God, the neighbour picked up the phone. By the grace of God, her daughter and son were at home. By the grace of God, they rushed up the hill and knocked on the door. But Ghayas was beginning to lose consciousness and mobility. With Talat guiding Ghayas over the phone he, in an uncoordinated manner, only just managed to unlock the front door, promptly falling to the ground before any other action could be taken. He lay upon the floor, unconscious.

In rapid succession, the teenagers called for an ambulance. Uzma arrived back home from work just as the ambulance arrived and she accompanied her father to hospital. On confirmation of what had happened, first Talat and then Faiza would find themselves on the next available flights to London.

It was later pieced together that hyperglycaemia had induced a fall earlier in the day and Ghayas had hit his head, which resulted in a hematoma. The hematoma had developed in Ghayas's brain and was affecting his coordination and speech. Fortunately, the doctors were able to locate and manage his treatment.

He would recover but for a shot to his confidence. His media appearances would be rolled back as he felt the quick responses of his mind required for news interview had taken a knocking. Ghayas lost none of his charm or sharpness to the hematoma. Most importantly, he could still smile. Unlike his contemporaries and predecessors, Ghayas had also left the infrastructure that would allow the rest of us to carry on with minimal interruption into the inevitable tomorrow that must be faced without Ghayas. As is the case with many other characters in this story, there will never be another Ghayas. *Insha'Allah* neither the community, nor the world will ever need another Ghayas. This feat must be accomplished in taking to heart the lessons learned through this life lived, for an infinity of other stories eagerly wait to be lived, and may they live towards the progress Ghayas spent his life working for.

For the time-being, by the Grace of Allah, Ghayas has a few more tales to tell and a few more adventures to live.

Cassandra Balchin, the champion of Muslim women's rights and by all accounts an incredible human being, lost a valiant battle to cancer in the summer of 2012. In her wake, she left a loving husband and two young sons. What little light can be drawn from such tragedies follows from Cassandra being given time in the end to be with those most important to her. During her last days, mostly confined to hospital, she limited her company so that she could spend as much time as possible with her husband and children. But there was one person in particular she still had business with. In her final days, Cassandra called for Ghayas-uddin Siddiqui to see her one last time. She had not forgotten the bearded feminist who stood and walked beside Cassandra in some of her finest hours fighting for the community. She had one more request to make of him.

From her hospital bed, Cassandra Balchin asked if Ghayas would deliver an oration at her funeral. Ghayas was taken aback. Him? Certainly, he was not an appropriate choice for such an honour? While his public speaking had improved vastly over the long course of his life at this point, he would certainly not regard himself amongst the great orators of his time. Besides, this should be performed properly by a holy man. He could easily arrange for his dear friend Mufti Barkatulla to give the oration for he knew the proper words and rituals for such ceremonies. Ghayas was many things, but an imam he was not. Cassandra stopped Ghayas. No, it must be you. This would not be a 'proper' funeral. There is nothing 'proper' in someone so young and with such potential to be taken from this world. She didn't want a 'religious' ceremony. It wouldn't be right. Something more spiritual would be more appropriate. She also desired to be cremated. The Hindu way, Ghayas might have thought. This burial is not permissible in accordance with Qur'anic law. It is most definitely not halal. But this was Cassandra's request. Would Ghayas be able to fulfil one more final request, his life being the resilient result of his dedication to others' final wishes?

Cassandra passed in July 2012. While the rest of the world was preparing to embark on a journey for the pursuit of glory and sporty fraternity in London for the Olympic Games, another gathering of global citizens would come to the old capital of the British Empire to celebrate the vacant seat of one of the greatest that humanity had to offer. Cassandra had left detailed instructions for the memorial service which went off without a hitch. Her husband began the ceremony with warm words and gratitude for everyone's time and presence for Cassandra's final send off. Various individuals spoke, regaling the assembled mourners with tales of Cassandra's great deeds. Her leadership in the pursuit of women's rights in an often hostile community. Her work across religious and cultural boundaries. Her work on the Muslim Marriage Contract and in starting the Open Democracy 50.50 project. Her contributions to law, gender and politics. Her dedication to justice. Her greatest success as a mother, as a wife, and as a loving human being. Readings from various sources accompanied recitations of Sufi poetry.

And then came the time for the oration. The collective turned as Ghayas stood. He walked to the podium, a paper in his hands. All that mattered was Cassandra and her final wishes. Ideology, religious devotion, politics; none of that mattered at this moment. Ghayas did not have to do this, but he chose to do this. And he spoke with a conviction that Ghayas's words had never held prior. Before the assembled he delivered what was described as a lovely speech. A proper eulogy fit for the woman Cassandra was. And so, her spirit and her memory were sent off from this earth.

Following the ceremony, a grand reception followed. People from all corners of the globe and a vast diversity of backgrounds and beliefs feasted together, sharing stories of the good times had with Cassandra. The memorial service occurred during Ramadan, so fasters and believers of other ideals all sat together, pork was served, alcohol was available, and most of all, there was harmonious peace in vast quantities—one last parting gift Cassandra would leave behind as she passed into the hereafter. The multicultural world in a cricket club. Unified in celebration of a good life. A kindred, restless soul. She was cremated, a final wish fulfilled and honoured.

"Oh! Ghayas-Sahib! *As-salamu alaykum!*" Indeed, the day had just gotten a whole lot more interesting for Ziauddin Sardar. It had been a long time. One phone call, over a quarter of a century in the making, was about to alter both the trajectory of one man's life and a community in need of a future. Hopefully this phone call could make up for a blemished history, something to laugh about down the road, another story to add beside the others that, collectively, might just make for the prologue of something greater.

Ghayas had piqued Ziauddin's intrigue by ringing him, but with the words "you were correct", he had captured Ziauddin's full curiosity.

A popular misconception was that the myth of the phoenix originated in ancient Greece. A similar solar bird, Bennu, was seen in Egyptian writings thousands of years before Heroditus put the phoenix down in writing, a creature he himself admitted came from the East. When we speak of ancient civilisations, we commonly compartmentalise them into isolation, ignoring the trade routes that not only provided for movement of goods, but exchanges of ideas long before anyone was studying multiculturalism and plural futures. The Bennu might just represent one of the earliest cases of cultural appropriation. Though it remains a point of contention for the historians, the similarities cannot be denied. A massive bird emanating from the sun described as having plumage of red, yellow and purple hues. And purple dyes were the specialty of the Phoenicians, the ancient Lebanese civilisation that the bird gets its Western moniker from. Both birds have close association to sun deities: Ra in the case of Egypt and Helios in Greece. Both travel with the sun, being born in the morning, dying at twilight, and doing it all over again in the morning.

It is almost forgivable when one sees the potential and brilliance contained within such a metaphor for the human condition. A beast able to will itself into existence is a powerful thing indeed, but to be able to cease to exist for an instance of pyrotechnic wonder, only to be reborn, made pure, made anew, to try again, is even more so. The idea that we can change is a power greater than anything garnered from conquest, revolution or domination. Today it permeates our society in ways we take for granted. From the games played, for example, sports or video games, which exist upon a plane of rules that state a finitude, an opportunity to go back, start again, and learn from each play or attempt. Religion derives a lot of its power over our hearts and minds in giving reassurance that change can happen and that there is a certain law of conservation of energy in regards to our existence. Karmatic balance or justice, if you will.

By 2008, Ghayas had made all the preparations for the Muslim Institute to undergo its own Bennu metamorphosis. It had been six years since that phone call to his old friend Ziauddin. Together, as if they had not experienced decades of radio silence, they were back at work again, this time to bring about the reconstitution of the Muslim Institute as it stands today. After hanging up with Ziauddin, Ghayas looked down at his address book, his finger sliding down to the next number of many to be dialled. These phone calls were not the official communication of the Leader of the Muslim Parliament or the Director of the Muslim Institute. They were not even phone calls from the student of chemical engineering or in any official capacity with any organised group or political party. This was just Ghayas. In one way, he was getting the band back together for one last concert. Though this was something more than a reunion. Ghayas knew the full extent of the change in direction he took on after Kalim's passing would mean preparing, where Kalim had failed, for a successful succession to the next generation. Who was to be the one who comes after me? Ghayas thought. So, between 2002 and 2008, Ghayas set up monthly brainstorming sessions at the Muslim Cultural Heritage Centre in Westbourne Park, West London. Old friends, intellectuals, activists, familiar faces and those long forgotten came together and, just like the old days, re-considered their positions on the ideas of Islam. Through these meetings, Ghayas was collecting the ashes of old ideas as the old worshipers did, taking myrrh to the temple of the sun in Heliopolis so that the Bennu may resuscitate itself and take flight once more.

The year was 2009, the UK had a new Prime Minister and the US a new President. Change was the zeitgeist echoing through the zephyrs all around the globe. There was to be a great gathering in Salisbury that winter. A stone's throw from Stonehenge, this gathering would take place at Sarum College, just across the street from the famous Salisbury Cathedral where the Bishop of Salisbury sits and the best-preserved copy of the Magna Carta is housed. The document that rebel barons forced King John of England to sign in 1215, establishing rights and liberties for the people of England. The document that symbolised a historical trajectory change, where the people (high class nobles, mind you) took power for themselves from an oppressive regime. This seemed as fit a place as any for Ghayas to give the future of the Muslim Institute to the next generation. Sarum College, an ecumenical Christian institution was the perfect place for a large gathering of Muslims to plan for their future.

Ghayas stood before the familiar, old friends and a new generation, a team he had meticulously compiled, asking forgiveness for those he had offended over the years and offering the proposition of building a new world. Before the judgement of a life lived, there was one failure he could correct. It would involve an Olympic level of humility gymnastics. The multi-decade legal battle for the future of the Muslim Institute was over. It could again take flight. He asked the assembled group to help him in reflecting and rebuilding the community each of them was a member of and dedicated to seeing progress into the future. This effort would not be for Ghayas, for he also managed to be ahead of the game in relation to the trend of abdications that became popular ten years after this gathering.

Ghayas's surrender of power to the future flew in the face of Muslim tradition. An elder stepping down before the shedding of his mortal coil was a very strange notion indeed. But to fully realise what he took on back in 1996, this was an essential milestone to be reached. The end. Ziauddin Sardar would be the Chairman of the new Muslim Institute and, being the futurist he was, he already had a plan for the handing of the mantle to the next generation beyond him. It was important for the Institute to grow and welcome new individuals to reflect the growing diversity of the community. The new Muslim Institute would not fall victim to being a dictating council of aged elders, but a dynamic body of constant flux, looking to the future and trying new things out constantly. To begin this project, the new Chairman Ziauddin would also edit a quarterly literary magazine, *Critical Muslim*. This provided an aptly named vehicle by which ideas could come together and be explored, assuring the future was safe in its plurality and open for the greater inclusivity and empowerment of the community, even extending beyond the British Muslim community to the larger community known as the human race. The works and acts of a life lived amount to nothing without leaving behind an infrastructure for the next generation to carry on where you left off, progressing into the unknown future. Ghayas trusted in Allah, but he tied his camel as well.

Ten more winter gatherings held, thirty issues of *Critical Muslim* (and counting), and a couple of bloodless and relatively peaceful regime changes. Numerous lectures organised, events coordinated, and ideas developed and tweaked in the last decade. A new generation of thinkers and friends, meeting for the common good of all their futures as a truly global community. Many of those now running the show had not even been born when Kalim and Ghayas and a handful of students started meeting back at the house in Slough all those years ago. The Muslim Institute had begun its latest Bennu cycle with resounding success. Ghayas could sit back in his chair, atop his hill in Chesham, watching the sun set into the moors beyond, Talat certainly at his side. A smile stretched along his jawline, contorting his close-cut beard into a shape best described as happiness.

Perhaps at this point you, fair reader, are expecting the oh-so-cliché happy fairytale ending. Next, Ghayas would ride off into the sunset, to roam the earth from community to community on a Möbius strip of adventures, helping and empowering the needy, to then continue with the wind to his next episode. Or perhaps the scene fades from the victorious Ghayas to a bust of his likeness in the library or a full-blown statue standing beside Winston in Parliament Square, followed by the floating text to offer the feel-good satisfaction of a conclusion. Forgive me, for I can offer no such solace here. It would be a disservice to Ghayas. Neat, tied-up endings are for epic fantasies and binge-watched television shows. A life does not have a conclusion. But the best lives, they have the more appropriate closure of a future.

So, where is Ghayas today? Well, I can almost guarantee not far from the life of the community. He is retired from his days as a talking head, no longer giving opinions or interviews. There is too much news and he is no longer a young man. Keeping up with it all cannot be managed at this time, so he has given up the limelight across the board. He certainly enjoys the company of his 11 grandchildren, watching them grow. But if you look closely at the next event, lecture or demonstration he will be there sitting quietly, listening. He may look out of place, but it would be abnormal for him to not stick out as a peculiarly odd addition to the assembled. It was not a new experience for Dr. Ghayas. There he sits, listening, absorbing what he can. The speakers range from all different corners of all different walks of life, and all the obscure opinions found elsewhere in the storm. Yet Ghayas patiently sits, listening, but more importantly, eager to learn what new voices can provide, watching in excitement as the next generation takes up the mantle of their parents. If there are no events at hand or the hour is especially obscure, he may be at home in Chesham, reading the latest issue of *Critical Muslim* or watching the evening news, both British and Pakistani. Again absorbing.

Learning whatever is available to add to his knowledge base. New facts. New ways of seeing old issues. New perspectives, words, insights. Later in life, his interest was especially piqued in examining the history of Mughal India, looking back to a moment where someone had appeared to get it right. Eighty years is a long time and, in that time, Ghayas has watched many people try to take the community in the direction they thought best for everyone. Postcolonialism, partition, nationalism, democracy, Islamism, authoritarianism, revolution, Islamic Republics, Islamic

States, Parliaments, activism, multiculturalism, plurality. Plenty of opportunities taken, plenty of opportunities missed. Potentialities realised and others left to wither into what could have been. Within each moment, a lesson. Each lesson to be learned or to struggle alongside. Wins and losses, yet in the grand scheme of things, simply plays taken and experiments conducted. Some successful and others, well, something else.

Born into one community that was torn asunder by the forces of history and corrupted, toxic structures, he found that life had delivered him into a new one, which he would watch grow into the British Muslims. In personal reflection, Ghayas would note that it all started with him as a curious young boy from a small village that most had never heard of in other parts of the world. He laughs now, not so much a boy but a curious man, ever eager to learn another fact, living in another small village that most outside of England have never heard of. That's the funny way in which it all plays out. Yet, Ghayas never stopped being the student. He would consider his studies the only place he had actually failed, but it was in failure that he learned that a process as important as education is never a project one completes or one that is simply personal. It is the continuous consciousness of a people, built by all the experiences and facts encountered over years and lifetimes. Thus, the restless spirit never grew sated. So, if the cries of injustice were heard, Ghayas would break from the text he was reading. Pluck off his reading glasses, place a marker in the book and get to work in correcting the wrong. If you were to meet this man, he might offer you a cup of tea after setting the book he was reading aside. The question of the day would be posed and a great conversation would be embarked upon. Perhaps biryani cooking in the kitchen and other eager minds around you would be ready to debate the issues of the day.

For Ghayas, the Bennu's journey is one that each of us must challenge ourselves to take on and, if possible, to complete each day as the legend states. It is in this self-reflection that we better ourselves and seek out building the best future for ourselves. But as I have stated, this is neither an individual's game nor a spectator's sport. This is one that includes us all and choosing to sit out is, in itself, a choice and thus a move. So it would seem that the story is told and all the revolutions have come to their conclusion, but there is one more revolution needing serious consideration and effort put in, that is beyond the revolution our planet will, hopefully, continue to make about the sun. There is a revolution that must occur within Islam, but more specifically its practitioners.

Following the collapse of the Mughal Empire in India in the early 19th century there was an intense debate over the causes of Muslim decline and defeat. One view was that whilst we were sleeping, a new body of knowledge had emerged elsewhere which now guides the destiny of mankind. Without excelling in it our future could not be secured. An alternative hypothesis is that we declined because we abandoned 'pure' Islam, and to reacquire former glory we should shun contact with the alien West, the new knowledge emerging and return to *aslaf* (the practices of the forebears). Sadly, the latter view prevailed and manifested itself in the form of oppression, conflict, extremism, poverty, illiteracy; diseases that plagued the Muslim world over the last two hundred years. Muslim orthodoxy still believes this was the right course but it denied Muslims any influence that they might have had in world affairs.

The world is changing again. The balance of power and order in the world is moving from the West to the East. If the 19th century belonged to Britain and the 20th century to America, then the 21st century belongs to the East. Some forecast that in 30 years, Asia will regain the dominant economic position it held 300 years ago, before the Industrial Revolution and during the Mughal Empire.[78] History, however, tends not to repeat itself fully. The Western world order will soon be replaced by a new global, multi-polar, multi-civilisational order with immense new powers that come with advancements in biotechnology and information technology never seen before in human history.[79] These will throw up new questions, inconceivable a generation ago, that humanity will need to grapple with. How will Muslims and Islam respond this time?[80]

New ways of thinking away from ideas of primordial purity and theological obscurantism will be required. God blesses all of the children of Adam so we must find ways to not just listen to one another but learn from each other in this more globalised and integrated world. Part of Ghayas's inspiration and energy comes from a man in whose honour he named an annual lecture series through the Muslim Institute, beginning in 2013. That man was Ibn Rushd, a very senior Muslim judge and thinker in Cordoba, Spain, from the 12th century. Ibn Rushd said that should reason and faith appear to contradict then what you find to be true on earth should prevail. Science (reason) and true faith can never contradict; any apparent contradictions were a result of human limitations in interpreting the Qur'an. This was how this great Andalusian scholar known in the West as Averroes masterfully harmonised the two. His writings were considered deeply blasphemous, heretical and evil. Long after he died, his followers were ruthlessly hunted down, banished and killed over several centuries by the powerful Roman Catholic Church and his ideas did not find fertile ground in the Muslim world. His thoughts, however, eventually led to the break-up of the Church's monopoly on knowledge and inspired the Renaissance and Enlightenment that dragged Europe out of its dark ages. The ideas that shook his world can shake ours too.[81]

From the ashes of past failures, the Bennu can again take flight. This is where 'we' will flourish and justice and freedom for all people can be achieved.

So how would we know if the world Ghayas worked for was realised? If the community would take up the challenge he left before them after he surrendered his power to the new British

Muslims? Now that is the question. What does the ideal British Muslim society look like?[82] Is this a society that is just, equal, or human? Is this society free? What does that even mean? What will that mean in twenty years? Is it one in which stereotypes and labels have disappeared? Is faith, ritual, and practice ubiquitous and open? Will it be something new? Or will it look very much like something very, very old? Is it an independent and free-thinking woman, university bound, to pursue her dreams wearing a hijab bearing the Union Jack? Is it a Muslim Prime Minister whose religious identity and skin tone have little to do with their politics? Is it a member of the Royal family dropping by for *jumu'ah*? Is it the flag of the United Kingdom flying proudly in front of a mosque? The powers that be in British high society amending the rules so that the full British breakfast must be halal? Maybe it is a Muslim family pausing their day to enjoy afternoon high tea? Or holding each other, crying in inconsolable joy at the next Royal conception announcement? Or posing as a Muslim family smiling in front of Tower Bridge? Perhaps, instead, it is something even more innocuous and subtle.

Perhaps the familiarity of images with which we associate this dream coming true is far simpler than we imagine, something we can't picture because we have never seen it. Yet, because of this, it must be constantly striven for. Let the dream be forgotten to those moments between regaining consciousness and the grasping of morning's reality. And as for what comes next. Well, that is for you, the community, to reach out and determine. Something unthought, but of course, not unthinkable.

REFERENCES

1 Thomas Pakenham, *The Scramble for Africa: White Man's Conquest of the Dark Continent from 1876–1912*, (Avon Books, New York, 1992).

2 Peter Hopkirk, *The Great Game: The Struggle for Empire in Central Asia*, (Kodansha International, Tokyo, 1992).

3 Larry Collins and Dominique LaPierre, *Freedom at Midnight: The Epic Drama of India's Struggle for Independence*, (Harper Collins, London, 1997).

4 Shashi Tharoor, *Inglorious Empire: What the British Did to India*, (Hurst, London, 2017).

5 Nisid Hajari, Midnight's Furies: *The Deadly Legacy of India's Partition*, (Mariner Books, Boston, 2016); Alex Von Tunzelmann, *Indian Summer: The Secret History of the End of an Empire*, (Picador, London, 2008)

6 William Dalrymple, "The Great Divide: The violent legacy of Indian Partition," *The New Yorker*. 22 June 2015.

7 A. N. Wilson, *Our Times: The Age of Elizabeth II*, (Arrow, London, 2008).

8 Andrew Roberts, *Eminent Churchillians* (Weidenfield & Nicolson, London, 1995).

9 For more on the dangers and fears immediately preceding the Paritition, see Anna Leach and Guardian Readers, "'Everything changed': Readers' stories of India's Partition," *The Guardian*, 14 August, 2017.

10 Muhammad Ali Jinnah, "Presidential Address to the Constituent Assembly of Pakistan," Delivered 11 August 1947, in G. Allana's Pakistan Movement Historical Documents (Karachi: Department of International Relations, University of Karachi, 1969), pp. 407–411.

11 Ibid.

12 A. R. Siddiqui, *Partition and the Making of the Mohajir Mindset: A Narrative*, (Oxford University Press, Oxford, 2008).

13 Seyyed Vali Reza Nasr, *Mawdudi & the Making of Islamic Revivalism*, (Oxford University Press, Oxford, 1996).

14 Haroon K. Ullah, *Vying for Allah's Vote: Understanding Islamic Parties, Political Violence, and Extremism in Pakistan*, (Georgetown University Press, Washington D.C., 2014).
15 M. A. Sherif, *Facets of Faith – Malek Bennabi and Abul A'la Maududi: The early life and selected writings of two great thinkers of the twentieth century*, (Islamic Book Trust, Kuala Lumpur, 2018).
16 Sayyid Abul A'la Maududi, *The Education*, translated and edited by S. M. A. Rauf (Markazi Maktaba Islami Publishers, New Dehli, 2009).
17 "Part 2: The Campus in Context: Opportunities + Constraints," University of Sheffield Master Plan, 2014, Feilden Clegg Bradley Studios, Grant Associates, and AECOM.
18 Humayum Ansari, *The Infidel Within: Muslims in Britain since 1800*, (Hurst, London, 2014)
19 Yahya Birt, "Ebrahimsa Mohamed (1937–2017) and Malcolm X's British Tour in 1964," Medium, 2 January 2018, https://medium.com/@yahyabirt/ebrahimsa-mohamed-1937-2017-and-malcolm-xs-british-tour-in-1964-3b43f2de9d09
20 Alex Haley and Malcolm X, *The Autobiography of Malcolm X*, (Ballantine Books, New York, 1992).
21 Malcolm X, "Oxford Union Debate," 3 December 1964, from http://malcolmxfiles.blogspot.com/2013/07/oxford-union-debate-december-3-1964.html
22 Stephen Tucker, *The Night Malcolm X Spoke at the Oxford Student Union: A Transatlantic Story*, (University of California Press, Berkeley, 2014).
23 Ebrahimsa Mohamed, "The Malcolm X I knew," *Impact International*, 24 September – 7 October 1971, https://medium.com/@yahyabirt/ebrahimsa-mohamed-1937-2017-and-malcolm-xs-british-tour-in-1964-3b43f2de9d09
24 Ghayasuddin Siddiqui, *The Impact of Nationalism on the Muslim World*, (The Open Press, London, 1986).
25 Michael Axworthy, *Revolutionary Iran: A History of the Islamic Republic*, (Oxford University Press, Oxford, 2016).
26 Vali Nasr, *The Shia Revival: How Conflict within Islam Will Shape the Future* (W.W. Norton & Co, New York, 2007).
27 Shirin Ebadi, *Iran Awakening*, (Random House, New York, 2006).
28 Lawrence G. Potter (editor), *Sectarian Politics in the Persian Gulf*, (Hurst, London, 2013).
29 Kalim Siddiqui, *Stages of Islamic Revolution*, (Islamic Book Trust, Kuala Lumpur, 1996).
30 Ali M. Ansari, *Confronting Iran: The Failure of American Foreign Policy and the Roots of Mistrust*, (Hurst, London, 2006).
31 Salman Rushdie, "Writer Rushdie recalls Indira, emergency," *Hindustan Times*, 07 April 2006. https://www.hindustantimes.com/

india/writer-rushdie-recalls-indira-emergency/story-6YjEPb2ryXg-DKEEUe9STTN.html

32 Daniel Pipes, *The Rushdie Affair: The Novel, the Ayatollah, and the West*, (Transaction Publishers, New Brunswick, 1990)

33 Christopher Hitchens, "Assassins of the Mind," *Vanity Fair*, 5 January 2009. https://www.vanityfair.com/news/2009/02/hitchens200902

34 Graeme Wood, "In Europe, Speech is an Alienable Right," *The Atlantic*, 27 October 2018. https://www. Theatlantic.com/ideas/archive/2018/10/its-not-free-speech-criticize-muhammad-echr-ruled/574174/

35 Ziauddin Sardar and Merryl Wyn Davies, *Distorted Imagination: Lessons from the Rushdie Affair*, (Grey Seal Books, London, 1990)

36 Pankaj Mishra, "Jospeh Anton by Salman Rushdie – review" *The Guardian*, 18 September 2012. https://www. Theguardian.com/books/2012/sep/18/joseph-anton-salman-rushdie-review

37 Associated Press, "Muslims in London Protest Rushdie Book, 84 Arrested," *Los Angeles Times*, 28 May 1989, https://www.latimes.com/archives/la-xpm-1989-05-28-mn-1613-story.html

38 Innes Bowen, *Medina in Birmingham, Najaf in Brent: Inside British Islam*, (Hurst, London, 2014)

39 Harriet Sherwood, "How halal meat became big business," *The Observer*, 24 June 2017. https://www. Theguardian.com/lifeand-style/2017/jun/24/halal-meat-big-business-islamic-food-goes-mainstream

40 Decca Aitkenhead, "The slaughter house rules: investigating the halal industry," *The Observer*, 14 September 2003. theguardian.com/world/2003/sep/14/religion.animalwelfare

41 Tim Wyatt, "EU court rules non-stunned halal and kosher meat cannot be marketed as organic," *The Independent*, 26 February 2019. https://www.independent.co.uk/news/world/europe/halal-kosher-meat-organic-stunning-eu-court-ruling-a8797761.html

42 The Week, "Halal meat: what is it and why is it so controversial?" 16 April 2019. https://www. Theweek.co.uk/58447/halal-meat-what-does-it-involve-and-is-it-cruel-to-animals

43 Daily Express UK, "Now KFC goes halal," 25 March 2010. https://www.express.co.uk/news/uk/165022/Now-KFC-goes-halal

44 Witness, "The day Iran buried Ayatollah Khomeini," *BBC News*, 3 June 2015. https://www.bbc.com/news/av/magazine-32938264/the-day-iran-buried-ayatollah-khomeini

45 James Buchan, "Ayatollah Khomeini's funeral," *New Statesman*, 12 March 2009. https://www.newstatesman.com/asia/2009/03/khomeini-funeral-body-crowd

46 Kemal Kurspahić, *As Long as Sarajevo Exists*, (Pamphleteers, Sarajevo, 1997).

47 Jonathan Bronitsky, "Crescent Over the Thames," *War on the Rocks*, 3 September 2014. https://warontherocks.com/2014/09/crescent-over-the-thames/

48 Paul Peachy, "Dozens of Muslim charities probed in UK," *The National*, 17 September, 2018. https://www. Thenational.ae/world/europe/dozens-of-muslim-charities-probed-in-uk-1.771226

49 Tahir Abbas, *Muslim Britain: Communities Under Pressure,* (Zed Books, London, 2005).

50 Anshuman A. Mondal, *Young, British Muslim Voices,* (Praeger, Westport, 2008); Philip Lewis, *Young, British & Muslim,* (Bloomsbury, London, 2007); Madeleine Bunting (ed.), *Race, Islam and Being British,* (The Guardian, London, 2005).

51 Miran Zupanič (director), *The Eyes of Bosnia,* Arsmedia. 1993.

52 Mike Corder and Amer Cohadzic, "Srebrenica 20 years after the genocide: The Dutch peacekeepers still haunted by memories of the massacre," *The Independent*, 9 July 2015. https://www.independent.co.uk/news/world/europe/srebrenica-20-years-after-the-genocide-the-dutch-peacekeepers-still-haunted-by-memories-of-the-10378913.html

53 Alan Taylor, "20 Years Since the Bosnian War," *The Atlantic*, 13 April 2012. https://www. Theatlantic.com/photo/2012/04/20-years-since-the-bosnian-war/100278/

54 Zafar Bangash, *A Life in the Islamic Movement: Dr. Kalim Siddiqui 1931-1996,* kalimsiddiqui.com/biography/

55 Jorgen S. Nielson, "Obituary: Kalim Siddiqui," *The Independent*, 20 April 1996. https://www.independent.co.uk/news/people/obituary-kalim-siddiqui-1305799.html

56 Zoe Williams, "The retelling of Diana's story has revealed the Britain we once were," *The Guardian*, 23 August 2017. https://www. Theguardian.com/commentisfree/2017/aug/23/diana-death-britain-stiff-upper-lip

57 Richard Powers Sayyed, *1997: The Future that Never Happened,* (Zed Books, London, 2017)

58 Terrance S. Carter, "The Impact of Anti-Terrorism Legislation on Charities: The Shadow of the Law," (Carter & Associates, Orangeville, 2005).

59 Patrick Cockburn, "British terror suspects seized in Yemen," *The Independent*, 28 January 1999. https://www.independent.co.uk/news/british-terror-suspects-seized-in-yemen-1076672.html

60 Anna Politkovskaya, *A Small Corner of Hell: Dispatches from Chechnya,* (University of Chicago Press, Chicago, 2007).

61 Steve Coll, *Ghost Wars: The Secret History of the CIA, Afghanistan, and Bin Laden, from the Soviet Invasion until September 10, 2001,* (Penguin Books, London, 2004).

62 Mansur Mirovalev "Chechnya, Russia and 20 years of conflict," *Al Jazeera*, 11 December 2014. https://www.aljazeera.com/indepth/features/2014/12/chechnya-russia-20-years-conflict-2014121161310580523.html

63 Lawrence Wright, *The Looming Tower: Al-Qaeda and the Road to 9/11*, (Vintage, New York, 2007).

64 Ghayasuddin Siddiqui, "A common struggle," *Socialist Worker*, Issue 1851, 17 May 2003. https://socialistworker.co.uk/art/3613/A%20common%20struggle

65 James Naughtie, "The friendship that shaped the post-9/11 world," *The Independent*, 12 September 2004, https://www.independent.co.uk/news/world/americas/the-friendship-that-shaped-the-post-911-world-545889.html

66 Steven Swann, "Who are the Guantanamo Brits?" *BBC News*, 2 March 2017. https://www.bbc.com/news/uk-39115761

67 BBC News, "'Million' march against Iraq war, 16 February 2003. http://news.bbc.co.uk/2/hi/uk_news/2765041.stm

68 Daniel P. Bolger, *Why We Lost: A General's Inside Account of the Iraq and Afghanistan Wars*, (Mariner Books, Boston, 2018).

69 Philip Lewis, *Young, British, and Muslim*, (Continuum, London, 2007).

70 Tahir Abbas, *Muslims in Britain: Communities Under Pressure*, (Zed Books, London, 2005).

71 Kamal Ahmed, Gaby Hinsliff, and Oliver Morgan, "Ministers plan to end forced marriages," *The Guardian*, 4 November 2001. https://www. Theguardian.com/politics/2001/nov/04/uk.politicalnews

72 Geeta Guru Murphy, "UK Politics: Forced marriage clampdown welcome," *BBC News*, 5 August 1999. http://news.bbc.co.uk/2/hi/uk_news/politics/412331.stm

73 Harriet Sherwood, "Most women in UK who have Islamic wedding miss out on legal rights," *The Guardian*, 20 November 2017. https://www. Theguardian.com/world/2017/nov/20/women-uk-islamic-wedding-legal-rights-civil-ceremony-marriage

74 Lucy Ward, "Campaign to stop forced marriages," *The Guardian*, 7 November 2001. https://www. Theguardian.com/politics/2001/nov/07/immigrationpolicy.politics

75 Shaista Gohir, "Information and Guidance on Muslim Marriage and Divorce in Britain," *Muslim Women's Network UK*, January 2016. http://www.mwnuk.co.uk/go_files/resources/MWNU%20Marriage_Divorce%20Report_WEB2.pdf

76 Rachel Donadio, "The Spotlight Effect: This Church Scandal Was Revealed by Outsiders," *The Atlantic*, 23 February 2019.

77 Robert Verkaik, "Muslim leaders fear thousands of children are abused at madrassas," *The Independent*, 22 March 2006. https://

www.independent.co.uk/news/uk/crime/muslim-leaders-fear-thou-sands-of-children-are-abused-at-madrassas-6105978.html

78 Peter Frankopan, *The New Silk Roads: The Present and Future of the World*, (Bloomsbury, London, 2018.

79 Parag Khanna, *The Future is Asian*, (Simon & Schuster, New York, 2019).

80 Ghayasuddin Siddiqui, "An Era of Change," Emel 96, September 2012. https://www.emel.com/article?id=109&a_id=2825

81 Ghayasuddin Siddiqui, "The Road to Muslim Dignity," *The Milli Gazette*. 15 September 2004. http://www.irfi.org/articles/articles_251_300/road_to_muslim_dignity.htm

82 "Islam and the voice of reason: Face to Face with Ghayasuddin Siddiqui," The Herald, 16 August 1999. https://www.heraldscotland.com/news/12269180.islam-and-the-voice-of-reason-face-to-face-with-dr-ghayasuddin-siddiqui

INDEX